OUT OF THE VINYL DEEPS

OUT OF THE VINYL DEEPS

Ellen Willis on Rock Music

Ellen Willis

EDITED BY
Nona Willis Aronowitz

FOREWORD BY
Sasha Frere-Jones

AFTERWORD BY
Daphne Carr AND **Evie Nagy**

University of Minnesota Press
Minneapolis
London

Unless otherwise noted, these essays were originally published in Ellen Willis's Rock, Etc. column in *The New Yorker* (1968–75).

Published by the University of Minnesota Press
111 Third Avenue South, Suite 290
Minneapolis, MN 55401-2520
http://www.upress.umn.edu

Library of Congress Cataloging-in-Publication Data

Willis, Ellen.
    Out of the vinyl deeps : Ellen Willis on rock music / Ellen Willis ; edited by Nona Willis Aronowitz ; foreword by Sasha Frere-Jones ; afterword by Daphne Carr and Evie Nagy.
        p.   cm.
    Essays originally published in *The New Yorker* magazine, 1968–75.
    Includes bibliographical references.
    ISBN 978-0-8166-7282-0 (hc : alk. paper) — ISBN 978-0-8166-7283-7 (pb : alk. paper)
    1. Rock music—1961–70—History and criticism.   2. Rock music—1971–80—History and criticism.   I. Aronowitz, Nona Willis, 1984–   II. New Yorker.   III. Title.
    ML3534.W612 2011
    781.66—dc22

                                                                    2010050856

Printed in the United States of America on acid-free paper

The University of Minnesota is an equal-opportunity educator and employer.

18 17 16 15 14 13 12 11   10 9 8 7 6 5 4 3 2 1

CONTENTS

Foreword

OPENING THE VAULT

Sasha Frere-Jones

In January 2004, I got a phone call from David Remnick, the editor-in-chief of *The New Yorker.* "We're doing a lousy job with pop music," he said. "I want to know if you can help. Come by when you have a minute." Three months later, I had a job—my first staff position as a writer. I was on the main stage and contracted to stay there. A blessing for any writer, but the assignment left me at sea. How was I going to write about pop for a magazine that usually crossed the street when confronted with the bumptious music of the great unwashed? And how could I do it for a readership that was probably content to leave the job undone?

During my first year at *The New Yorker,* I heard from many people who were surprised that an alleged coven of tweedy, high-minded types would even want a pop critic. (After my first column, a friend said, "You get to do *another* one?") But I wasn't the first person thrown at the task.

I decided to look into how the job had been handled before my arrival. I went to the magazine's librarian, Jon Michaud, and asked him who the first official pop critic of the magazine had been.

"Ellen Willis," he said. "She was the first." I assumed her stint had been as short as Nick Hornby's, Elizabeth Wurtzel's, everyone else's, and had resulted in maybe five or six pieces.

"How many columns did she run?" I asked. Jon went away and came back several minutes later with several typewritten index cards.

"Fifty-six," he said.

I xeroxed all fifty-six pieces and took them to my office. It was like finding a missing Beatles album.

In most discussions of pop criticism between 1968 and 1975, the focus has been on the work of men: Richard Goldstein and Robert Christgau at the *Village Voice*, Greil Marcus and Lester Bangs at *Rolling Stone*, Dave Marsh at his own *Creem* magazine, and John Rockwell at the *New York Times*. Yet other names, though not as common now, were also read at the time. Christgau told me that, in the late sixties, Ellen Sander was writing regularly about rock in the *Saturday Review* (a circulation of 510,000 in 1967); Peter Winkler was tracking pop for the independent *Cheetah*; and Michael Thomas covered pop for *Eye* magazine, a bid by the Hearst Corporation to capture the youth market that began in 1968, published fifteen issues, and then folded in 1969. There are more, many of whom simply moved on to other topics and left before pop criticism was its own category.

Even if influential types were following small magazines and new alt weeklies, Willis was writing for a larger audience than almost any other critic—475,000, while *Rolling Stone* reached only 75,000. At the dawn of pop criticism, when the field was barely a field and certainly not a well-paying gig, a woman wrote seven years' worth of serious, politically engaged pieces about pop for a national magazine. In 2004, however, almost everyone younger than forty I approached had only a vague of idea who Willis was. Most identified her as a "feminist writer." That's not entirely history's fault, and it's not an inaccurate reading of Willis's own priorities: this response reflects Willis's handling of her own criticism. In 1981, Knopf published a compilation of Willis's pieces, *Beginning to See the Light*. For the collection, Willis chose only eight of her music pieces (four from *The New Yorker*) and twenty pieces about culture, politics, and feminism. After 1981, she wrote only a handful of pieces about music, mostly in the *Voice* or in the form of liner notes; seven of these later writings are included here. Willis's life's work was an examination of freedom, power, and gender; her take on pop music is a subset of that work. But her writing on pop was a model for music criticism and deserves a prominent spot in the canon of pop criticism.

Willis's pieces retain the mark of their time without being hostage to it. Her criticism is striated with details of personal struggles as well as clear and calm examinations of the day's icons. Her piece about Elvis in Vegas refuses to make fun of Elvis and Vegas (a move most writers at the magazine would go for in a heartbeat, especially now) while also holding both of them to the coals. The piece on Woodstock debunks the specifics of an overhyped festival without forsaking the ideals ostensibly embodied by that festival. Willis's dance of competing ideas and emotions is a critical triumph; she resisted punch lines or easy, unifying themes and earned her reader's engagement with comprehensive honesty. This quality is easily seen in two pieces not written for *The New Yorker,* "Beginning to See the Light," a piece for the *Village Voice* on the dialectic of pleasure and politics as experienced through a moral wrestling match with punk and coffeehouse folkies, and "Dylan," the piece written for *Cheetah* magazine that got her hired by *The New Yorker* in the first place, her only piece of music writing at the time. If you have ever struggled to reconcile your support of the rebellion in rap with its inhuman and misogynist commonplaces, "Beginning to See the Light" will feel like it was written yesterday. "Dylan," as Christgau reports, took Willis almost five months to write and "taxonomizes an alternative culture from within in the moment in a fairly accurate way." If you have ever read about authenticity in pop or wondered about which part of an artist's work is mere sound and which bits are fury, then "Dylan" is your essay. It is not your answer, though: one of Willis's gifts, and not something many editors could handle now, was an acceptance of ambiguous conclusions, no matter how much she craved the intellectual resolution.

After reading Willis's work, I felt like I had to call her. She had done the job I was trying to do when it was infinitely harder, and she had likely done a better job than I would. She was teaching in the Cultural Reporting and Criticism program at New York University, which she founded in 1997. We met at a restaurant on Sullivan Street, near her office. She seemed baffled by the idea of our meeting. It was clear that her experience as a pop critic was a distant episode, and her interest in that body of work was minor at best. She couldn't recall how or why *The New Yorker* had hired her, though she remembered why she had left. After publishing a long feature on a rape case for *Rolling Stone* in 1975, she ran into *The New Yorker*'s editor-in-chief, William Shawn. He expressed his admiration for the piece, then added that *The New Yorker* "could never run something like that." Willis left soon after. Our lunch ended soon after she told this story. I had the sensation of not adding any value to Ellen's day, no matter how lucky I felt to have met her. Willis died on November 9, 2006, of lung cancer.

After she died, her story returned to her family and friends. I was no longer interested in how she had affected my day job—I simply wanted to find out who she had been. At the 2007 EMP conference in Seattle, Bob Christgau delivered a brief, emotional tribute to his mentor, protégé, lover, and friend. Here is an excerpt from that talk:

> Ellen was one of the few people I've ever known who I'd say un-equivocally was smarter than me. Another candidate would be her second husband, the political theorist Stanley Aronowitz—who at Ellen's funeral said she was smarter than him. Students and colleagues fondly describe her as shy, but she wasn't shy—she was thinking, and ignoring you.
>
> Because Ellen was always thinking, she was intoxicating and addictive. But once we broke up I broke away. My fervent and explicit belief in marriage as an institution and monogamy as a way of living was developed—with input from the most ex-traordinary woman, or person, I've known—in conscious contra-distinction to Ellen's ideology of sexual freedom, which most of her admirers value far more than they do the rock criticism she quit in 1975.
>
> For me, of course, that rock criticism is her most important work. As a writer and a thinker, she set out many of the ideas that define my calling to this day. The persona she established was pretty cool too—skeptical, sexual, and political; affection-ate, vulgar, and very smart.

During the weeks when I worked on this foreword, I contacted Richard Goldstein. He wrote to me several times, and below is an edited, con-densed version of his e-mails:

> For me Ellen was the model of the radical humanist who abhorred reflexive thinking. She was an anti-Stalinist by temperament, but hardly a red-baiter. She hated liberals for their cowardice and their failure to examine their own duplicities. (Just try getting a liberal to admit to having racist, sexist, or homophobic drives.)

She achieved that rare balance between militant activism and paradoxical reasoning.

I first met her when she was going out with Christgau, back in maybe 1967. She was less confident in those days, more easily bollixed. I remember a rock event in Toronto that we both covered, she for *The New Yorker*. She was xeroxing her copy (since it was in typescript—no computers, and so, no duplicate or archive). The Xerox machine was eating her copy without sending it, crumpling it page by page, but she kept feeding in pages even though they came out unreadable. It seemed to me that she had lost control of the situation. Such a vivid contrast with her intellectual rigor.

Ellen was, more than anything, a liberationist. She taught me that gay liberation was an "epiphenomenon" of feminism, and that's something I still believe. Finally, she believed that for any leftist agenda to succeed it has to be based on pleasure, on realizing desire. This is a lesson the left has largely forgotten; indeed, the right has appropriated it, though they use social sadism the way we used orgiastic ecstasy. Ellen would surely agree that we won't see a revival of revolutionary sentiment until we learn to make it fun. In that respect, Ellen, Emma Goldman, and Abbie Hoffman are part of a lost tradition—radicals of desire.

My most extensive discussions of Ellen were with Karen Durbin, her coworker at *The New Yorker* and longtime friend, one of the people to whom *Beginning to See the Light* was dedicated. What follows is a condensed version of several exchanges:

Ellen's hiring was all down to Jake Brackman, who made his name at *The New Yorker* with two long fact essays, one on pop (a fresh subject in those days) and one on *The Graduate*. Jake didn't know Ellen but he read her great piece on Dylan in *Cheetah*, and it moved him to find Shawn and tell him that the magazine needed to cover rock, pop, and folk music, that the music coming out then was truly important, and that Ellen was the person to write about it. Shawn read the piece and invited her to come in. I remember when she passed my office door to go into his office. I was wildly curious and dying of envy. I saw this girl with long wild hair and, as I recall it, jeans. I may well be wrong about that; she might have had a minidress on (Ellen loved minidresses, the shorter the better), but she did come to *The New Yorker* in jeans at times, and women were forbidden to wear trousers of any kind at the magazine then. But Ellen didn't know that, and if she had, I very much doubt she would have run home to change.

Ellen was that wondrous creature, an intellectual who deeply valued sensuality, which is why she wrote with such insight about rock and roll but also with such love. She respected the sensual; in a fundamentally puritanical culture, she honored it. She saw how it could be a path to transcendence and liberation, especially for women, who, when we came out into the world in the early to midsixties, were relentlessly sexualized and just as relentlessly shamed. Rock and roll broke that chain: it was the place where we could be sexual and ecstatic about it. Our lives were saved by that fine, fine music, and that's a fact.

Ellen reminds us all that these arguments had to be proven once, that vocations and disciplines needed to be established to get bigger work done. This isn't that hard to imagine, despite how ubiquitous pop criticism has become, how cheap and plentiful the spin-offs. She never set a sorry word to paper. To do that would have betrayed the collective possibility and the individual reality, two of her intellectual passions.

Unless you've been struck by a car, or lightning, this collection will change your idea of rock criticism, Ellen Willis, and, in a minor way, *The New Yorker,* that old broad side of a barn. Don't read these pieces once. Like great singles, they get better if you ask more of them. Play them again and again.

Introduction

WAKE-UP CALL

Nona Willis Aronowitz

It was the eve of December 13, the night before my mother's birthday, and I was hurting for gift ideas. I was twelve years old. Tower Records and I were new neighbors in the Village in New York City. Clutching my allowance money, I ventured inside, hoping to find a good addition to my mom's meager CD collection (it was 1996; CDs were still a relatively new medium). Finally, I found the perfect gift: the Janis Joplin box set. I'd grown up with the sounds of Janis's soulful wheeze, and amid the ceiling-high stacks of records at my house, my mom still kept hers in constant rotation. It was obvious she felt a special connection to Janis—they even had the same hair. She was sure to love the set.

The next day, my mom gently dropped a bomb. Not only did she already own the collection, but she had written the liner notes for it.

Well. After that wake-up call, slowly but surely I began to see my mother, Ellen Willis, the way the rest of the world did: as a brilliant and versatile writer, thinker, educator, feminist, and radical leftist activist with a huge body of work—including years' worth of writing on rock and roll. During high school, I lazily thumbed through her first book, *Beginning to See the Light,* mostly focusing on essays about sex and women.

But it wasn't until my senior year when I finally began to read my mother's pop music criticism, mainly because I crawled out from under my hip-hop rock and revisited the tunes that had been background noise in my household for years. In college, I read a good chunk of it when I was toiling on a term paper on how rock–and-roll music and '60s and '70s political activism intertwined. I interviewed legendary critic Bob Christgau, consulted another legend, Greil Marcus—two of my mother's good friends and intellectual allies—and pored over dozens of books about the time period. Few of the books mentioned my mom. I remember feeling indignant. Wasn't she a big expert on the rock music of the sixties and seventies? Wasn't she the first pop music critic *The New Yorker* ever had? Wasn't she, like, *a big deal?*

When I came to her outraged, she shrugged.

"I didn't make a career out of rock criticism," she said to me with her characteristic, matter-of-fact modesty. "I was interested in writing about rock and roll as an expression of a radical cultural and political force. To be honest, it became divorced from all those things for me in the eighties. I moved on to feminism and politics."

I started writing cultural reporting myself my junior year, almost unconsciously, doing arts pieces for my college newspaper and writing event reviews for Popmatters.com. Mom edited them all. In fact, I seldom handed in a paper without filtering it through my mother's watchful eye. I realized her impact on my writing when I handed her a 3,000-word piece on an international hip-hop festival in Hartford, when the original assignment had been to write only 1,500. It mercilessly evaluated the evolution of hip-hop, offering not only observation but blunt commentary on the syrupy mess that I saw indie hip-hop becoming.

She handed me her *New Yorker* column on Woodstock in response, a piece that calls out the more sinister capitalist intentions of the famously utopian rock festival. It was then that I realized I'd absorbed it all: the stacks of records, the visits to the *Village Voice* office on Take Your Daughters to Work Day, those filing cabinets in my mom's office crammed with old *Rolling Stone* articles. I realized more than ever—*my mom is a serious badass!*

Emboldened by my mother's approval, I wrote more. A few months after graduation, I was knee-deep into my internship at Salon.com (with, incidentally, my mom's former student Lauren Sandler) when my mother died of lung cancer on November 9, 2006. A flurry of public tributes and eulogies ensued. In the grand tradition of posthumous fame, the press and the blogosphere seemed to finally understand the far-reaching influence of the role of Ellen Willis in the history of rock criticism. Robert Christgau anointed her the "godmother" of rock journalism in *Rolling Stone.* "[Willis] was an intellectual who valued pop culture, even the male-dominated bastion of rock," proclaimed Ken Tucker, writing in *Entertainment Weekly.* "Her place in the history of pop criticism should be modified, and now," asserted *New Yorker* pop music critic Sasha Frere-Jones, who wrote the foreword to this anthology. "Her contribution was early, big, and deserves rereading, every bit of it."

These acknowledgments are long overdue. My mother was named *The New Yorker*'s first pop music critic in 1968, when she was twenty-six and was one of the only women to elbow through the exclusive, testosterone-fueled rock criticism scene. Her column, Rock, Etc., unlike the rest of the magazine's formal style, brought forth a voice that was sharp, thoughtful, and ecstatic all at once, a voice that later moved on to contemplate not simply music but politics, culture, religion, war, and social movements. She assessed rock and roll in terms of not only musical form and cultural impact but how it made her *feel,* a style that is now a wistful artifact of the long-form New Journalism from the sixties and seventies. When I did the research for this collection in the tiny microfilm room at Northwestern University, I couldn't help feeling insanely jealous—not only because my mother's clear, shrewd writing style is enviable, but because there simply isn't a space for this kind of in-depth cultural journalism anymore.

My mother's interest in music ends with punk and the Reagan era, although she occasionally couldn't resist commenting on the latest works of the Stones or Bob Dylan. She eventually stopped using music as a springboard for social commentary; as she said back when I was in college, rock and roll ultimately betrayed her high hopes for a cultural revolution. But her contribution is resonant and needs to take its rightful place in pop culture history. Willis's writing should be considered alongside that of critics like Lester Bangs, Dave Marsh, Greil Marcus, and Robert Christgau—writers who chose to deepen and develop their love of music into a lifelong career of music criticism, the last two of whom fervently cite my mother as an early and important influence of theirs.

It can be hard to read some of my mother's longer, headier, more directly political essays anthologized in her other books, *No More Nice Girls* and *Don't Think, Smile,* if only because every sentence feels so important that you have to read it twice, or dog-ear and underline it, or look something up on Wikipedia. Not so with this collection. *Out of the Vinyl Deeps* is pop sensibility at its finest, a volume that could single-handedly prove just how effective a mass medium like rock and roll is for revealing human desires and both a national and countercultural identity. It is a reminder that pop criticism needn't live inside its own music-nerd echo chamber; Willis, in fact, as a cultural journalism professor at New York University, was always intent on making sure that it didn't.

I have put together *Out of the Vinyl Deeps* to rewrite the reigning narrative of rock criticism, both by gathering my mother's writing in one place and by bookending her work with essays by writers who are all indebted to her. We—Frere-Jones, rock writer Daphne Carr, Evie Nagy, who is an editor at *Billboard* and Mom's former student, and I—are all her successors, the writers and thinkers who have inherited her legacy of pop culture criticism.

I have organized *Out of the Vinyl Deeps* by category, with the exception of the first section. "Before the Flood" comprises a single piece of writing: my mother's trailblazing essay on Bob Dylan. It's an essay that demystifies Dylan's transformation from "proletarian assertiveness to anarchist angst to pop detachment." (And it will make you really pissed that Mom never got to put in her two cents worth about Todd Haynes's Dylan biopic, *I'm Not There.*) It appeared in early 1968 in one of the first issues of the fledgling *Cheetah*—a magazine originally expected to be mainstream by its advertisers, only to be taken over by countercultural troublemakers like Christgau and Willis herself. It is the piece that scored her the *New Yorker* gig.

The rest of this anthology is a collection of those Rock, Etc. *New Yorker* columns, along with writing published after her seven-year stint at the magazine. I have divided her writing into six subsections: The World-Class Critic, The Adoring Fan, The Sixties Child, The Feminist, The Navigator, and The Sociologist. My mother wrote criticism that was part of the "cultural conversation," as she called it, which required many approaches—a keen reporting eye at Woodstock and Newport; a sociologist's take on Springsteen and class clash; a feminist's lens to untangle the psyche of Janis; a fan's passion to describe dancing to a Creedence album. Here we get an unflinchingly honest assessment of punk and misogyny, a probing look into the lure of the Velvets, and a rumination on women in rock, among others. Within each section, the writing is arranged chronologically, with the exception of the liner notes from Lou Reed's

Rock and Roll Diary and "Velvet Underground," which appear one after another in the World-Class Critic section. (To read the liner notes right after the "Velvet" piece would be the equivalent of spilling your life story to someone and then saying, "Nice to meet you.")

The section called The Sixties Child may need a little explaining, as it's the least obviously coherent section in this book. Willis wrote the bulk of her music writing in the seventies, but her political and cultural transformation as a writer, a rock-and-roll fan, and (at least provisionally) a feminist took place in the sixties. In each of these pieces, Willis points out and picks apart generational chasms, and whether or not she invokes the decade implicitly, she is informed by her sixties experience. This lens should not be mistaken as nostalgia but, rather, a reference point, a way to contextualize the seventies as reflective and a kind of sobering reality check.

Seven *New Yorker* columns were omitted from these sections, either because they were short concert reviews not written for posterity or because they overlapped with longer pieces later written for *Rolling Stone* or other anthologies. In the case of the aforementioned Janis Joplin liner notes, a portion has been omitted that appears in a piece on Joplin written for the *Rolling Stone Illustrated History of Rock 'n' Roll* (that piece is in this volume, directly before the liner notes). In some cases, the Rock, Etc. columns were printed with titles; I provided one when a title did not originally appear. Unless otherwise indicated, the footnotes were added by Willis in 1981 for *Beginning to See the Light.*

This anthology is less a survey of sixties and seventies rock music than it is Willis's picks for the most culturally valuable, influential, or fascinating artists and moments. She never stressed much about coverage while writing her Rock, Etc. column and especially in her writing that followed; she tracked every move of the Who, Bob Dylan, the Stones, Janis, and the Velvet Underground as she blatantly ignored others. Since, as rock critic Georgia Christgau said at the 2008 EMP Pop Conference, "[Willis] cared less about rock than she did about movements," covering the new It band was just not that important to her.

As her daughter, I have received an enormous amount of feedback, requested or offered, from my mother's contemporaries, colleagues, former students, and friends on how her life's work has influenced them. Frere-Jones, Carr, and Nagy employ the words of some of these people amid their own assessments of her work, to provide insight into the kind of impact she has had on rock criticism, on journalism, and on the "cultural conversation." I probably could have assembled an entire book based solely on testimonials from the past few years in the form of e-mails, blog posts, or confessions at drunken parties.

Ultimately, though, my mother's work speaks for itself. This book is legions more than simply a stack of reviews, and more than even an assessment of pop culture. There is burgeoning social and political philosophy present in these pages; her positions on race, class, gender, counterculture, sex, and utopia are all channeled through the prism of rock music and what it stood for. *Out of the Vinyl Deeps* is not only a prequel to the immensely layered writing career of Ellen Willis—it's a belated recognition of a true cultural phenomenon.

BEFORE THE FLOOD

Dylan
FROM *CHEETAH*, 1967

I

Nearly two years ago, Bob Dylan had a motorcycle accident. Reports of his condition were vague, and he dropped out of sight. Publication of his book, *Tarantula*, was postponed indefinitely. New records appeared, but they were from his last album, *Blonde on Blonde*. Gruesome rumors circulated: Dylan was dead; he was badly disfigured; he was paralyzed; he was insane. The cataclysm his audience was always expecting seemed to have arrived. Phil Ochs had predicted that Dylan might someday be assassinated by a fan. Pete Seeger believed Dylan could become the country's greatest troubadour, if he didn't explode. Alan Lomax had once remarked that Dylan might develop into a great poet of the times, unless he killed himself first. Now, images of James Dean filled the news vacuum. As months passed, reflex apprehension turned to suspense, then irritation: had we been put on again? We had. Friends began to admit, with smiles, that they'd seen Bobby; he was rewriting his book; he was about to

1

sign a contract with MGM Records. The new rumor was that the accident had been a cover for retreat. After *Blonde on Blonde*, his intensive foray into the pop demimonde, Dylan needed time to replenish his imagination. According to a less romantic version, he was keeping quiet till his contracts expired.

The confusion was typical. Not since Rimbaud said "*I* is another" has an artist been so obsessed with escaping identity. His masks hidden by other masks, Dylan is the celebrity stalker's ultimate antagonist. The original disparity between his public pose as rootless wanderer with southwestern drawl and the private facts of home and middle-class Jewish family and high school diploma in Hibbing, Minnesota, was a commonplace subterfuge, the kind that pays reporters' salaries. It hardly showed his talent for elusiveness; what it probably showed was naïveté. But his attitude toward himself as a public personality was always clear. On an early recording he used the eloquent pseudonym "Blind Boy Grunt." "Dylan" is itself a pseudonym, possibly inspired by Dylan Thomas (a story Dylan now denies), possibly by a real or imaginary uncle named Dillon, who might or might not be the "Las Vegas dealer" Dylan once claimed was his only living relative.

In six years Dylan's stance has evolved from proletarian assertiveness to anarchist angst to pop detachment. At each stage he has made himself harder to follow, provoked howls of execration from those left behind, and attracted an ever-larger, more demanding audience. He has reacted with growing hostility to the possessiveness of this audience and its shock troops, the journalists, the professional categorizers. His baroque press conference inventions are extensions of his work, full of imaginative truth and virtually devoid of information. The classic Dylan interview appeared in *Playboy*, where Nat Hentoff, like a housewife dusting her furniture while a tornado wrecks the house, pursued the homely fact through exchanges like: "Do you have any unfulfilled ambitions?" "Well, I guess I've always wanted to be Anthony Quinn in *La Strada*. . . . I guess I've always wanted to be Brigitte Bardot, too; but I don't really want to think about *that* too much."

Dylan's refusal to be known is not simply a celebrity's ploy, but a passion that has shaped his work. As his songs have become more introspective, the introspections have become more impersonal, the confidences of a no-man without past or future. Bob Dylan as identifiable persona has been disappearing into his songs, which is what he wants. This terrifies his audiences. They could accept a consistent image—roving minstrel, poet of alienation, spokesman for youth—in lieu of the "real" Bob Dylan. But his progressive self-annihilation cannot be contained in a game of let's pretend, and it conjures up nightmares of madness, mutilation, death.

The nightmares are chimerical; there is a continuing self, the Bobby Dylan friends describe as shy and defensive, hyped up, careless of his health, a bit scared by fame, unmaterialistic but shrewd about money, a professional absorbed in his craft. Dylan's songs bear the stigmata of an authentic middle-class adolescence; his eye for detail, sense of humor, and skill at evoking the archetypal sexual skirmishes show that some part of him is of as well as in the world. As further evidence, he has a wife, son, and house in Woodstock, New York. Instead of an image, Dylan has created a magic theater in which the public gets lost willy-nilly. Yet he is more—or less—than the sum of his illusions.

Many people hate Bob Dylan because they hate being fooled. Illusion is fine, if quarantined and diagnosed as mild; otherwise it is potentially humiliating (Is he laughing at me? Conning me out of my money?). Some still discount Dylan as merely a popular culture hero (How can a teen-age idol be a serious artist? At most, perhaps, a serious demagogue). But the most tempting answer—forget his public presence, listen to his songs—won't do. For Dylan has exploited his image as a vehicle for artistic statement. The same is true of Andy Warhol and, to a lesser degree, of the Beatles and Allen Ginsberg. (In contrast, James Dean and Marilyn Monroe were creatures, not masters, of their images.) The tenacity of the modern publicity apparatus often makes artists' personalities more familiar than their work, while its pervasiveness obscures the work of those who can't or won't be personalities. If there is an audience for images, artists will inevitably use the image as a medium—and some images are more original, more compelling, more relevant than others. Dylan has self-consciously explored the possibilities of mass communication just as the pop artists explored the possibilities of mass production. In the same sense that pop art is about commodities, Dylan's art is about celebrity.

This is not to deny the intrinsic value of Dylan's songs. Everyone interested in folk and popular music agrees on their importance, if not their merit. As composer, interpreter, most of all as lyricist, Dylan has made a revolution. He expanded folk idiom into a rich, figurative language, grafted literary and philosophical subtleties onto the protest song, revitalized folk vision by rejecting proletarian and ethnic sentimentality, then

all but destroyed pure folk as a contemporary form by merging it with
pop. Since then rock-and-roll, which was already in the midst of a creative
flowering dominated by British rock and Motown, has been transformed.
Songwriters have raided folk music as never before for new sounds, new
images, new subject matter. Dylan's innovative lyrics have been enthusiastically imitated. The folk music lovers who managed to evolve with him,
the connoisseurs of pop, the bohemian fringe of the literary community,
hippies, and teenagers consider him a genius, a prophet. Folk purists and
political radicals, who were inspired by his earlier material, cry betrayal
with a vehemence that acknowledges his gifts.

Yet many of Dylan's fans—especially ex-fans—miss the point. Dylan
is no apostle of the electronic age. Rather, he is a fifth-columnist from the
past, shaped by personal and political nonconformity, by blues and modern poetry. He has imposed his commitment to individual freedom (and
its obverse, isolation) on the hip passivity of pop culture, his literacy on
an illiterate music. He has used the publicity machine to demonstrate his
belief in privacy. His songs and public role are guides to survival in the
world of the image, the cool, and the high. And in coming to terms with
that world, he has forced it to come to terms with him.

II

By 1960 the folk music revival that began in the fifties had expanded
into an all-inclusive smorgasbord, with kitschy imitation-folk groups at
one end, resurrected cigar-box guitarists and Ozark balladeers at the
other. Of music that pretended to ethnic authenticity, the most popular
was folk blues—Lead Belly, Sonny Terry and Brownie McGhee, Lightnin'
Hopkins. The response to blues was in part a tribute to the ascendancy
of rock-and-roll—Negro rhythms had affected the consciousness of every
teenager in the fifties. But blues, unlike rock, was free of identification with
the dominant society. Its sexuality and rebelliousness were undiluted, and
it was about people, not teenagers. Besides, the Negro, always a dual symbol of suffering and life force, was gaining new political importance, and
folk blues expressed the restlessness of activists, bohemians, déclassé
intellectuals. Since younger Negro performers were not interested in
preserving a genre they had abandoned for more distinctly urban forms,
white city singers tried to fill the gap. Patronized unmercifully by blues

purists, the best of them did not simply approximate Negro sounds but evoked personal pain and disenchantment with white culture.

At the same time there was a surge of folk composing. The Weavers, in the vanguard of the revival, had popularized the iconoclastic ballads and talking blues of Woody Guthrie, chronicler of the dust bowl and the Depression, the open road, the unions, the common man[1] as intrepid endurer. Pete Seeger, the Weavers' lead singer in the early days and the most prestigious folk musician in the country, had recorded albums of topical songs from the thirties and forties. With the emergence of the civil rights movement, freedom songs, some new, some updated spirituals and union chants, began coming out of the South. Northern musicians began to write and perform their own material, mainly variations on the hard-traveling theme and polemics against racism, the bomb, and middle-class conformity. Guthrie was their godfather, Seeger their guru, California songwriter Malvina Reynolds their older sister. Later, they were to acquire an angel—Joan Baez, who would record their songs and sing them at racial demonstrations and peace rallies; an organ—*Broadside,* a mimeographed magazine founded in 1962; and a sachem—Bob Dylan.

Gerde's Folk City, an unassuming, unbohemian cabaret in Greenwich Village, was the folk fans' chief New York hangout. On Monday, hootenanny night, blues interpreters like Dave Van Ronk, bluegrass groups like the Greenbriar Boys, the new topical songwriters—Tom Paxton, Phil Ochs, Len Chandler—would stop in and perform. Established singers came because Gerde's was part of the scene, because they enjoyed playing to the aficionados who gathered after midnight. The young ones came for a showcase and for contact with musicians they admired.

When Bob Dylan first showed up at Gerde's in the spring of 1961, fresh-skinned and baby-faced and wearing a schoolboy's corduroy cap, the manager asked him for proof of age. He was nineteen, only recently arrived in New York. Skinny, nervous, manic, the bohemian patina of jeans and boots, scruffy hair, hip jargon, and hitchhiking mileage barely settled on nice Bobby Zimmerman, he had been trying to catch on at the

---

1. When I wrote this piece (and a few others in the book), I had not yet stopped using *man, he,* etc., as generic terms applying to both sexes. In the interest of historical accuracy I've left these locutions intact, though they grate on me aesthetically as well as politically. For the same reason I have not changed *Negro* to *black.*

coffeehouses. His material and style were a cud of half-digested influences: Guthrie-cum-Elliott; Blind Lemon Jefferson-cum-Lead Belly-cum-Van Ronk; the hillbilly sounds of Hank Williams and Jimmie Rodgers; the rock-and-roll of Chuck Berry and Elvis Presley. He was constantly writing new songs. Onstage, he varied poignancy with clownishness. His interpretations of traditional songs—especially blues—were pretentious, and his harsh, flat voice kept slipping over the edge of plaintiveness into strident self-pity. But he shone as a comedian, charming audiences with Charlie Chaplin routines, playing with his hair and cap, burlesquing his own mannerisms, and simply enjoying himself. His specialty was composing lightly sardonic talking blues—chants to a bass-run guitar accompaniment, a favorite vehicle of Woody Guthrie's: "Them Communists were all around / in the air and on the ground / . . . I run down most hurriedly / and joined the John Birch society."

That fall, *New York Times* folk music critic Robert Shelton visited Gerde's and gave Dylan an enthusiastic review. Columbia Records signed him and released a mediocre first album in February 1962. It contained only two Dylan compositions, both nonpolitical. Dylan began publishing his topical songs in *Broadside*. Like his contemporaries, he was more propagandist than artist, his syntax often barbarous, his diction crude. Even so, his work stood out—it contained the most graphic descriptions of racial atrocities. But Dylan also had a gentler mood. Road songs like "Song to Woody" strove—not too successfully—for Guthrie's expressive understatement and simple, traditional sound.

In May 1962, *Broadside* published a new Dylan song, "Blowin' in the Wind." Set to a melody adapted from a spiritual, it combined indignation with Guthriesque simplicity and added a touch of original imagery. It received little circulation until nearly a year later, when Peter, Paul, and Mary heard Dylan sing it at a coffeehouse. Their recording of the song sold a million copies, inspired more than fifty other versions, and established topical song as the most important development of the folk revival. The relative subtlety of the lyrics made the topical movement aesthetically self-conscious. It did not drive out direct political statements—Dylan himself continued to write them—but it set a standard impossible to ignore, and topical songs began to show more wit, more craftsmanship, more variety.

"Blowin' in the Wind" was included on Dylan's second album, *The Freewheelin' Bob Dylan*, which appeared in May 1963. This time, nearly all the songs were his own; five had political themes. It was an extraordinary record. The influences had coalesced; the voice, unmusical as ever, had found an evocative range somewhere between abrasion and sentimentality; the lyrics (except for "Masters of War," a simplistic diatribe against munitions makers) were vibrant and pithy. The album contained what may still be Dylan's best song—"It's a Hard Rain's A-Gonna Fall," a vivid evocation of nuclear apocalypse that owed much to Allen Ginsberg's biblical rhetoric and declamatory style. Its theme was modern, its spirit ancient. At first hearing, most of the *Freewheelin'* songs sounded less revolutionary than they were: so skillfully had Dylan distilled the forms and moods of traditional music that his originality took time to register.

Freewheelin' illuminated Dylan's America—or, rather, two Americas. "Hard Rain" confronted the underside, "where the executioner's face is always well-hidden," "where black is the color and none is the number," a world of deserted diamond highways, incipient tidal waves, clowns crying in alleys, children armed with guns and swords, "10,000 whisperin' and nobody listenin'" and occasional portents of redemption: "I met a young girl, she gave me a rainbow." The satirical "Talking World War III Blues" toured the country's surface: hot dog stands, parking meters, Cadillacs, rock-and-roll singers, telephone operators, cool females, officious doctors. Dylan's moral outrage coexisted with a grudging affection for American society and its foibles. If there was "Masters of War," there was also "I Shall Be Free": "My telephone rang, it would not stop, it was President Kennedy callin' me up. / He said my friend Bob, what do we need to make this country grow? / I said my friend John, Brigitte Bardot."

For a time the outrage predominated. Dylan's output of bitter protest increased and his humor receded. He was still learning from Woody Guthrie, but he often substituted despair for Guthrie's resilience: his finest ballads chronicled the disintegration of an unemployed miner's family; the killing of a Negro maid, punished by a six-month sentence; the extremity of a penniless farmer who shot himself, his wife, and five kids. At the same time his prophetic songs discarded the pessimism of "Hard Rain" for triumph in "The Times They Are A-Changin'" and vindictiveness in "When the Ship Comes In": "Then they'll raise their hands, say we'll meet all your demands, and we'll shout from the bow, your days are numbered."

It was Dylan's year. Stimulated by the wide acceptance of his work, inspired by his ideas and images, topical songwriters became more and

more prolific. Dylan songs were recorded by dozens of folk singers, nota-
bly Joan Baez (at whom he had once sneered, "She's still singing about
Mary Hamilton. Where's that at?"). No folk concert was complete without
"Hard Rain," or "Don't Think Twice," or a protest song from Dylan's third
album, *The Times They Are A-Changin'.* The college folk crowd imitated
Dylan; civil rights workers took heart from him; masochistic journalists
lionized him. And in the attenuated versions of Peter, Paul, and Mary, the
Chad Mitchell Trio, even Lawrence Welk, his songs reached the fraternity
house and the suburb.

Then Dylan yanked the rug: he renounced political protest. He put
out an album of personal songs and in one of them, "My Back Pages,"
scoffed at his previous moral absolutism. His refrain—"Ah, but I was
so much older then, I'm younger than that now"—seemed a slap at the
thirties left. And the song contained scraps of uncomfortably private
imagery—hints of aesthetic escapism?

Folk devotees were shocked at Dylan's apostasy. Folk music and social
protest have always fed on each other, and the current revival had been
political all along. For children of Depression activists growing up in the
Eisenhower slough, folk music was a way of keeping the faith. When they
converged on the Weavers' Town Hall hootenannies, they came as the anti-
McCarthy resistance, pilgrims to the thirties shrine. The Weavers were
blacklisted for alleged Communist connections; Pete Seeger had been
there, singing for the unions, for the Spanish Republic. It didn't matter
what they sang—in the atmosphere of conspiratorial sympathy that permeated those performances, even "Greensleeves" had radical overtones.
Later, as the left revived, folk singing became a badge of involvement,
an expression of solidarity, and most important, a history-in-the-raw of
struggle. Now, Dylan's defection threatened the last aesthetically respectable haven for believers in proletarian art.

Dylan had written personal songs before, but they were songs that
accepted folk conventions. Narrative in impulse, nostalgic but restless
in mood, their central image the road and its imperative, they comple-
mented his protest songs: here was an outlaw, unable to settle for one
place, one girl, a merely private life, committed to that symbolic onward
journey. His new songs were more psychological, limning characters and
relationships. They substituted ambition for the artless perfection of his
best early songs; "It Ain't Me, Babe," a gloss on the spiritual possessiveness of women, took three stanzas to say what "Don't Think Twice, It's

All Right" had suggested in a few phrases: "I'm thinkin' and wonderin', walkin' down the road / I once loved a woman, a child I'm told / gave her my heart but she wanted my soul."[2] Dylan's language was opening up— doves sleeping in the sand were one thing, "crimson flames tied through my ears" quite another. And his tone was changing: in his love songs, ingenuousness began to yield to self-possession, the spontaneity of the road to the gamesmanship of the city. They were transitional songs, full of half-realized ideas; having rejected the role of people's bard, Dylan had yet to find a new niche.

III

In retrospect, Dylan's break with the topical song movement seemed inevitable. He had modeled himself on Woody Guthrie, whose incessant traveling was an emotional as well as economic necessity, whose commitment to radical politics was rooted in an individualism as compulsive as Dylan's own. But Guthrie had had to organize or submit; Dylan had other choices. For Guthrie, the road was habitat; for Dylan, metaphor. The closing of the iron mines had done to Hibbing what drought had done to Guthrie's Oklahoma, but while Guthrie had been a victim, Dylan was a bystander. A voluntary refugee from middle-class life, more aesthete than activist, he had less in common with the left than with literary rebels— Blake, Whitman, Rimbaud, Crane, Ginsberg.

The beauty of "Hard Rain" was that it exploited poetry while remaining a folk lyric, simple, repetitive, seemingly uncontrived. Now Dylan became self-consciously poetic, adopting a neo-Beat style loaded with images. Though he had rejected the traditional political categories, his new posture was if anything more scornful of the social order than before. "It's Alright, Ma (I'm Only Bleeding)" attacked both the "human gods" who "make everything from toy guns that spark to flesh-colored Christs

---

2. Here as elsewhere in this prefeminist essay I refer with aplomb if not outright endorsement to Dylan's characteristic bohemian contempt for women (which he combined with an equally obnoxious idealization of female goddess figures). At the time I did not question the idea that women were guardians of oppressive conventional values; I only thought of myself as an exception. *I* was not possessive; I understood men's need to go on the road because I was, spiritually speaking, on the road myself. That, at least, was my fantasy; the realities of my life were somewhat more ambiguous.

that glow in the dark" and their acquiescent victims. "Gates of Eden,"
like "Hard Rain," descended into a surreal netherworld, the menace this
time a psychic bomb, the revolt of repressed instinct. As poetry these
songs were overrated—*Howl* had said it all much better—and they were
unmusical, near-chants declaimed to a monotonous guitar strum. Yet the
perfunctory music made the bohemian commonplaces work—made them
fresh. Perhaps it was the context: though few people realized it yet, the civil
rights movement was losing its moral force; the Vietnam juggernaut was
becoming the personal concern of every draftable man; a new generation
of bohemians, more expansive and less cynical than the Beats, was about
to blossom. The time was right for a reaffirmation of individual revolt.

But Dylan had also been exposed to a very different vision: in May
1964, he had toured an England transformed by mod fashion and the
unprecedented excitement over the Beatles and the Rolling Stones. When
his new record came out the following spring, its title was *Bringing It All
Back Home.* On the album jacket a chiaroscuro Dylan, bright face emerging from ominous shadows, stared accusingly at the viewer. In black suit
and striped shirt, he perched on a long divan, hugging a cat, behind him
a modish, blank-faced beauty in scarlet lounging pajamas. The room,
wreathed in light and dominated by a baroque mantelpiece, abounded
with artifacts—*Time,* a movie magazine, a fallout shelter sign, folk and
pop records (including earlier Dylan), a portrait, a candlestick, a few mysterious objects obscured by the halo.

Most of side one was devoted to "Gates of Eden" and "It's Alright,
Ma." But the most arresting cut on the side was "Mr. Tambourine Man,"
a hymn to the psychedelic quest: "Take me disappearing through the
smoke-rings of my mind. . . . take me on a trip upon your magic swirling
ship." Drug-oriented bohemians loved it; it was another step away from
the sober-sided politicals. It was also more like a folk song than anything
Dylan had written since giving up politics, a spiritual road song with a
lilting, singable melody.

The other side was rock-and-roll, Dylan on electric guitar and piano
backed by a five-man band. It was not hard rock. There was no over-
dubbing, and Dylan played his amplified guitar folk-style. But the beat
was there, and the sound, if not overwhelming, was big enough to muffle
some of the lyrics. These dispensed a new kind of folk wisdom. Chaos had
become a condition, like the weather, not to analyze or prophesy but to
gripe about, cope with, dodge: "Look out, kid, it's somethin' you did / God

knows when but you're doin' it again." The message was pay attention to what's happening: "Don't follow leaders, watch the parkin' meters."

One rock song, "Subterranean Homesick Blues," was released as a single. As Dylan's pop debut, it was a modest success, hovering halfway up the *Cash Box* and *Billboard* charts. That summer, Dylan cut "Like a Rolling Stone," the most scurrilous and—with its powerful beat—the most dramatic in a long line of non–love songs. It was a number-one hit, as "Blowin' in the Wind" had been two years before—only now it was Dylan's own expressive snarl coming over radio and jukebox.

"Like a Rolling Stone" opened Dylan's first all-rock album, *Highway 61 Revisited.* More polished but less daring than *Bringing It All Back Home,* the album reworked familiar motifs. The title song, which depicted the highway as junkyard, temple, and battlefield, was Dylan's best face-of-America commentary since "Talking World War III Blues." The witty and scarifying "Ballad of a Thin Man," which derided the rationalist bewildered by the instinctual revolt, was an updated "Times They Are A-Changin'," with battle lines redrawn according to pop morality. Dylan did not hail the breakdown of sanity he described but merely kept his cool, mocking Mr. Jones (the pop equivalent of Mr. Charlie) for committing squareness: "The sword-swallower he comes up to you and then he kneels / . . . and he says here is your throat back, thanks for the loan / and something is happening but you don't know what it is, do you, Mr. Jones?" "Desolation Row" was Dylan's final tribute to the Götterdämmerung strain in modern literature—an eleven-minute freak show whose cast of losers, goons, and ghosts wandered around in a miasma of sexual repression and latent violence underscored by the electronic beat.

The violent hostility of traditionalists to Dylan's rock-and-roll made the uproar over "My Back Pages" seem mild. Not only orthodox leftists but bohemian radicals called him a sellout and a phony. At the July 1965 Newport Folk Festival he appeared with his electric guitar and was booed off the stage. Alan Lomax, America's foremost authority on folk songs, felt Dylan had chucked his artistry for a big audience and forsaken a mature culture for one that was evanescent and faddish. Tom Paxton, dean of the new crop of topical songwriters, commented: " 'Where it's at' is a synonym for 'rich.' "

Defiantly, Dylan exacerbated the furor, insisting on his contempt for message songs and his indifference to causes, refusing to agonize over his wealth or his taxes ("Uncle Sam, he's my *uncle*! Can't turn your back on a member of the family!"). In one notorious interview he claimed he had written topical songs only to get published in *Broadside* and attract attention. Many former fans took the bait. Actually, Dylan's work still bristled with messages; his "opportunism" had absorbed three years of his life and produced the finest extensions of traditional music since Guthrie. But the purists believed in it because they wanted to. Their passion told less about Dylan than about their own peculiar compound of aristocratic and proletarian sensitivities.

Pure folk sound and idiom, in theory the expression of ordinary people, had become the province of middle-class dissidents who identified with the common man but whose attitude toward common men resembled that of White Russian expatriates toward the communized peasants. For them popular music—especially rock-and-roll—symbolized the displacement of the true folk by the masses. Rock was not created by the people but purveyed by the communications industry. The performer was incidental to engineer and publicity man. The beat was moronic, the lyrics banal teenage trivia.

These were half-truths. From the beginning, there was a bottom-up as well as top-down movement in rock-and-roll: neighborhood kids formed groups and wrote songs; country singers adopted a rhythm-and-blues beat. Rock took a mechanized, acquisitive society for granted, yet in its own way it was protest music, uniting teenagers against adults' lack of sympathy with youthful energy and love and sex. The mediocrity of most performers only made rock more "authentic"—anyone could sing it—and one of the few remaining vindications of the American dream— any kid from the slums might become a millionaire. (The best singers, of course, were fine interpreters; Elvis Presley and Chuck Berry did not have golden voices, but neither did Lead Belly or Woody Guthrie.) Rock-and-roll was further from the grass roots than traditional music, but closer than any other kind of pop. If folk fans did not recognize this, the average adult did and condemned the music for its adolescent surliness and its sexuality, covert in the lyrics, overt in the beat and in the intense response to idols.

But it remained for the British renaissance to prove that the mainstream of mass culture could produce folk music—that is, antiestablishment music. The Beatles, commercial without apology, delighted in the Americanized decadence of their environment. Yet their enthusiasm was subversive—they endorsed the reality of the culture, not its official myths. The Rolling Stones were iconoclastic in a different way: deliberately ugly, blatantly erotic, they exuded contempt for the public while making a fortune. Their cynicism, like Lead Belly's violence or Charlie Parker's heroin, was part of their charisma. Unlike traditional folk singers, they could cheerfully censor their lyrics for Ed Sullivan without seeming domesticated—the effect was more as if they had paraded a sign saying "Blank CBS." British rock was far superior to most early rock-and-roll.[3] Times had changed: electronic techniques were more sophisticated, radio stations and record companies less squeamish about sexual candor, and teen culture was merging into a more mature, less superficial youth culture with semibohemian tastes. Most important, the British groups successfully assimilated Negro music, neither vitiating rhythm-and-blues nor imitating it, but refining it to reflect their own milieu—white, urban, technological, materialistic, tough-minded.

Most folk fans—even those with no intrinsic objections to rock, who had perhaps listened to it when they were teenagers and not obliged to be serious—assumed that commercial exploitation automatically gutted music. Yet the Stones were creating blues as valid as the work of any folk singers, black or white. After *Bringing It All Back Home,* the contradiction could no longer be ignored, and those not irrevocably committed to the traditional folk ethos saw the point. Phil Ochs praised *Highway 61*; Joan Baez cut a rock-and-roll record; more and more folk singers began to use electronic instruments. Folk-rock generated an unaccustomed accord between the folk and pop worlds. In *Crawdaddy!* Richard Fariña lauded "this shift away from open-road-protest-flat-pick-style to more Nashville-Motown-Thameside, with the strong implication that some of us had been listening to the AM radio." Malvina Reynolds pronounced the new rock-and-roll "a wonder and delight." By November 1966, folk-rock had received the final imprimatur—Pete Seeger recorded an album backed by three members of the Blues Project.

---

3. This statement now strikes me as absurd, a confusion of aesthetic sophistication and self-consciousness with merit in some absolute sense. It makes even less sense when applied to the best midsixties British rock versus the best early rock-and-roll. Precisely because they had a more spontaneous, direct relation to their material and their audience, performers like Elvis Presley, Chuck Berry, Little Richard, and Jerry Lee Lewis got to places that the Beatles, the Stones, and the Who never even tried to reach. The reverse is also true, of course.

Folk-rock was never a form, but a simpleminded inspiration responsible for all sorts of hybrids. At first it was mostly rock versions of Dylan folk songs, social protest rock, and generational trauma rock, a weekend-hippie version of the classic formula, children against parents. Then, self-styled musical poets Simon and Garfunkel began imitating Dylan's apocalyptic songs ("The words of the prophets are written on a subway wall"), starting a trend of elaborate and, too often, sophomoric lyrics. The Lovin' Spoonful invented the "good-time sound," a varying mixture of rock, blues, jug, and old pop. Donovan wrote medieval fantasies and pop collages like "Sunshine Superman" and "Mellow Yellow." And there was acid-rock, the music of new bohemia.

Psychedelic music, like folk-rock, was a catch-all label; it described a variety of products shaped by folk, British rock, Chicago blues, jazz, Indian music. Psychedelic lyrics, heavily influenced by Dylanesque imagery, used the conventions of the romantic pop song to express sexual and mystical rather than sentimental love and focused on the trip—especially the flight—the way folk music focused on the road. The Byrds, who had started folk-rock moving with their hit record of "Mr. Tambourine Man," launched the California psychedelic sound with "Eight Miles High," which picked up on the Beatles' experiments with Indian instrumentation and was ostensibly about flying over the London airport (it was banned anyway by right-thinking disc jockeys). Though the Byrds were from Los Angeles, the scene soon shifted north, and a proliferation of underground rock groups—some, like Jefferson Airplane, the Grateful Dead, and Country Joe and the Fish, quickly surfaced—made San Francisco the new center of avant-garde pop, superseding Britain.

The California groups came closest to making the term *folk-rock* say something. For hippie culture, bastard of the Beat generation out of pop, was much like a folk culture—oral, naive, communal, its aphorisms ("Make love, not war," "Turn on, tune in, drop out") intuited, not rationalized. Pop and Beat, thesis and antithesis of the affluent society, contained elements of synthesis: both movements rejected intellect for sensation, politics for art, and Ginsberg and Kerouac glorified a grassroots America that included supermarkets and cars as well as mountains and apple pie. The hippies simplified the Beats' utopian anarchism and substituted psychedelic drugs for Zen and yoga; they also shared the pop enthusiasm for technology and the rainbow surface of affluence—their music was rock, their style mod. Like Dylan, they bridged old culture and new—they were still idealists—and they idolized him. But he did not consider himself their spokesman. At twenty-five, he was too old ("How can I be the voice of their generation? I'm not their generation") and, though he did not admit it publicly, too well read. While "Mr. Tambourine Man" was becoming the hippie anthem, he was saying "LSD is for mad, hateful people" and making fun of drugs in "Memphis Blues Again." Dylan was really at cross-purposes with the hippies. They were trying to embody pop sensibility in a folk culture. He was trying to comprehend pop culture with—at bottom—a folk sensibility.

IV

It is a truism among Dylan's admirers that he is a poet using rock-and-roll to spread his art: as Jack Newfield put it in the *Village Voice*, "If Whitman were alive today, he too would be playing an electric guitar." This misrepresentation has only served to discredit Dylan among intellectuals and draw predictable sniping from conscientious B-student poets like Louis Simpson and John Ciardi. Dylan has a lavish verbal imagination and a brilliant sense of irony, and many of his images—especially on the two *Blonde on Blonde* records—are memorable. But poetry also requires economy, coherence, and discrimination, and Dylan has perpetrated prolix verses, horrendous grammar, tangled phrases, silly metaphors, embarrassing clichés, muddled thought; at times he seems to believe one good image deserves five others, and he relies too much on rhyme. His chief literary virtue—sensitivity to psychological nuance—belongs to fiction more than poetry. His skill at creating character has made good lyrics out of terrible poetry, as in the prerock "Ballad in Plain D," whose portraits of the singer, his girl, and her family redeem lines like: "With unseen consciousness I possessed in my grip / a magnificent mantelpiece though its heart being chipped."

Dylan is not always undisciplined. As early as *Freewheelin'* it was clear that he could control his material when he cared to. But his disciplines are songwriting and acting, not poetry; his words fit the needs of music and performance, not an intrinsic pattern. Words or rhymes that seem gratuitous in print often make good musical sense, and Dylan's voice, an extraordinary interpreter of emotion though (or more likely because) it is almost devoid of melody, makes vague lines clear. Dylan's music is not inspired. His melodies and arrangements are derivative, and his one technical accomplishment, a vivacious, evocative harmonica, does not approach the virtuosity of a Sonny Terry. His strength as a musician is his formidable eclecticism combined with a talent for choosing the right music to go with a given lyric. The result is a unity of sound and word that eludes most of his imitators.

Dylan is effective only when exploiting this unity, which is why his free-verse album notes are interesting mainly as autobiography (or mythology) and why *Tarantula* is unlikely to be a masterpiece. When critics call Dylan a poet, they really mean a visionary. Because the poet is the paradigmatic seer, it is conventional to talk about the film poet, the jazz poet. Dylan is verbal, which makes the label even more tempting. But it evades an important truth—the new visionaries are not poets. Dylan is specifically pessimistic about the future of literature. Far from Desolation Row, "The Titanic sails at dawn / . . . Ezra Pound and T. S. Eliot fighting in the captain's towers / while calypso singers laugh at them and fishermen hold flowers." The infamous Mr. Jones, with his pencil in his hand, his eyes in his pocket, and his nose on the ground, is a literary man. With the rock songs on *Bringing It All Back Home,* Dylan began trying to create an alternative to poetry. If Whitman were alive today, he might be playing electric guitar; then again, he might be writing advertising copy.

In May 1966, Dylan recorded *Blonde on Blonde,* a double album cut in Nashville with local musicians. Formally, it was his finest achievement since *Freewheelin',* but while the appeal of the *Freewheelin'* songs was the illusion of spontaneous folk expression, the songs from *Blonde on Blonde* were clearly artifacts, lovingly and carefully made. The music was rock and Nashville country, with a sprinkling of blues runs and English-ballad arpeggios. Thematically, the album was a unity. It explored the subworld pop was creating, an exotic milieu of velvet doors and scorpions, cool sex ("I saw you makin' love with him, / you forgot to close the garage door"), zany fashions ("it balances on your head just like a mattress balances on a bottle of wine, / your brand-new leopard-skin pillbox hat"), strange potions ("it strangled up my mind, / now people just get uglier and I have no sense of time"), neurotic women ("she's like all the rest / with her fog, her amphetamine, and her pearls").

The songs did not preach: Dylan was no longer rebel but seismograph, registering his emotions—fascination, confusion, pity, annoyance, exuberance, anguish—with sardonic lucidity. Only once, in "Just Like a Woman," did his culture shock get out of control: "I can't stay in here /

ain't it clear / that I just can't fit." Many of the songs were about child-women, bitchy, unreliable, sometimes vulnerable, usually one step ahead: "I told you as you clawed out my eyes / I never really meant to do you any harm." But there were also goddesses like Johanna and the mercury-mouthed, silken-fleshed Sad-Eyed Lady of the Lowlands, Beatrices of pop who shed not merely light but kaleidoscopic images.

The fashionable, sybaritic denizens of *Blonde on Blonde* are the sort of people despised by radicals as apologists for the system. Yet in accepting the surface that system has produced, they subvert its assumptions. Conservative and utopian ideologues agree that man must understand and control his environment; the questions are how, and for whose benefit. But pop culture defines man as a receiver of stimuli, his environment as sensory patterns to be enjoyed, not interpreted (literature and philosophy are irrelevant) or acted upon (politics is irrelevant). "If you want to understand me, look at my surface," says Andy Warhol. And "I like my paintings because anybody can do them." The bureaucrat defends standardization because it makes a complex society manageable. Yet he thinks of himself as an individualist and finds the idea of mass-produced, mechanized art incomprehensible, threatening—or a put-on. The pop artist looks at mass culture naively and sees beauty in its regular patterns; like an anthropologist exhibiting Indian basket-weaving, Warhol shows us our folk art—soup cans. His message—the Emperor has no clothes, but that's all right, in fact it's beautiful—takes acceptance of image for essence to its logical extreme. *Blonde on Blonde* is about this love of surface.

Dylan's sensitivity to pop comes straight out of his folk background. Both folk and pop mentalities are leery of abstractions, and Dylan's appreciation of surface detail represents Guthriesque common sense—to Dylan, a television commercial was always a television commercial as well as a symbol of alienation. From the first, a basic pragmatism tempered his commitment to the passionate excesses of the revolutionist and the *poète maudit* and set him apart from hipster heroes like James Dean. Like the Beats, who admired the total revolt of the hipster from a safe distance, Dylan is essentially nonviolent. Any vengefulness in his songs is either impersonal or funny, like the threats of a little boy to beat up the bad guys; more often, he is the bemused butt of slapstick cruelty: "I've got a woman, she's so mean / sticks my boots in the washing machine / sticks me with buckshot when I'm nude / puts bubble gum in my food."

Dylan's basic rapport with reality has also saved him from the excesses of pop, kept him from merging, Warhol-like, into his public surface. *John Wesley Harding,* released after twenty months of silence, shows that Dylan is still intact in spirit as well as body. The songs are more impersonal—and in a way more inscrutable—than ever, yet the human being behind them has never seemed less mysterious. For they reveal Dylan not as the protean embodiment of some collective nerve, but as an alert artist responding to challenge from his peers. If Dylan's first rock-and-roll songs were his reaction to the cultural changes the new rock represented, *John Wesley Harding* is a reaction to the music itself as it has evolved since his accident. The album is comprehensible only in this context.

As Dylan's recovery advanced, he began making the papers again. He signed a new contract with Columbia—the defection to MGM never came off—and the company announced that he was recording. Dylan was still revered, his near-mythic status only solidified by his long absence from the scene. But whether he could come back as an active performer was another question. Shortly after the appearance of *Blonde on Blonde,* three important albums—the Beatles' *Revolver,* the Stones' *Aftermath,* and the Beach Boys' *Pet Sounds*—had all set new standards of musical ambition and pretension. Ever since, the "serious" rock groups had been producing albums that said, in effect, "Can you top this?"—a competition that extended to album covers and titles. In the spring of 1967 the Beatles released *Sgt. Pepper's Lonely Hearts Club Band,* possibly the most elaborate rock album ever made and certainly the most celebrated. It was reported that Dylan had listened to the first few cuts of *Sgt. Pepper* and snapped "Turn that off!"; perhaps the new developments in rock—which he had done so much to inspire—had left him behind. On the other hand, perhaps he was leaving rock behind. Many of Dylan's associates—notably Tom Wilson, his former A&R man—had always insisted that Dylan was much more sophisticated musically than he let on. And in May a New York *Daily News* reporter quoted Dylan as saying he was at work on "two new sounds."

By Christmas the Stones were first in the pretensions sweepstakes: *Their Satanic Majesties Request,* with its 3-D cover, was almost a parody of the whole art-rock phenomenon. How was Dylan going to top *that*? Everyone waited for a revolutionary masterpiece or an extravagant flop. What we got was *John Wesley Harding* in a plain gray jacket with a Polaroid snapshot of Dylan and three Indians in the country. The first sound to greet the eager listener was the strumming of an acoustic guitar. The first line of the first song was "John Wesley Harding was a friend to the poor." Dylan had done it again.

The new melodies are absurdly simple, even for Dylan; the only instruments backing his guitar, piano, and harmonica are a bass, a drum, and in two songs an extra guitar; the rock beat has faded out and the country and English ballad strains now dominate. The titles are all as straight as "John Wesley Harding": most are taken from the first lines of the songs. The lyrics are not only simple but understated in a way that shows Dylan has learned a trick or two from Lennon–McCartney, and they are folk lyrics. Or more precisely, affectionate comments on folk lyrics— the album is not a reversion to his early work but a kind of hymn to it. Nearly all the songs play with the clichés of folk music. The title song, for instance, seems at first hearing to be a second-rate "Jesse James" or "Pretty Boy Floyd." It starts out with all the catch phrases about the benevolent outlaw, then goes into the story: "It was down in Cheney County the time they talk about / With his lady by his side he took a stand." But the next line goes right out of it again: "And soon the situation there was all but straightened out." You never learn what happened in Cheney County or why it wasn't *entirely* straightened out, and the song ends with more stock lines about the bandit's elusiveness and the helplessness of the law. It is not about John Wesley Harding, but about a familiar formula: and this, friends, is how you write the generic outlaw song.

Several of the songs are folk-style fantasies. "Frankie Lee and Judas Priest" is both a folk ballad (based on another stock situation, the gambler on the road) and one of Dylan's surrealist dream songs; "As I Walked Out One Morning" describes a run-in with an Arthurian enchantress as if she were a revenue agent or the farmer's daughter. This juxtaposition of the conventional and the fantastic produces an unsettling gnomic effect, enhanced in some cases by truncated endings: in "The Drifter's Escape," the drifter's trial for some unknown offense ends abruptly when lightning strikes the courthouse and he gets away in the confusion; "All along the Watchtower" ends with a beginning, "Two riders were approaching, the wind began to howl." The aura of the uncanny that these songs create is probably what Dylan meant when he remarked, years ago, that folk songs grew out of mysteries.

But some of the album is sheer fun, especially "Down along the Cove," a jaunty blues banged out on the piano, and "I'll Be Your Baby Tonight," a thirties-type pop tune that rhymes "moon" with "spoon" for the benefit of those pundits who are always crowing over the demise of "Tin Pan Alley pap." And "Dear Landlord," the best cut musically, is further evidence that Dylan has—well, the only word for it is—mellowed: "Now each of us has his own special gift and you know this was meant to be true, / And if you don't underestimate me I won't underestimate you." In the end, what this album is about is Dylan's reconciliation with his past, with ordinary people, and even—warily, ambivalently—with his archenemies, the landlords of the world.

Of course, being Bob Dylan, he has turned this reconciliation into a rebellion. His sudden removal of the mask—see, it's me, a songwriter, I just want to write nice songs—and the apparent step backward could be as traumatic for the public as his previous metamorphoses; Dylan is still in the business of shaking us up. *John Wesley Harding* does not measure up to *Blonde on Blonde*. It is basically a tour de force. But it serves its purpose, which is to liberate Dylan—and the rest of us—from the *Sgt. Pepper* straitjacket. Dylan is free now to work on his own terms. It would be foolish to predict what he will do next. But I hope he will remain a mediator, using the language of pop to transcend it. If the gap between past and present continues to widen, such mediation may be crucial. In a communications crisis, the true prophets are the translators.

Chapter 1

THE WORLD-CLASS CRITIC

Two Soul Albums

NOVEMBER 1968

Among the more interesting developments in pop music has been the emergence of the LP record as the basic aesthetic and economic unit of serious white rock. Black musicians (not counting those who are also part of the white scene—bohemians like Jimi Hendrix and Buddy Miles, or newly canonized folk heroes like B. B. King) remain largely unaffected by this phenomenon. Most soul albums still consist of one or two hits padded with enough undistinguished cuts to fill out a twelve-inch record—a logical extension, after all, of the traditional B-side on a 45. Of course, there are exceptions, notably almost any album by Otis Redding or James Brown. But in general the singles orientation of the R&B labels (particularly Motown and the smaller companies; Atlantic, though it is No. 1, tries harder) is frustrating both for a reviewer and for anyone interested in accumulating a compact, representative record collection. To keep track of and evaluate the enormous number of R&B singles on the market is a full-time job in itself. Yet reviewing black albums too often means being depressingly and misleadingly negative.

Luckily, if an R&B performer is big enough, the company that records him will break down and issue a Greatest Hits album or its de facto equivalent, a recording of the artist in concert. Aretha Franklin's current album, *Aretha in Paris*, was cut live at the Olympia Theatre and contains all her most popular songs—"I Never Loved a Man," "Baby, I Love You," "Respect," "Dr. Feelgood," "Since You've Been Gone," "A Natural Woman," "Chain of Fools." Since her renaissance on Atlantic, her albums—especially *Lady Soul*—have been better than the average R&B product. But if I had to choose one to own, it would be *Aretha in Paris*. For the most part, the performance as well as the material is excellent. I have never heard the gospel elements in Aretha's voice used to greater effect than in this particular rendition of "Dr. Feelgood"—a song that also exploits to the fullest her warm, non–femme fatale sexuality. At times, out of insecurity, or perhaps boredom, she pushes too hard and makes the mistake of choking up her delivery. Her speeded-up, breathless performance of "Respect" (she does it as a finale and sounds as if she couldn't wait to get off the stage) desecrates a magnificent arrangement. I could also do without her interpretation of "Satisfaction"; like Otis Redding's, it is embarrassingly campy. The Rolling Stones may base their music on blues, but make no mistake: they have a quintessentially white sensibility, and the post-Kinsey-adolescent lyrics of "Satisfaction" sound ridiculous coming from a mature black singer. Nor is Aretha's version a convincing feminine translation of an assertively masculine song. To make matters worse, as if she knew something was lacking, she does all sorts of fancy, tasteless things with her voice. Aside from those two cuts, my only complaint is the gentility of the audience, which provides a lot of disconcerting silences and polite applause where shouting and stomping are called for. Whether Parisian audiences always act that way or whether this was just an off night I don't know.

I wish Atlantic would put out a Greatest Hits record by Sam and Dave. Except for James Brown, they are the most exciting soul act in existence. At last summer's Soul Together memorial for Martin Luther King Jr. in Madison Square Garden, they took the show away from Aretha Franklin, although she was brilliant. What makes their performance so distinctive is the tension between their immense exuberance, on the one hand, and their tight arrangements and beautifully choreographed dancing, on the other. This tension is much more difficult to project on records than James Brown's frenzy or Wilson Pickett's arrogant sexuality or Otis Redding's rough tenderness. It comes across best on their great single "Hold On, I'm Comin'," which was moderately successful; unfortunately, their biggest hit—the record the white audience knows them by—is the meretricious "Soul Man," one of the worst songs they've ever done. Their new album, *I Thank You*, like the one before it, is disappointing. Not that it isn't pleasant to listen to; it just doesn't generate much electricity. Which is to say that none of the songs touches "Hold On" or "When Something Is Wrong with My Baby." The only cut that comes close is, predictably, the hit title song. Second best is "These Arms of Mine" (an Otis Redding song, so my emotion is probably suspect). The already converted should enjoy this album. As for the rest of you, save your money and go see Sam and Dave live; they are truly spectacular. I understand that they will be playing the Fillmore East sometime in December.

The Who Sell
JULY 1969

Early in 1966, I got hold of two 45s a tourist friend had brought back from England—"Anyway Anyhow Anywhere" and "Substitute," by an unknown (in the States) rock group called the Who. The records turned out to be driving, snarling, harder-than-Stones rock and roll, with tough, sophisticated lyrics. "Substitute" was—though I didn't think in such terms then—the best rock-as-paradox song ever written. ("Street Fighting Man" is second.) It embodied the tension between the wildness of rock and its artificiality: "But I'm a substitute for another guy. / I look pretty tall but my heels are high. . . . / I was born with a plastic spoon in my mouth. . . . / I look all white, but my dad was black." In addition, these musicians I had never heard of were using the feedback from their amplifiers to make unheard-of noises, adding chaos to the steady violence of the beat. It seemed an odd case of cultural lag that the Who hadn't caught on here. They were obviously superstar material, they were apparently making it big in England, and "Substitute" was a sure hit if I had ever heard one. I went looking for more Who records. I had to look pretty hard, but within a few weeks I had found an American version of "Substitute," recorded on Atco (with the reference to interracial parentage deleted), and the Who's first album, *My Generation* (Decca), both of which I immediately bought.

As funny as the Beatles, as arrogant as the Stones, the Who specialized in an unbohemian youth-prole defiance that was much closer to the spirit of fifties rock. As Peter Townshend, the group's lead guitarist, chief songwriter, and presiding genius put it recently, "Mick Jagger was a beatnik. I only became one later." The unadorned message of the album's title song ("Why don't you all f-f-fade away? / Don't try to dig what we all s-s-say") was familiar, though the anarchic electronic noise was new. That summer, when the Beatles amazed us with *Revolver,* I decided that the Who had missed their chance. They were wonderful, but too provincial and unpolished for the great studio-rock era then emerging. Neither Atco, which had not yet learned how to promote the new rock, nor Decca, an easy-listening, country-oriented label, had recognized the Who's potential, and now it was too late. By rights, the Who should have been up there with the Beatles and the Stones—international celebrities, cosmopolites. Instead, I figured, they would wind up in some Birmingham factory. In taking the Who's image so literally, I was badly underestimating Townshend's brilliance—but also paying it unwitting tribute.

Months later, the Who finally had their first Stateside success. "Happy Jack," a medium-sized hit, was soon followed by an album of that name. In accordance with the times, the Who's music had grown more complex and subtle; the violence was balanced by playfulness, and the suggestion of the fifties was gone. Generational polemics had given way to narratives and character sketches, often infused with whimsy. I missed the crude energy but liked what had replaced it. The major achievement of the album was "A Quick One While He's Away," a series of brief songs about a woman, her late-arriving lover, and her temporary comforter, Ivor the Engine Driver. The mini-opera, as Townshend called it, ended with a transcendent, *Messiah*-like chorus of "You are forgiven!"—energy transformed into love and exaltation.

The Who toured the United States and established themselves as fine live performers. Roger Daltrey, the blond lead singer, made angel faces for the Who's newer, gentler songs, with their freaky characters—"Tattoo," "I'm a Boy," "Happy Jack"—but could switch to convincing j.d. truculence for old standards like "My Generation." Keith Moon gave a nonstop, manic show on the drums. Townshend kept up and elaborated his cathartic smash-the-guitar (and sometimes the sound equipment) finale. The Who were enthusiastically received at the Monterey Pop Festival and began to gather an underground following, "underground" in that Decca wasn't pushing them. The group's managers pushed them instead and, aided by the hip community's efficient grapevine, generated another hit single, "I Can See for Miles," and made a best-seller out of the Who's next LP, *The Who Sell Out.*

The album was presented as a Top Forty program, complete with commercials and disc-jockey patter, on Radio London, one of the illegal offshore radio stations that had been challenging the BBC's monopoly and, not incidentally, providing England with its first authentic rock radio. *The Who Sell Out* was not a satire—as many American bohemians, with their anticommercial reflexes, assumed—but a tribute. It was also the Who's first direct acknowledgment of the pop consciousness that had always informed their style and their music, from Townshend's British-flag jackets to footnotes on mass culture like "Substitute" to songs like "Anyway Anyhow Anywhere," which, as Townshend explains, "looked, felt, and sounded like pop records but were deliberately polished up to make them more exciting." *The Who Sell Out* emphasized the tender aspect of pop—its humanity, rather than its aggressive vulgarity. The characters portrayed in the songs were all more or less unworldly—misfits in some way—but nonetheless the kind of people who eat Heinz baked beans and sign up for instruction from Charles Atlas. In a sense, the record was a protest against the idea of mass man; the characters in the beautifully crafted singing commercials (Spotted Henry, who found salvation in Medac pimple-remover, and the actress whose deodorant let her down in "Odorono") had the uniqueness and the spiritual dignity of, say, Mary-Anne with the Shaky Hands or Silas Stingy or the religious crusader of "Rael." Townshend's message seemed to be that people's foibles made them worthy of love. As in "A Quick One," with its theme of sin and redemption, the Christian overtones were there but deflated to the level of the ridiculously, banally human. People might be too preoccupied with acne, money, sex, or crazy religious wars on islands, but "You are forgiven!"

The fourth Who album was a debacle. Without the Who's knowledge or permission, Decca, which still hadn't caught on to what was happening—or didn't care—took their current single, "Magic Bus," threw in whatever old Who tracks were available, some of them from previous albums, and created a mediocrity called *Magic Bus: The Who on Tour.* From Decca's standpoint, this was perfectly logical: when you have a hit record, you squeeze extra money out of it by putting out a padded album—right? Right—five years ago. The group was furious, and the resulting showdown apparently blew some cobwebs out of Decca's offices. In any case, the Who's new rock opera, *Tommy,* has been packaged with as much care, and released with as much fanfare, as it deserves—which is plenty.

As befits an opera, *Tommy* has a highly melodramatic plot. Little Tommy Walker sees his father kill his mother's lover and goes blind, deaf, and dumb when his parents exhort him, "You didn't hear it, / You didn't see it. / You won't say nothing to no one." He is bullied by a cousin, raped by an alcoholic uncle, and pitied by his parents but develops a rich inner life. He takes LSD, becomes a famous pinball champion, is finally cured of his afflictions, and is hailed by thousands as a new messiah. But when he insists that his followers seek enlightenment by playing pinball with their eyes covered and their ears and mouths stopped, the people reject him, and he reverts to a solipsistic existence. *Tommy* succeeds purely as rock; like most of the Who's work, it combines maximum breakout frenzy (which they perfected long before the white blues bands came along) with maximum economy and restraint. But there is an added dimension, first hinted at in "A Quick One"—a quiet, melodic lyricism that represents spirituality. The melodies in *Tommy* are the most compelling that Townshend has written, especially in the songs that go on wholly or partly inside Tommy's head—"Amazing Journey," "Sensation," "Go to the Mirror." The result is a dramatic—even operatic—tension, expressed as noise versus music, between the outside world's destructiveness toward Tommy and his inner peace and growth.

Although Tommy is clearly sympathetic and, in fact, a hero, struggling out of a hopeless situation to attain near-divinity, Townshend is too much of a populist simply to glorify mysticism. Tommy's version of enlightenment has its ludicrous side—it's hard to blame the people for backing out. And he is ultimately a failure, a wounded ego going back into himself instead of out into the world. The people's point of view is best articulated in a song about a groupie named Sally Simpson: though she reaches out to Tommy because he serves a need, for sex or love or rebellion against her father, "She knew from the start / Deep down in heart / That she and Tommy were worlds apart." Townshend's basic skepticism about transcendental solutions comes through in one of the opera's key songs, "The Acid Queen." Not only does acid fail to cure Tommy, as advertised, but there is a suggestion that the trip is a torture much like nasty Cousin Kevin's or dirty Uncle Ernie's: "He's never been more alive. / His head it shakes, his fingers clutch. / Watch his body writhe!"

Tommy works both as a long coherent piece and as a collection of songs. Although rock opera is a dangerously pretentious concept, the album is neither arty nor boring, because each cut—except for one rather monotonous instrumental—is short, self-contained, excellent—it's a pop song. "Pin Ball Wizard" is even more than excellent—it's one of the great rock songs of the decade. With those two exceptions, this record is too uniformly good for one track or another to be singled out for mention.

So the Who have finally made it, both critically and commercially, and everyone is happy for them, and especially for Townshend. Yet the years of struggle did have their positive side. For rock musicians, freedom is the recognition of commercial necessity; no one knows that better than Pete Townshend. From the beginning, the Who knew they had it ("All the groups knew they had it," says Townshend, "but we *really* knew we had it") and were determined to break through, differentiate themselves from the hundreds, maybe thousands, of British groups that had been inspired by the Beatles. Townshend created and exaggerated an image ("American bands don't understand about image; that's why you can't tell one from the other"), and the image *became* the Who and became a myth. Pete's guitar-smashing climax started as an assault on indifference: "There was magic in the group, and we weren't communicating it; I had to do something." Decca's neglect and the elusiveness of success in America forced the Who to keep honing and refining the image, the music, the act.

The group's evolution has also been a function of Townshend's personal growth: "Look, rock and roll is above all an expression of the frustrations of youth. Well, this is 1969, I'm an adult, I don't have the same frustrations anymore. My concerns now are mainly spiritual." Nevertheless, the Who remain the Who, and at the core of their music, however spiritualized, is rock and roll. They look all white, but their dad was black. They are no longer kids, but they have not forgotten.

Songs of Innocence and Experience
FEBRUARY 1970

A deepening sense of incipient disaster is making many of us turn inward—less in an attempt to evade external reality than in renewed appreciation of simple pleasures we have taken too much for granted. In recent months, thousands of young people have migrated to the country; others have migrated in their heads. In a way, to choose a rural environment over the hyperadrenergic, cynical, demanding metropolis is to return to childhood. And it is not surprising that the rock records that have meant the most to me lately are very much concerned with childhood, innocence, world-weariness, and rebirth.

It took me a long time to get into the Velvet Underground's third album *(The Velvet Underground),* because I couldn't quite believe in it. The Velvet Underground—weren't they part of Andy Warhol's freak show? Remember the album cover with the yellow banana that you could peel off to reveal a pink banana? The record inside was all about death, junkies, Delmore Schwartz—stuff like that. Well, this album is about Jesus, putting jelly on your shoulder, wearing your red pajamas, seeing the light, closing your door so that the night will last forever, and stuff like that—all expressed in gentle music dominated by a haunting and very electric guitar and artless, androgynous, childlike voices. *The Velvet Underground* is a religious record, and the group's theology is basically that innocence is grace and sophistication is sin: "Candy says / 'I've come to hate my body and all that it requires in this world. . . . / I'm gonna watch the bluebird fly over my shoulder.'" The last cut on the second side is called "Afterhours" and features what sounds like a four-year-old girl singing, very flat, lines like "Oh, someday I know someone will look into my eyes and say hello, you're my very special one." This kind of thing could get sticky, but it works because the songs are so good—especially "Pale Blue Eyes," "I'm Beginning to See the Light," and the instrumental passages in "What Goes On"—and because the Underground has enough of a sense of humor to twist things around a bit by incorporating into several songs a child's-eye view of traditional religion and morality: "It was good what we did yesterday, and I'd do it once again. / The fact that you are married only proves you're my best friend. / But it's truly, truly a sin." The one bad cut on the album is a pseudo–Frank Zappa electronic thing called "The Murder Mystery," which, unfortunately, is eight minutes long. If only groups would put their unsuccessful experiments at the end of a side, so that we could reject them with no hassle.

Abbey Road has given me more pleasure than any other Beatles album since *Sgt. Pepper.* For the first time in a long while, the Beatles seem to have a real sense of themselves. They have transcended both pretentiousness and exaggerated simplicity, and have avoided moralizing about politics and pontificating about Indian philosophy. The basic message of *Abbey Road,* like that of *Nashville Skyline,* is joy in living from day to day, but this album is a lot less smug and image-conscious than Dylan's, and its version of happiness is less bourgeois: Dylan celebrates maturity; the Beatles proclaim, "One two three four five six seven, / All good children go to Heaven." The spirit of the album is epitomized by "Here Comes the Sun," which is a classic and the best song George Harrison has ever written. If that's where the Maharishi was leading, maybe we all judged too soon. "Sun" is a distillation of everything the Beatles have learned about the studio, assimilated so well that although there is an incredible amount of musical activity going on throughout the song, it sounds totally simple and straightforward. The word that best describes it is *mellow.* The thaw it talks about is the calm after an emotional storm, the mental plateau after a heavy acid trip, the satisfied exhaustion after hard physical labor. "Little darling, I feel that ice is slowly melting. / Little darling, it seems like years since it's been clear. / Here comes the sun. / Here comes the sun. / (And I say) It's all right"—and, in contrast to "Revolution," where the optimism sounded completely false, it *is* all right; that is, on some level deep beneath all the chaos, we are together, children going to Heaven. Other favorite tracks are "Because" ("Because the world is round / It turns me on"), Ringo's song "Octopus's Garden" (son of "Yellow Submarine"), and "I Want You (She's So Heavy)," which after repeating the same few bars *x* number of times cuts off abruptly, to end side one; I always try to wait it out and be on top of it, and I always forget and am shocked, which I guess is another lesson in accepting life. My only complaints about the album are a little too much whimsy and another atrocious imitation of fifties rock ballads ("Oh! Darling"). I'm not complaining very hard.

Sweet Thursday is an English quintet that has just put out a first album of the same name. It is the best new group I've heard since the Band, and the only group I know that synthesizes the best tendencies in British and American rock. Most British rock bands, as opposed to blues bands, are very pop-oriented and have little understanding of the romantic idealism that has infused American rock since Dylan. On the other hand, post-Dylan bands in this country have tended toward a folkier sound, and often the beat has disappeared altogether. *Sweet Thursday* is very hard, very tender, and uncannily American; several of the songs would have fit perfectly into the sound track of *Easy Rider,* and the Dylan influence—particularly on intonation and the use of rhymes—is pervasive. The musicianship is excellent, especially Nicky Hopkins on organ and piano and Harvey Burns on drums, and the melodies are good, though to some extent they all seem to be variations on one or two basic tunes. But mainly *Thursday* is a big beat and powerful, bittersweet emotion. The record is uneven, but four cuts make it worth buying. "Dealer" is about trying to stay sane and play out the game when "the tree has long since fallen where you sheltered from the rain, / And the dealer, he pays twenty-one." "Jenny" is an attempt to recover innocence and simplicity: "Jenny, take me home. / I can't make it on my own." "Laughed at Him" is one of those wise-fool songs about a man who has seen too deeply to get along in ordinary society, but in spite of the trite theme it is very moving, mainly because of the singing and guitar work. "Gilbert Street," a ten-and-a-half-minute cross between "Penny Lane" and "Desolation Row," is a poignant evocation of wandering and searching, with a suggestion that the search involves drugs but only as one more metaphor for travel. I hope the group will tour the United States soon. I suspect they are fantastic live performers.

New Morning: *Dylan Revisited*
DECEMBER 1970

I played *Self-Portrait* enough to give any ten records a fair hearing and never got to like it much—which is not what I would have predicted. When I first heard that a Dylan album was coming out, I thought of it without excitement, as an event that required my professional attention. Even before I'd heard the album, a possible first line for a review floated into my mind: " 'He not busy being born is busy dying'—Bob Dylan said that." My pessimism was based mostly on preconceptions about Dylan's recent lifestyle and the direction he had been taking since *John Wesley Harding.* I had to admit I'd liked him better as an enfant terrible, the Robert Frost act turned me off, and what else was new? But I had an opposite prejudice that was even stronger: Dylan could not make a bad album—never had and never would—and if I listened long enough I'd figure out what the genius was doing. As time passed and the album still left me cold, one of Dylan's new songs, "Minstrel Boy," began to bother me. It was one of the better cuts, both musically (the Band did some of the singing) and lyrically. The refrain went, "Who's gonna throw that minstrel boy a coin?" Was Dylan talking about his relationship with his audience? Or was I oversensitive? Finally, I decided that *Self-Portrait* was really a loser, after all.

The worst thing about the album was that it was a two-record set. This painfully emphasized the thinness of the material, which consisted of a few original songs and instrumentals outnumbered by Nashville tunes, folkie standards, old Dylan, old ballads and blues that had been polished up and copyrighted by Dylan, Paul Simon's "The Boxer," and (!) "Blue Moon." The album was, for the most part, indifferently performed and produced, as if it had been slapped together from homemade tapes cut in Dylan's famous basement or at concerts where he was either bored or shy. It sounded like———. But, of course, *Self-Portrait* was Dylan's answer to all those bootleg records, a comment on the aesthetics of amateur production. "Copper Kettle," an old bootlegging song, was even thrown in as a clue. A clever idea, but the result was as dull, even irritating, as those twenty seconds of Dylan and his producer cackling over a mistake on "Bringing It All Back Home." Most of the old songs—including "Like a Rolling Stone" and "She Belongs to Me"—sounded canned and lifeless; the new stuff tended to be pleasant, featureless background music.

The album did have some high points. "All the Tired Horses," one of the few new Dylan compositions, was beautiful, hypnotic music—the best track on the album. And Dylan's version of "Take a Message to Mary" was great—a simple, unaffected expression of feeling (Dylan's voice can still convey emotion more convincingly than any other pop voice around) that rendered the song's frontier morality valid and human. (This is exactly what he failed to do with most of the country music on *Self-Portrait*—the clichés remained clichés, the feelings stereotyped.) These two cuts, along with "Days of 49" and the two versions of "Little Sadie," showed promise of saying something interesting about the Western myth, but the theme was never developed.

Self-Portrait was a paradoxical title. Dylan had always striven to annihilate, or at least conceal, himself—to make his music impersonal—and in *Self-Portrait* he came nearer to achieving that goal than ever before. Yet at the same time the album proved that no matter what is put on a Dylan record—and "Blue Moon" is about as absurd as anything this side of a reading of the phone book—it ends up a self-portrait, because

Dylan himself is so much more important than any record of his could ever be. Several times, I asked myself how I would react to *Self-Portrait* if it weren't Dylan's—would I be less harsh, or, on the contrary, would I not bother to listen to it at all?—but I simply couldn't perform that separation.

Now we have *New Morning*, a new Dylan LP after only four months, which these days is just a flash of superstar time. If this unaccustomed productivity represents Dylan's (or Columbia's) haste to distract us from *Self-Portrait*, it works. *New Morning* is an excellent album. On the front cover is a large photograph of Dylan. Is he telling us that here is another self-portrait, this time done right? One of the songs on the album confides, "The man in me will hide sometimes to keep from being seen, / But that's just 'cause he doesn't want to turn into some machine." *New Morning* is a retreat from anonymity, a distillation of earlier Dylan. It has the casual feel (but little else) of *Self-Portrait*. It plays with the ideas and the generic songwriting of *Nashville Skyline*. It has the warm vibes of "I'll Be Your Baby Tonight" and the first underground tape. Some of the lyrics resemble the spare, cryptic poetry of *John Wesley Harding*; the way Dylan handles his voice and experiments with different musical styles is reminiscent of *Blonde on Blonde*. He plays the piano for the first time since *Highway 61 Revisited*, and it sounds great. This album is also funnier than any that Dylan has done since he decided to grow up. The wittiest cut is "Day of the Locusts," which may be about Dylan's getting his honorary degree and is certainly about the Midwest in the summertime and how it feels to be finally getting out of school: "The weather was hot, nearly ninety degrees. / The man standin' next to me, his head was exploding; / Well, I was prayin' the pieces wouldn't fall on me." "Three Angels" is a combined spoof of bathetic talk songs in the "Are You Lonesome Tonight?" vein, of religious country-and-western, and of image-chain songs like "Gates of Eden": "Three angels up above the street, / Each one playing a horn, / Dressed in green robes with wings that stick out; / They've been there since Christmas morn." And "If Dogs Run Free" sounds like Lewis Carroll: "If dogs run free / Then what must be / Must be, and that is all."

Dylan is still very much preoccupied with finding happiness in the pastoral life. The title song is his definitive statement on the subject ("So happy just to be alive underneath the sky of blue / On this new morning . . . with you") and one of those perfect songs he manages to toss off every so often. At the risk of sounding ungrateful, though, I must say I find it the least exciting perfect song in his repertoire; Dylan describes joy eloquently but fails to make it contagious, as, say, the Beatles did in "Good Day Sunshine." "Winterlude" and "If Not for You" belong on *Nashville Skyline*. Both cuts fall flat for me; they do what they're supposed to do, but we've already had an album's worth of nice little country songs, and that was enough to make the point. In other songs, Dylan displays a more complex, and more interesting, attitude toward the country. "Time Passes Slowly" evokes the stasis of rural existence and makes it sound at once beautiful and a little boring. "One More Weekend," a honky-tonk rocker (shades of "Leopard-Skin Pill-Box Hat"), is about getting away, or, you can take a swinging couple out of the city but you can't take the city, et cetera. In "Sign on the Window," a song I like better with each hearing, the protagonist is suffering over his girl, who has gone to California with another man. He concludes, "Build me a cabin in Utah, / Marry me a wife, catch rainbow trout, / Have a bunch of kids who call me 'Pa.' / That must be what it's all about." You know he wishes it were and knows it isn't, and you know the same goes for Dylan. Life isn't all a new morning. It's also empty houses. And California.

Yes, *New Morning* is fine work—Dylan showing his best, doing what he wants to do—and that makes it all the more obvious how much the Dylan mystique has eroded. One day recently, I was playing a stack of records that included Arlo Guthrie's new album. I wasn't even listening; I was reading a book. But one cut on the Guthrie record caught my attention. I thought it was the most powerful song I'd heard in a month. It happened to be "Percy's Song," by Bob Dylan, circa 1964. That's the kind of crude impact he used to have, and I miss it. "I got nothin', Ma, to live up to"—Bob Dylan said that, too. He's right. But I still miss it.

Breaking the Vinyl Barrier
JULY 1971

After the split with Big Brother, Janis Joplin began to move in new directions, and her style was still in transition—if such a word is relevant—when she died. Like her third album, *Kozmic Blues*, her fourth, and last, *Pearl*, has a tentative quality, though the new band, Full-Tilt Boogie, is a big improvement. Probably Janis didn't get a chance to finish the album; still, I'd guess that its loose-ends feel is an accurate expression of where Janis was—is—will be at. As a last testament, *Pearl* is frustrating. But then so are all of Janis's albums. She was an incredible performer, and none of her records can duplicate the effect she had on an audience. Each of them (except for the early Mainstream fiasco, which, for the dedicated, was recently reissued by Columbia) does have one great cut that breaks the vinyl barrier. On *Cheap Thrills,* it is "Ball and Chain"; on *Kozmic Blues,* "Maybe"; on *Pearl,* "Me and Bobby McGee." Solo performers playing acoustic guitar and singing soft, country-flavored songs are very much in vogue these days, but I would never have imagined that Janis, of all people, could get into this genre, create something memorable in it, and—what is most amazing—remain totally herself while doing it. Kristofferson's song is wonderful, of course, and very germane to Janis's hang-ups; her performance is indicative of her evolution. No longer the betrayed innocent, she sings of choices made and regretted without losing her resilience: life goes on, and memories are good, even if the present isn't. The long la-la ending underscores this basic optimism. In general, Janis is hanging looser and easier on this record. In "Get It While You Can," another of my favorite cuts, she sounds almost like a soul singer. On the other hand, "A Woman Left Lonely" is, no mistake, the old Janis, inadequately disguised by polished production and a control that threatens to break down at any moment. These three cuts are superb; "Cry Baby" is almost as good; "Buried Alive in the Blues," an instrumental, is a bit of a drag; the rest are mostly listenable but less than earthshaking. Then, there is "Mercedes Benz," which Janis wrote and sings a cappella. Like most novelties, it wears thin very quickly. Still, I'm glad it's there. When the metaphysics of Janis's life and death begin to overwhelm me (did she have to turn the suicidal drive of her early music into the ultimate channel?), I like to stop and listen to her appeal: "Worked hard all my life-time, / no help from my friends, / So, Lord, won't you buy me a Mercedes Benz?" To which I can only say amen.

Morrison Live
JUNE 1972

The other night, at Carnegie Hall, before an ebullient sellout crowd: Van Morrison comes onstage wearing sunglasses. A girl two rows in front of me is wearing a green glass heart with a silver arrow through it. She stands up and screams like a siren, her voice rising and falling. Morrison is poker-faced and poker-legged, not simply cool but downright cold. After the first few songs, he begins playing games—burlesquing sexiness, exaggerating his usual vocal idiosyncrasies and supplementing them with what I can only attempt to describe as hard-edge scatting. (A parody? A technical exercise?) He holds his body aloof, kicking one leg from the knee. The shades stay on. The two blonde women in long white dresses who make up two-thirds of the backup trio look as if they put the *astral* in "Astral Weeks"; one of them is Janet Planet, Van's wife, who has bleached her hair since appearing on the *Tupelo Honey* album cover. During "Caravan," Morrison digresses to aver that sometimes the only thing between him and insanity (or did he say sanity?) is the radio. He recalls Rosko, the original late-night d.j. on WOR-FM. "Rosko got me through a lot of bad periods. Wherever you are, Rosko, thank you very much." Later, he sings "Tupelo Honey" and pronounces *oceans* "oshunzah." But the big moment of the show comes near the end. During the pause between two phrases of a song, Morrison lights a little cigar and drags on it; then he resumes singing without missing a beat or changing expression. I am sure this is not an easy thing to do. When the concert is over, the shades come off.

I'm as big a *Moondance* freak as the next *Moondance* freak, and I even like *Tupelo Honey,* now that I've gotten over being annoyed that the title song is just "Crazy Love" with new words, but I find Morrison's stage persona hard to take. His effectiveness for me has always depended on the way the emotional impact of his songs—which often revolve around little epiphanies about the wonder of simple things and the recovery, or rediscovery, of innocence—balances his controlled, stylized white soul singing. His performing stance upsets the balance by emphasizing everything that is mannered and artificial about his singing while making the content of many of the songs either absurd or unintelligible. All in all, I'd rather sit home with his albums. A new one, *Saint Dominic's Preview,* is due out this summer.

I went to the concert not only to see Morrison but to get my first look at the supporting act—Nils Lofgren and his rock-and-roll band, Grin. The group has released two impressive albums, *Grin* and *1+1,* which feature Lofgren as composer, lead singer, guitarist, and piano player. Lofgren writes two kinds of songs. On *1+1* he labels them "dreamy" and "rockin'," and that about sums it up. The dreamy songs combine the most singable melodies I've heard in a long time with lyrics that have both a deliberately childlike directness and a grown-up resonance: "Don't let life get you down, / Oh, life is so beautiful, / And when you feel all alone, / Don't sell your heart, / it's your home." The rockin' songs are not as consistently successful, but in some ways they are even more interesting. They apply the naive sensibility of the dreamy songs to rock and roll and, in the process, make a Beatle-like affirmation of rock-and-roll-as-fun. "Slippery Fingers" ("Well, I ain't really that good lookin'. . . . / It ain't 'cause I'm short and funny, aw no, honey, / It's my slippery fingers, that's all") is the 1972 equivalent of "I Want to Hold Your Hand." The Beatles were saying, Isn't the romantic fantasy in pop songs fun—and silly? Lofgren is saying the same about less ethereal fantasies. Rock history goes on: the sexual posturing of, say, the early Stones, which was then an extension of and a comment on fifties music, has now become a convention in its own right, material for younger musicians to amuse themselves with. Grin is one of a number of groups that are creating contemporary rock and roll, a form that can be clearly distinguished both from the endless varieties of hyphenated rock and from the back-to-the-roots rock of groups like Redwing and J. Geils Band. Unlike the first category, it is crude energy before it is music; unlike the second, it has assimilated the language of late-sixties white blues, transmitted through bands like Led Zeppelin, Blue Cheer, and Iron Butterfly—particularly the emphasis on volume for its own sake, a jarring, staccato beat, and lots of distortion. Grand Funk uses this language to express anger and rebellion; Grin uses it to express good-humored punkiness. There are obviously many possibilities.

Lofgren's performance was pretty good, though it didn't quite measure up to his records. He still has a lot to learn about generating excitement in an audience, but he is hip about image. He looks like a cross between Donovan and the lead singer of the McCoys and comes on like an imp from Astoria or somewhere, with grungy, stringy hair, and a red sash tied to his guitar.

"Elvis Presley? In Person?"
JULY 1972

It just happened that during the weekend Elvis Presley was to appear at Madison Square Garden—taking on New York for the first time in his career—my college class was in town celebrating its tenth reunion. Never one to waste a metaphor, I invited two classmates to the opening concert. I wasn't sure they would want to go, since neither one was a rock-and-roll nut; to my surprise, they were not only interested but excited. In fact, both had exactly the same reaction: "Elvis Presley? *In person?*"

You don't, of course, have to be a rock-and-roll nut to love Elvis. He is at once a rock legend and a mainstream pop star—a unique combination. The Beatles came close to achieving that dual status, but ultimately they could not resolve their divergent aesthetics and lifestyles. Elvis is John and Paul in one package. This does not mean that he is necessarily at war with himself, though I used to like to think so. It would probably be closer to the truth to suggest that for Elvis—as for most of his original audience, after all—rock and roll was a way to get through adolescence rather than a way of life, and that he now regards the music as a crucial and beloved part of his history rather than as his self-definition. All of which may explain why the concert I saw was not just another rock-revival number but a genuine, contemporary mass-cultural event.

There was a full house Friday night. Most of the fans were in their twenties and thirties, though I saw plenty of older people—more men than women, oddly—and gaggles of teenagers, who screamed, and even necked, in the higher reaches of the balconies. The audience was relatively straight looking but—in spite of the ten-dollar-top ticket prices—not at all classy. It was very much a New York crowd, which is to say uninhibited, demanding, and critical. The Sweet Inspirations, who opened the show, passed muster, but the second act, a pathetic comedian, was relentlessly booed until, in the most excruciating moment of truth since Tiny Tim was hit with a shoe at the Fillmore East, he bowed out, observing that there were twenty thousand of us and only one of him. Then, after a short intermission, Elvis came on, in a spectacular white jumpsuit and cape, heralded by screams, strobe-like flashbulbs, and "Thus Spake Zarathustra." From the first minute, he was in complete control. No other rock star—not Dylan, certainly not Mick Jagger—has such easy authority. Elvis has it not only because he is Elvis but because he really isn't a rock star anymore. A rock concert is generally an overt or covert invitation to rebellion, and since rebellion against the performer is one of the possibilities, the relationship between superstar and audience is characteristically uneasy. Presley, secure in his postrock persona, could afford to keep his distance. But the old energy was still there, no less effective for being so well contained.

After beginning with an Arthur Crudup blues, Elvis devoted the first third of his performance to other people's hits—rock-and-roll songs like "Proud Mary," ballads like "You Don't Have to Say You Love Me," rock ballads like "You've Lost That Lovin' Feelin'." The second third was a Presley retrospective. Elvis sang the old hits straightforwardly, making no attempt either to recapture his youth or to parody it, except at the climax, when he coyly started and stopped several times before going into "Hound Dog." All this was certainly enjoyable enough, but it was the last part of the concert that moved me most. When Elvis began singing "Bridge over Troubled Waters," I knew something important was happening: here was this schlocky song I absolutely despised, and Elvis not only was making it work but nearly had me in tears. Later, during an emotional medley of "Dixie" and "Battle Hymn of the Republic" ("What's he trying to do? Bring the nation together, or what?" one of my friends asked), I realized that the task Presley had set himself was to establish his identity as a pop—not necessarily rock—singer, and to do it in such a way as to wring assent from the deepest-dyed, hardest-core rock fan. Such a bold self-affirmation ("Accept me as I am, not as your fantasies of the past want me") would have been unnecessary anywhere but in New York, a city that cherishes its rock legends and doesn't have a whole lot of use for mainstream pop stars. At the Garden, it was an act of courage. No one but Elvis could have got away with it—and now that I'm feeling a little more detached, I'm not so sure he did. Toward the end of the concert, a female fan leaped from her seat onto the stage. The jump was a long one, and it looked as if she couldn't possibly make it in one piece. She did, though, and the cops carried her off. Then Elvis sang "I Can't Help Falling in Love with You" (yeah, me too, Elvis), and the lights went up. Well, call it a draw.

Bowie's Limitations

OCTOBER 1972

In England, David Bowie may become—may already be—a real star, but in the American context he looks more like an aesthete using stardom as a metaphor. I'm not entirely happy with this conclusion; it seems almost ungrateful. A week ago, I went to see Bowie's New York debut at

Carnegie Hall and ended up standing on my seat; at that, he was subdued by a virus and was much less exciting than when I saw him perform at a British rock club three months ago. Bowie is personally appealing, his act is entertaining theater, his band rocks, and Mick Ronson, the guitarist, is so sexy he crackles. Yet after both concerts I felt unsatisfied; more than that, I felt just the slightest bit conned. Something was being promised that wasn't being delivered.

Part of the problem is Bowie's material. *Hunky Dory,* the first of his albums to get much critical attention, has become one of my favorite records, but his more recent stuff bores me. When *Hunky Dory* came out, I took one look at the album cover—a soft, vague picture of the artist looking soft and vague—and anticipated a soft, vague sensibility. Instead, Bowie turned out to be an intelligent, disciplined, wry Lou Reed freak. To say that his current opus, *The Rise and Fall of Ziggy Stardust and the Spiders from Mars* (suggested alternate title: *Jefferson Starship vs. Powerman & Moneygoround*), fulfills the threat of the *Hunky Dory* cover would be unfair, but not very. Some of the songs are okay—"Hang On to Yourself," "Starman," even "Five Years" when it manages to transcend the self-pity inherent in its theme (the end of the world). But the idea of a pop star from outer space (read pop star as explorer, prophet, poet of technology, exotic on the outside but merely human on the inside, and so on) just doesn't make it, except maybe as a spoof, and Bowie—or should I say Ziggy?—takes it seriously. "We got five years, my brain hurts a lot. / Five years, that's all we've got"? Ouch! Onstage, "Ziggy's" deficiencies are obscured by Bowie's flash and Mick's crackle. Still, Bowie is at his best doing other people's songs—"Waiting for the Man," "White Heat/White Light," "I Feel Free." On the other hand, the worst song in his repertoire isn't anything from "Ziggy." It's "Amsterdam," by Jacques Brel.

A lot of nonsense has been written about Bowie. The ubiquitous comparisons to Alice Cooper, in particular, can only be put down to willful incomprehension. There is nothing provocative, perverse, or revolting about Bowie. He is all glitter, no grease, and his act is neither overtly nor implicitly violent. As for his self-proclaimed bisexuality, it really isn't that big a deal. British rock musicians have always been less uptight than Americans about displaying, and even flaunting, their "feminine" side. Androgynousness is an important part of what the Beatles and the Stones represent; once upon a time Mick Jagger's bisexual mannerisms and innuendos were considered far out. Bowie's dyed red hair, makeup, legendary dresses, and onstage flirtations with his guitarist just take this tradition one theatrical step further. In any case, Bowie's aura is not especially sexual; Ronson is the turn-on of the group, and his attractiveness— platinum hair, high heels, and all—is very straight, if refreshingly non-macho. What Bowie offers is not "decadence" (sorry, Middle America) but a highly professional pop surface with a soft core: under that multicolored Day-Glo frogman's outfit lurks the soul of a folkie who digs Brel, plays an (amplified) acoustic guitar, and sings with a catch in his voice about the downfall of the planet.

I've been thinking about all this ever since July, when RCA Records, with unusual promotional zeal, flew a bunch of American journalists to London to see Bowie on his home ground. As it happened, Lou Reed was also in town to see Bowie, who is producing Reed's second solo album. The night of our arrival, Lou was scheduled to perform at the Kings Cross Cinema, a proletarian Fillmore that features weekend shows lasting from midnight till six in the morning, and a number of us dedicated fans, undeterred by the fact that we hadn't slept in some thirty hours, decided to go. The performance could have been better; Reed's new band not only wasn't the Velvet Underground but wasn't even barely competent. Lou wore black eye makeup, black lipstick, and a black velvet suit with rhinestone trimming. (The Reed-Bowie influence, it seems, has gone both ways.) His voice had an unaccustomed deadpan quality, but it still conveyed that distinctive cosmic sadness. It occurred to me that one reason I loved Reed was that he didn't invite us to share his pain—he simply shared ours. I went to bed at 4 A.M. feeling somber and drained. The next night, our party was bused to the Bowie concert, which was held at a club called Friars Aylesbury, thirty miles away. Friars was considerably more middle class than the Kings Cross, and it was mobbed by pink-cheeked teenagers. They were crazy about Bowie. I was susceptible but confused. Afterward, a group of us went back to the Kings Cross to see some American expatriates—Iggy Pop and the Stooges, one of the original Detroit high-energy bands. Iggy's thing is hostility; he leaps into the audience and grabs people by the hair. His best song is called "Hungry." He is also a great rock-and-roll dancer. Unlike David Bowie, he sweats.

On Sunday afternoon, I went for a walk in Hyde Park with Iggy and Dave Marsh, the editor of *Creem*. We spent a long time trying unsuccessfully to hunt down a vender who would sell Iggy a cold Coke. "This country is weird, man," said Iggy. "It's *unreal*." Later, Dave and I talked about Bowie: What was it that was missing? "Innocence," Dave suggested. But maybe it's just that unlike Lou Reed (who will never be a star here, either) or Iggy (who just might) Bowie doesn't seem quite real. Real to me, that is—which in rock and roll is the only fantasy that counts.

Frankenstein at the Waldorf
NOVEMBER 1973

New York hasn't been doing so well lately. The Mets lost the World Series, and the Dolls' first album languishes in the nether regions of the LP charts. No matter that *New York Dolls* has virtually no competition as the most exciting hard-rock album to come out this year, or that more than half the cuts are or should be instant classics. ("Frankenstein," "Looking for a Kiss," "Subway Train," "Bad Girl," and Bo Diddley's "Pills" are only great; "Personality Crisis" and "Trash" are transcendent.) The people are all buying *Goats Head Soup* instead. The chief complaints I hear from the unconverted are that the Dolls aren't good musicians (they should maybe drown Johnny Thunders and hire Mick Taylor?) and that they are one of those decadent glitter bands. Anyone who has seen the Dolls in the past year knows that makeup and transsexual cavorting are not all that crucial to their act, but the album cover—a picture of the band in drag, *New York Dolls* autographed in lipstick—does its best to perpetuate a stereotype that is at best limiting, at worst misleading. This piece of reverse public relations could be attributed to either stupidity or monumental chutzpah, and since the Dolls have never struck me as stupid, I'd bet on the latter. In any case, it seems clear that the real source of anti-Dolls sentiment is their aggressive lower-middle-class, Queens Boulevard-cum-Lower East Side (and proud!) identity. Your average American rock-and-roll fan can stand the Dolls' brand of high-strung urban grunge only if it comes from somewhere besides New York—preferably England. I'm convinced that David Johansen's poignant question "Do you think that you could make it with Frankenstein?" was first addressed to some blonde California surfer.

Locally, of course, the Dolls' unabashed nativism—together with their talent and energy—has given us all something to occupy our souls besides

Watergate, health foods, survival on the street, and the quest for the hundred-dollar-a-month apartment. So it is entirely fitting that their most recent gathering of the tribes, a midnight Halloween costume party at the Waldorf-Astoria, resulted in a small riot. The doors were supposed to open at eleven, and by ten-forty-five more than a thousand people, many of them elaborately costumed as everything from King Kong to Todd Rundgren, had gathered at the entrance to the Grand Ballroom, in a relatively narrow space between a wall and a bank of elevators. As crowds do, they began to push. It was very hot. I wondered how, in the face of this ravening mob, the guards expected to separate the seven-fifty-a-ticket customers from the crashers. The management may have been wondering the same thing; half an hour later, the doors were still closed and the crush was getting worse. A kid in a clown suit pinched a girl who had squeezed in front of him; she tried to kick him in the groin and missed. An argument developed between the standpatters and the activists: "Waddya mean, stop pushing? You wanna be out here another hour in this heat?" At that point, someone opened a lone door at the side. Where I was, the surge was successfully contained, but later I heard that there had been at least one fight and that a number of ticket holders had been turned away.

The rest of the party was a bit of an anticlimax. For one thing, it was badly paced. Everyone was keyed up to hear the Dolls, who had been away for three months on a national tour, but the program began with a costume contest. The panel of judges was announced and prizes were enumerated (my favorite was second prize, a weekend for three at the Newark Motor Inn); the contestants paraded onstage in their peacock feathers, Christmas-tree lights, and horse heads. The judges took an inordinate amount of time picking the winners, and then there was a long intermission. When the Dolls finally came on, it was almost 2 A.M., and a certain edge was off the evening; two hours of beer and dope had begun to cool out the crowd. If time was one problem, space was another. There were too many tables near the stage, cutting into dancing room and making it impossible for anyone who wasn't standing on a table to see.

The concert itself was an equivocal success, mainly because it included only one new Dolls song, "Lone Star State" ("For Janis Joplin and another Texan we won't mention, 'cause it might incriminate him"). To know the Dolls' repertoire is to love it, but I've already heard it live half a dozen times (not to mention on the record, which I play compulsively), and some fresh material would have been nice. The Dolls' next album, according to Johansen, is tentatively titled *Too Much Too Soon.* I hope so, but one new song per set is more like too little too late.

The Rolling Stones Now
DECEMBER 1973

There was a time when a new Rolling Stones album was an automatic, instant rush, fueled by Mick Jagger's phenomenal power to create and control his universe—a power as exciting as it was at times offensive. But then the Stones began to sing about their own nervous breakdowns instead of other people's; the hysteria of "Gimme Shelter" and the resignation of "You Can't Always Get What You Want" converged in the impotent horror of Altamont. Subsequent Stones records, instead of taking immediate command, have tended to confirm a kind of domino theory of album listening: if I feel compelled to play one cut over and over, chances are I'll end up loving the rest. When I first heard *Exile on Main St.,* I hated it. I found the mix, with its recessed vocals, alienating; I concluded that the Stones, seduced by Mick Taylor, had finally abandoned the rock-and-rollers and gone over to the musicians. Yet I found myself obsessed by "Tumbling Dice," with its chaotic music and maddeningly elusive lyrics and desperate mood. The next domino to fall was "Rocks Off," which, I discovered with a shock, was "Satisfaction" updated. Then I heard the love in "Shine a Light" and began to realize that if *Exile*'s surface was alienating—as alienating as exile itself—its undercurrents of rebellion and transcendence were no less potent for being submerged. I now think that *Exile* is arguably the Stones' best work. My conversion to *Goats Head Soup* was less dramatic—partly because it isn't nearly as rich as *Exile,* partly because I'd given up expecting that instant rush—but the process was similar. The song that first drew me in was the obvious one, "Star Star," which would have been a gigantic hit if Jagger had exercised his fabled talent for slurring obscenities. Most of the others followed soon afterward. But only a month ago I was listening to "Angie," a song I'd dismissed as an irritating whine, and suddenly heard it as exactly the opposite—a victory over self-pity. Given enough time, I may even get to like "Can't You Hear the Music."

It's Only Rock & Roll is yet another low-key album that yields its pleasures slowly. In order of discovery, they include "It's Only Rock & Roll (But I Like It)," wherein Jagger-Richard prove that they can write a better rock-and-roll anthem than anyone else while making fun of the whole idea *and* throwing in some maybe serious comment on the star-fan relationship; the melancholic nastiness of "Till the Next Goodbye" (refrain: "Till the next time that we say goodbye, I'll be thinking of you"); Mick Taylor's brilliant guitar in "Time Waits for No One"; the "Gimme Shelter"-cum-"Superfly" sinister urgency of "Fingerprint File"; the triple edge of "Luxury," a reggae song in which multimillionaire pop star assumes the persona of harassed refinery worker complaining about the inequities of capitalism while cherishing his own lubricious fantasies of wealth; "If You Really Want to Be My Friend," a powerful, if somewhat ambiguous, dialogue between a woman (Bianca?) and a rock-and-roll star (guess who) on the subject of—well, call it open marriage. But the album as a whole is interesting in a way that transcends particulars: it suggests not only that Mick Jagger is as insecure about the current state of relations between the sexes as you and I but that he has come to regard his celebrity less as a source of power in his dealings with women than as an added complication. His straightforward performance of the Temptations' "Ain't Too Proud to Beg"—which seems to announce both a new humility in love and the black influence that is more conspicuous on this album than on any other Stones record since 1965—establishes a tone of uncharacteristic vulnerability; "Time Waits for No One," which is rescued from triteness by its wonderful music, implies that that vulnerability has a lot to do with the question of what happens to a forty-year-old Rolling Stone. When, in the title song, Mick addresses his teenage fans with a mixture of disdain, attraction, mockery, and, ultimately, recognition of the secret bond he pretends to deny ("It's only rock & roll"), his sardonic tone admits that he'd *better* like it—while it lasts.

Listening to this album, I can't help wondering about Jagger's marriage, which is opaque to me in a way that his turbulent affair with Marianne Faithfull was not. Bianca's public image is that of a party-going, costume-wearing, expensive shell, and as a couple they give the impression of having an alliance (what its terms are is unclear) rather than a relationship. But after hearing these songs I'm not so sure. It just could be that Mick has finally met his match. "Short and Curlies" may be a crude, infuriating display of male paranoia, but it says something that Jagger's presumption of control and his anatomical metaphors have undergone a reversal since "Under My Thumb." And in "If You Really Want to Be My Friend" it is the woman who demands freedom, the man who pleads for an end to power games: "I know you think life is a thriller; / you play the vamp, I play the killer. . . . / By the last reel we'll be cryin.'" She responds on several levels of wonderful condescension, with "People tell me you are a vulture, / Say you're a sore in a cancer culture, / Now, but you got a little charm around ya." It's only human, and I like it.

With the emergence of *The Harder They Come* as a midnight-movie staple, Jimmy Cliff could hardly be in a better position to make his move. Unfortunately, Cliff doesn't have nearly as good an instinct for self-promotion as the charismatic singer-outlaw he portrays. His recent concert at Carnegie Hall was so dull that my annoyance at its brevity was purely abstract. Appearing in an unassuming white suit rather than one of his outrageous Johnny Too Bad outfits, he put on an unassuming performance of mostly interchangeable songs. His new album, *Music Maker,* also suffers from a lack of excitement and variety. So, come to think of it, do the two other albums that have come out since the movie sound track. You can get it if you really want, but, Jimmy, you gotta want it more. . . . Maybe I'm just a Blue Meanie, but in my opinion Tom O'Horgan's *Sgt. Pepper* extravaganza, at the Beacon Theatre, represents some sort of apotheosis of pointless, mindless theatrics. I did enjoy the giant octopus puppet—which should have been in the Macy's Parade—and John Lennon, who was sitting three rows behind me, looking sexier than ever.

The Best of '74
JANUARY 1975

Since New Year's, I've received several letters from readers asking why I haven't come across with a ten-best-albums list. One letter wondered acerbically if I regarded such a project as too frivolous for a serious critic. Perish the thought! The list game is as integral to rock as statistics are to baseball. In fact, it's not criticism I've been taking too seriously all these years but list making. I worry over my criteria. (Do I pick the albums I play most or the ones I admire most?) Then I worry over the imperatives of the list itself, which transcend the merits of particular records. (To be truly satisfying, for instance, a ten-best list should have some sort of aesthetic and historical balance; if it doesn't, something is wrong with the year's output of albums or the reviewer's listening habits, or both. And I hate to make arcane choices of albums that only I and three other critics have heard; sometimes it's necessary, but it makes the list less elegant.) Before I know it, it's May, and a ten-best list in May has all the appeal of a baseball game in January. But this, folks, is next year—inspired by those letters and the *Village Voice* critics' poll, I've gotten it together. Here, with apologies for past derelictions but no promises for the future, are my ten favorite albums of 1974.

(1) Bob Dylan, *Planet Waves*. I listen to it all the time, love it more and more, and hear new subtleties in it (especially in view of those on-again, off-again divorce rumors). Dylan's extraordinary singing has all the emotional range and complexity that the lyrics here (except for "Wedding Song") lack. I think that the words on *Planet Waves* are meant mainly as filler—that Dylan is trying to get out from under his reputation as a poet and force us to concentrate on his music. He should know better than to imagine that any lyric he writes can escape close attention; still, the more I am seduced by his voice, the less the verbal shortcomings matter.

(2) Van Morrison, *It's Too Late to Stop Now*. Few live albums are really successful; in most cases they sacrifice the discipline of the studio without achieving anything like the immediacy of a performance. This one, miraculously, does fine on both counts. Obviously, Morrison is as capable as ever of both passion and control. Which makes me wonder why his most recent studio albums have been so pallid, and why his concerts are so self-indulgent that they put me to sleep.

(3) Bob Dylan and The Band, *Before the Flood*. I never could talk about "psychedelic music" without feeling a little silly, but this record of the Dylan-Band tour may be the first album that actually deserves the phrase. I suspect that to fully appreciate that comment—or the album—you have to have been there, but for me, at least, *Before the Flood* comes so close to re-creating a religious experience that it's scary. In places, this album is the aural equivalent of an enlarged photograph—a record of a performance, with all its details magnified and clarified. When I saw Dylan

and the Band at the Garden, I was too excited about Dylan to realize how amazing the Band's performance was. I realize it now.

(4) Eric Clapton, *461 Ocean Boulevard.* An album with the texture of rock and the feeling of country blues, relaxed without being limp, modest without being diffident, sensual without being especially sexy, white without being racist, good-humored yet ever-cognizant of the link between blues and pain. Particularly brilliant: Clapton's version of "Willie and the Hand Jive"; his guitar on "Let It Grow."

(5) New York Dolls, *In Too Much Too Soon.* Some people think the Dolls are a rip-off of the Rolling Stones. Then again, some people think the Stones are a rip-off of Chuck Berry. Does this album really capture the spirit of the seventies? Or just the seventies as I wish they were?

(6) Rolling Stones, *It's Only Rock & Roll.* They said it; I didn't.

(7) Stevie Wonder, *Fulfillingness' First Finale.* I don't like this record quite as much as *Talking Book* or *Innervisions,* but that may be because they came first. And though I continue to be ambivalent about Wonder's religious pretensions, anyone who can compel me to love a song called "Heaven Is 10 Zillion Light Years Away" must be synching into *some* sort of cosmic reality. At the other extreme, "You Haven't Done Nothin'" is the most cathartic diatribe to come along since "You're So Vain."

(8) Bachman-Turner Overdrive, *Not Fragile.* No, I haven't forgiven Randy Bachman for writing "American Woman," and I'm still not crazy about his sensibility, but even if this album's exuberant version of heavy weren't irresistible I would have to consider it on the basis of the title alone. My favorite cut, "Roll On Down the Highway," would qualify the group as the American Slade if it weren't Canadian.

(9) Gladys Knight and the Pips, sound track from *Claudine.* The movie, in spite of being about a black welfare family, was in certain respects a very middle-class saga; Gladys Knight, a woman who has shown, among other things, that it's possible to be a frankly middle-class soul singer without being gutless, does a fine job of interpreting Curtis Mayfield's score. Though nothing on this record is as exciting as the best songs on

Imagination—an album that would also have been on my list, aesthetic balance or no, if it hadn't been released at the tail end of 1973—it's more consistent; the only bad cut is a boring instrumental.

(10) Gram Parsons, *Grievous Angel*. There are albums I played more last year, and albums I admired more, but none that moved me more. Parsons was one of the few singers who could make me feel an emotional connection to country music. It wasn't just that he brought an urban bohemian's sensibility to the songs he wrote or selected but that he went beneath the genre's provincial surface—which is exactly what most country-rockers dig on—straight to the bleak loneliness and vulnerability at its core. His singing on this album has made me shiver more than once. It sounds like glib hindsight to suggest that he was hinting at his death, but how else can I take lines like "Put out the flames and set this cold heart free"?

Liner Notes from Lou Reed's Rock and Roll Diary, 1967–1980
1980

For those of us who are always confronting our own history through rock and roll, this album is more than the summation of one artist's career; it is the spiritual record of a decade in the life. During the '70s, virtually every significant development in rock and roll has borne Lou Reed's imprint. As composer and lead singer for the Velvet Underground, Reed more or less invented the genre of rock and roll—"avant-punk," as Robert Christgau has aptly labeled it—that became the basis of the punk rock/ new wave explosion. On his own, he has struggled with the confusions of contemporary life, and of his own evolving persona, in ways that implicitly criticize the music he inspired.

Because Reed's music so brilliantly evokes the bleakness and constriction that seemed to define the '70s, it is easy to forget that his prophetic early work made a radical break with the prevailing musical and social atmosphere. The mid-'60s were above all an era of good feeling. The utopian mood spread from the West Coast, even penetrating the skeptical marrow of New Yorkers. We were all getting high with a little help from the Beatles and the San Francisco acid rock bands, digging their promises of expanded consciousness, universal love, limitless possibility. Who could resist?

In the midst of all this euphoria the Velvet Underground began performing in New York's East Village with Andy Warhol's mixed media show, the Exploding Plastic Inevitable. Their publicity, which ran to phrases like "a total bombardment of the senses," suggested that the Velvets were yet another psychedelic band—and in a way they were. But their brand of sensory bombardment could not have been more at odds with the era of good feeling. Their terrain was the city at its hardest and sleaziest. Their music was as painful as it was compelling, assaulting the ear with excruciating distortion and chaotic noise barely contained by the repetitive rhythms of rock and roll. Their themes were perversity, desperation, and death. Instead of celebrating psychedelic trips, they showed us the devastating power, horror, and false transcendence of heroin addiction; they dared to intimate that sadomasochism might have more to do with their—and our—reality than universal love. Musically as well as verbally, they insisted that the possibility, far from being limitless, was continually being stifled and foreclosed. At a time when hippie rock musicians were infatuated with the spontaneous jam, the Velvets' music was cerebral, stylized. They maintained a poignant ironic tension between the tight, formal structure of the songs and their bursts of raw noise, between their high artfulness and their street-level content, between fatalism and rebellion.

Though the Velvets' overall sound owed nearly as much to John Cale, Sterling Morrison, and Maureen Tucker as to Lou Reed, it was Reed who defined the band's sensibility, embodied its contradictions. He was a romantic alienated bohemian and an antiromantic pop ironist, a middle-class Jewish kid from Brooklyn who came on like a streetwise punk in tight jeans and shades, a classical piano student turned rock and roller, Bob Dylan-cum-Nelson Algren-cum-Jean Genet. He talked his songs in an expressive semi-mumble that made you think of James Dean without the naïveté.

Not that Lou did not display his own kind of innocence. His songs hinted, when you least expected it, that underneath the meanness and paranoia, the affectless brutality that smothered pain, there was after all the possibility of love. His depictions of urban hell contained occasional glimpses of redemption. Still, the inhabitants of Reed's universe experienced love mainly through its absence; the glimpses were not only rare but as likely as not to be illusory.

The group's first album, *The Velvet Underground and Nico,* came out in 1967, the same year the Beatles released *Sgt. Pepper.* It offered an extended tour of the urban underworld that included the now-classic "Waiting for the Man" and "Heroin." The latter, a saga of a man on his way to spiritual death, fighting and embracing it at once, is the most profoundly moving and disturbing drug song ever written. LP number two, *White Light/White Heat,* was even darker in its vision and more relentlessly, abrasively discordant; the title song epitomized the album's tone of rising hysteria. This least accessible and most overtly experimental of the Velvets' albums was also the last to which John Cale contributed. *The Velvet Underground,* made without Cale and released in 1969, was markedly different in both its sound and its mood. The music was almost folk-like in its simplicity; the lyrics emphasized a theme that had for the most part remained implicit in the earlier albums—the yearning for an all too elusive innocence and spiritual freedom. In songs like "Pale Blue Eyes" and that joyful, goofy hymn to/parody of enlightenment, "Beginning to See the Light," Lou Reed acknowledged the vulnerability his supercool punks, junkies, and androgynes could deny but never quite extinguish.

Loaded was again a departure from the Velvets' previous work. Formally it was closer to classic rock and roll, pared down to its most basic structures. It commented on earlier rock genres, urban life, and romantic fantasies with a playful, deadpan wit. *Loaded* is probably the Velvets' most influential record; two cuts in particular, "Sweet Jane" and "Rock & Roll" may well be Reed's most influential songs. It was also the group's last studio album. In August 1970, in the wake of the Velvets' legendary gig at Max's Kansas City (tapes of which were later released as an "official bootleg"), Lou Reed abruptly quit the band, effectively breaking it up: soon afterward he went off to England for two years. Posthumously the Velvets released *1969 Velvet Underground Live,* a two-record set that contains some fine performances, among them the version of "Heroin" included in this anthology. And that—much to the dismay of the Velvets' small but passionate cult—was that.

It made sense for Reed to choose England as his temporary base for building a new identity as a solo performer: it was a change of scene, and at the same time more receptive than any other place outside of New York to formal experiments with rock and roll. Lou's first solo album, *Lou Reed,* sounded tentative, as if he had not quite settled on a voice (though several of its cuts—"Lisa Says," "I Love You," "Wild Child"—are sentimental favorites of mine). Then he hired David Bowie (who had included a musical tribute to the Velvets on *Hunky Dory*) to produce his second album. The album, *Transformer,* referred directly and explicitly to gay life and transvestitism. The subject matter was not new but Reed's attitude toward it was—he was now openly identifying with a subculture he had always viewed obliquely, from a protective ironic distance.

Both lyrically and musically, *Transformer* was less intellectual and more pop than Reed's work with the Velvet Underground. At first I thought it was disappointingly conventional, lacking in the Velvets' subtlety. That judgment turned out to be a joke on me: *Transformer* is as easy to take as medicine that tastes like honey and kicks you in the throat. Take a song like "Perfect Day," a lovely, soft ode to an idyll in the park . . . or is it? But the album's deceptively ordinary surface had commercial appeal, which was no doubt part of the point. The Velvets' critically acclaimed obscurity had been frustrating for Reed. Is there such a thing as a rock and roller who does not dream of connecting with the mass audience? Propelled by the hit single "Walk on the Wild Side," *Transformer* went gold, and in 1973 Lou Reed was finally a pop star.

Berlin followed that fall. The metaphor of the divided city—which has been picked up by '70s rock and rollers from David Bowie to Johnny Rotten—and a loose narrative line provided the framework for a stark record of emotional destruction closer in tone and spirit to the Velvets' first album than anything Reed had done since. *Berlin* was full of insights you'd just as soon not have into the painful nuances of the war between the sexes. It was not easy to take on any level, and it was not popular.

Nonetheless Reed continued to broaden his audience with two live albums and *Sally Can't Dance.* He then did his best to discourage it with *Metal Machine Music,* a double album of electronic noise that some critics pronounced an interesting experiment, others a moral outrage. ("It's the only record I know that *attacks* the listener," was Lou's proud assessment.) Next came *Coney Island Baby,* with its luminescent title song, to remind us that Reed had a tender underbelly; then a switch of record labels and *Rock and Roll Heart.* In much of his mid-'70s work, Reed seems once again to be casting around for a direction, trying on stances. If *Metal Machine Music* attacks the listener, Lou's studio albums from this period are if anything a bit restrained and polite. Not coincidentally, these were the worst of times for rock and roll: New York's early '70s punk/glitter scene had not quite recovered from the breakup of the Dolls. Jonathan Richman had gone acoustic, Iggy Pop had disappeared, Mott the Hoople had drowned in self-pity. The middlebrow complacency of mainstream rock acted even on those of us who rejected it as a kind of cultural novocaine. Since it was no longer necessary to define himself against the grain of the '60s, or possibly to draw on—and contribute to—the energy of a vital rock and roll community, Lou Reed was, like so many lesser artists, thrown back on himself, and his isolation showed.

But rebellion was brewing, and in 1977 the new wave broke. The punk rockers were clearly the Velvets' children, a tribute to and vindication of Lou Reed's genius. At the same time, like all kids, they were not an unmixed blessing. For one thing their arrival made Reed, willy-nilly, a grand old man, posing an implicit challenge: are you over the hill? Besides, though Reed and his aesthetic offspring shared a hard-nosed iconoclasm, their outlooks were very different. The punks assumed an aggressively nihilistic pose—life was meaningless, love a bad joke. Reed was a pessimist, not a cynic. He saw nihilism as a seductive but evil escape and believed that however desperate the odds, the struggle for love was a moral and spiritual necessity.

Reed's first post–new wave album, *Street Hassle,* was and is both an answer to the challenge and a magnificent restatement of Reed's fundamental humanism. In my opinion its title song is (along with "Heroin") his greatest work. During this eleven-minute exploration of sex, death, and love, Reed nails himself and the punks and you and me to the wall—then frees us. *Take No Prisoners,* a two-record live set, is a further reaffirmation. "So now everybody's gonna say Lou Reed's mellowed, he's older," Lou complains to the audience, before launching into a performance of "Street Hassle" that's as mellow as a razor blade.

In his most recent albums, *The Bells* and *Growing Up in Public,* Reed has continued—as if he were picking a scab—to expose his/our need for love and stubborn defenses against it. He is angry, sad, and compassionate about the awful failures of empathy that pass for love between women and men, parents and children, even friends. He wants to believe in the most sentimental, romantic clichés and can't quite pull it off. Nor can he believe, finally, that the clichés are entirely false. The song that says it best, I think, is "All Through the Night": *Have you ever played with an all-night band and gone through it all through the night?*

　　With a daytime of sin and a nighttime of hell, everybody's gonna look for a bell to ring all through the night.

　　Could anyone but Lou Reed get away with suggesting that our lives—or at least our souls—may still be saved by rock and roll? On to the '80s.

The Velvet Underground
FROM GREIL MARCUS'S *STRANDED*, 1979

I'LL LET YOU BE IN MY DREAM

A change of fantasy: I have just won the first annual Keith Moon Memorial Essay Contest. (This year's subject was "Is Ecstasy Dead?") The prize is a fallout shelter in the bowels of Manhattan, reachable only through a secret entrance in CBGB's basement. It is fully stocked: on entering the contest I was asked to specify my choice of drugs (LSD), junk food (Milky Way), T-shirt ("Eat the Rich"), book *(Parade's End)*, movie *(The Wizard of Oz)*,[1] rock-and-roll single ("Anarchy in the U.K."), and rock-and-roll album. The album is *Velvet Underground,* an anthology culled from the Velvets' first three LPs. (My specially ordered version of this collection is slightly different from the original; for "Afterhours," a song I've never liked much, it substitutes "Pale Blue Eyes," one of my favorites.) The songs on *Velvet Underground* are all about sin and salvation. As luck would have it, I am inspecting my winnings at the very moment that a massive earthquake destroys a secret biological warfare laboratory inside the Indian Point nuclear power plant, contaminating New York City with a virulent, radioactive form of Legionnaires' disease. It seems that I will be contemplating sin and salvation for a long time to come.

Originally published in *Stranded: Rock and Roll for a Desert Island,* edited by Greil Marcus. New York: Knopf, 1979. The anthology was a compilation of critics' responses to the question "What rock-and-roll album would you take to a desert island?"

1. On second thought, I'd rather have *Gone With the Wind,* or maybe *The Harder They Come.*

I LOVE THE SOUND OF BREAKING GLASS

In New York City in the middle sixties the Velvet Underground's lead singer, guitarist, and auteur, Lou Reed, made a fateful connection between two seemingly disparate ideas—the rock-and-roller as self-conscious aesthete and the rock-and-roller as self-conscious punk. (Though the word *punk* was not used generically until the early seventies, when critics began applying it to unregenerate rock-and-rollers with an aggressively lower-class style, the concept goes all the way back to Elvis.) The Velvets broke up in 1970, but the aesthete-punk connection was carried on, mainly in New York and England, by Velvets-influenced performers like Mott the Hoople, David Bowie (in his All the Young Dudes rather than his Ziggy Stardust mode), Roxy Music and its offshoots, the New York Dolls and the lesser protopunk bands that played Manhattan's Mercer Arts Center before it (literally) collapsed, the antipunk Modern Lovers, the archpunk Iggy Stooge/Pop. By 1977, the same duality had surfaced in new ways, with new force, under new conditions, to become the basis of rock-and-roll's new wave.

There are important differences, both temperamental and musical, that divide today's punks and punkoids from the Velvets and other precursors and from each other; American punk (still centered in New York) and its British counterpart are not only different but in a sense opposed. Yet all this music belongs to a coherent genre, implicitly defined by the tension between the term *punk* and the more inclusive *new wave*, with its arty connotations. If the Velvets invented this genre, it was clearly anticipated by the Who: Pete Townshend, after all, is something of an aesthete, and Roger Daltrey something of a punk. It was not surprising that the impulse to make music that united formal elegance and defiant crudity should arise among working-class Englishmen and take shape among New York bohemians; each environment was, in its own way, highly structured and ridden with conflict. And as a vehicle for that impulse, rock-and-roll had unique advantages: it was defiantly crude, yet for those who were tuned in to it, it was also a musical, verbal, and emotional language rich in formal possibilities.

The Who, the Velvets, and the new wave bands have all shared this conception of rock-and-roll; their basic aesthetic assumptions have little to do with what is popularly known as "art rock." The notion of rock-as-art inspired by Dylan's conversion to the electric guitar—the idea of making rock-and-roll more musically and lyrically complex, of combining elements of jazz, folk, classical, and avant-garde music with a rock beat, of creating "rock opera" and "rock poetry"—was from the rock-and-roll fan's perspective a dubious one. At best it stimulated a vital and imaginative eclecticism that spread the values of rock-and-roll even as it diffused and diluted them. At worst it rationalized a form of cultural upward mobility, concerned with achieving the appearance and pretensions of art rather than the reality—the point being to "improve" rock-and-roll by making it palatable to the upper middle class. Either way, it submerged rock-and-roll in something more amorphous and high-toned called rock. But from the early sixties (Phil Spector was the first major example) there was a countertradition in rock-and-roll that had much more in common with "high" art—in particular avant-garde art—than the ballyhooed art-rock syntheses: it involved more or less consciously using the basic formal canons of rock-and-roll as material (much as the pop artists used mass art in general) and refining, elaborating, playing off that material to produce what might be called rock-and-roll art. While art rock was implicitly based on the claim that rock-and-roll was or could be as worthy as more established art forms, rock-and-roll art came out of an obsessive commitment to the language of rock-and-roll and an equally obsessive disdain for those who rejected that language or wanted it watered down, made easier. In the sixties the best rock often worked both ways: the special virtue of sixties culture was its capacity for blurring boundaries, transcending contradictions, pulling off everything at once. But in the seventies the two tendencies have increasingly polarized: while art rock has fulfilled its most philistine possibilities in kitsch like Yes (or, for that matter, Meat Loaf), the new wave has inherited the countertradition, which is both less popular and more conscious of itself *as* a tradition than it was a decade ago.

The Velvets straddled the categories. They were nothing if not eclectic: their music and sensibility suggested influences as diverse as Bob Dylan and Andy Warhol, Peter Townshend and John Cage; they experimented with demented feedback and isolated, pure notes and noise for noise's sake; they were partial to sweet, almost folk-like melodies; they played the electric viola on "Desolation Row." But they were basically rock-and-roll artists, building their songs on a beat that was sometimes implied rather than heard, on simple, tough, pithy lyrics about their hard-edged urban demimonde, on rock-and-roll's oldest metaphor for modern city life—anarchic energy contained by a tight, repetitive structure. Some of the Velvets' best songs—"Heroin," especially—redefined how rock-and-roll was supposed to sound. Others—"I'm Waiting for the Man," "White Light/White Heat," "Beginning to See the Light," "Rock & Roll"—used basic rock-and-roll patterns to redefine how the music was supposed to feel.

The Velvets were the first important rock-and-roll artists who had no real chance of attracting a mass audience. This was paradoxical. Rock-and-roll was a mass art, whose direct, immediate appeal to basic emotions subverted class and educational distinctions and whose formal canons all embodied the perception that mass art was not only possible but satisfying in new and liberating ways. Insofar as it incorporates the elite, formalist values of the avant-garde, the very idea of rock-and-roll art rests on a contradiction. Its greatest exponents—the Beatles, the Stones, and (especially) the Who—undercut the contradiction by making the surface of their music deceptively casual, then demolished it by reaching millions of kids. But the Velvets' music was too overtly intellectual, stylized, and distanced to be commercial. Like pop art, which was very much a part of the Velvets' world, it was antiart art made by antielite elitists. Lou Reed's aesthete-punk persona, which had its obvious precedent in the avant-garde tradition of artist-as-criminal-as-outlaw, was also paradoxical in the context of rock-and-roll. The prototypical rock-and-roll punk was the (usually white) working-class kid hanging out on the corner with his (it was usually his) pals; by middle-class and/or adult standards he might be a fuck-off, a hell-raiser, even a delinquent, but he was not really sinister or criminal. Reed's punk was closer to that bohemian (and usually black) hero, the hipster: he wore shades, took hard drugs, engaged in various forms of polymorphous perversity; he didn't just hang out on the corner, he lived out on the street, and he was a loner.

As white exploitation of black music, rock-and-roll has always had its built-in ironies, and as the music went further from its origins, the ironies got more acute. Where, say, Mick Jagger's irony was about a white middle-class English bohemian's (and later a rich rock star's) identification with and distance from his music's black American roots, his working-class image, and his teenage audience, Lou Reed's irony made a further leap. It was not only about a white middle-class Jewish bohemian's identification with and distance from black hipsters (an ambiguity neatly defined when Reed-as-junkie, waiting for his man on a Harlem street corner, is challenged, "Hey white boy! Whatchou doin' uptown?") but about his use of a mass art form to express his aesthetic and social alienation from just about everyone. And one of the forms that alienation took pointed to yet another irony. While the original, primal impulse of rock-and-roll was to celebrate the body, which meant affirming sexual and material pleasure, Reed's temperament was not only cerebral but ascetic. There was nothing resembling lustiness in the Velvets' music, let alone any hippie notions about the joys of sexual liberation. Reed did not celebrate the sadomasochism of "Venus in Furs" any more than he celebrated heroin; he only acknowledged the attraction of what he saw as flowers of evil. Nor did he share his generation's enthusiasm for hedonistic consumption—to Reed the flash of the affluent sixties was fool's gold. Like Andy Warhol and the other pop artists he responded to the aesthetic potency of mass cultural styles; like Warhol he was fascinated by decadence—that is, style without meaning or moral content; but he was unmoved by that aspect of the pop mentality, and of rock-and-roll, that got off on the American dream. In a sense, the self-conscious formalism of his music—the quality that made the Velvets uncommercial—was an attempt to purify rock-and-roll, to purge it of all those associations with material goodies and erotic good times.

Though it's probable that only the anything-goes atmosphere of the sixties could have inspired a group like the Velvets, their music was prophetic of a leaner, meaner time. They were from—and of—hardheaded, suspicious New York, not utopian, good-vibes California. For all Lou Reed's admiration of Bob Dylan, he had none of Dylan's faith in the liberating possibilities of the edge—what he had taken from *Highway 61 Revisited* and *Blonde on Blonde* was the sound of the edge fraying. Like his punk inheritors, he saw the world as a hostile place and did not expect it to change. In rejecting the optimistic consensus of the sixties, he prefigured the punks' attack on the smug consensus of the seventies; his thoroughgoing iconoclasm anticipated the punks' contempt for all authority—including the aesthetic and moral authority of rock-and-roll itself.

Throughout this decade rock-and-roll has been struggling to reclaim its identity as a music of cultural opposition, not only distinct from but antagonistic to its own cultural conglomerate, rock. The chief accomplishment of the punks has been to make that antagonism explicit and public in a way that is clearly contemporary—that is, has nothing to do with "reviving" anything except the spirit of opposition itself. What is new in rock-and-roll—what is uncomfortable and abrasive and demanding—is the extent to which it insists on a defensive stance; the authentic late seventies note is nothing so much as cranky. Though the British punk movement was in some respects a classic revolt of youth—a class-conscious revolt, at that—its self-mocking nihilism is a classic crank attitude, while the American new wave makes up in alienated smart-assism for what it lacks in shit-smearing belligerence. The power and vitality of the crank posture are attested to by the way it makes less discordant sensibilities sound corny, even to those of us who might prefer to feel otherwise. Bruce Springsteen may still pull off a credible mélange of fifties teenage-street-kid insurgency, sixties apocalyptic romance, and early/mid-seventies angst, but he is an anomaly; so is Graham Parker, whose stubborn and convincing faith in traditional rock-and-roll values recalls John Fogerty's. Patti Smith, on the other hand, is a transitional figure, half cranky messiah, half messianic crank. The rock-and-rollers who exemplify the current aesthetic do so with wide variations in intensity, from Johnny Rotten (maniacal crank) to Elvis Costello (passionate crank) to Nick Lowe or Talking Heads (cerebral cranks) to the Ramones (cranks of convenience). (The Clash, one convolution ahead, is boldly anti- or postcrank—the first eighties band?) The obvious core of their crankiness is their consciousness of themselves as a dissident minority, but it's more complicated than that. Real, undiluted rock-and-roll is almost by definition the province of a dissident minority (larger at some times than at others); it achieved its cultural hegemony in the sixties only by becoming rock—by absorbing competing cultural values and in turn being absorbed, making a new rebellion necessary. What is different now is that for the first time in the music's twenty-five-year history, rock-and-rollers seem to accept their minority status as given and even to revel in it. Which poses an enormous contradiction, for real rock-and-roll almost by definition aspires to convert the world.

In some ways the crankiness of current rock-and-rollers resembles the disaffection of an earlier era of bohemians and avant-gardists convinced they had a vision the public was too intractably stupid and complacent to comprehend. But because the vision of rock-and-roll is inherently populist, the punks can't take themselves seriously as alienated artists; their crankiness is leavened with irony. At the same time, having given up on the world, they can't really take themselves seriously as rock-and-rollers, either. They are not only antiart artists but antipeople populists—the English punks, especially, seem to abhor not only the queen, America, rich rock stars, and the uncomprehending public, but humanity itself. The punks' working-class-cum-lumpen style is implicitly political; it suggests collective opposition and therefore communal affirmation. But it is affirmation of a peculiarly limited and joyless sort. For the new wave's minimalist conception of rock-and-roll tends to exclude not only sensual pleasure but the entire range of positive human emotions, leaving only what is hard and violent, or hard and distanced, or both: if the punks make sex an obscenity, they make love an embarrassment.

In reducing rock-and-roll to its harshest essentials, the new wave took Lou Reed's aesthete-punk conceit to a place he never intended. For the Velvets the aesthete-punk stance was a way of surviving in a world that was out to kill you; the point was not to glorify the punk, or even to say fuck you to the world, but to be honest about the strategies people adopt in a desperate situation. The Velvets were not nihilists but moralists. In their universe nihilism regularly appears as a vivid but unholy temptation, love and its attendant vulnerability as scary and poignant imperatives. Though Lou Reed rejected optimism, he was enough of his time to crave transcendence. And finally—as "Rock & Roll" makes explicit—the Velvets' use of a mass art form was a metaphor for transcendence, for connection, for resistance to solipsism and despair. Which is also what it is for the punks; whether they admit it or not, that is what *their* irony is about. It may be sheer coincidence, but it was in the wake of the new wave that Reed recorded "Street Hassle," a three-part, eleven-minute anti-nihilist anthem that is by far the most compelling piece of work he has done in his post-Velvets solo career. In it he represents nihilism as double damnation: loss of faith that love is possible, compounded by denial that it matters. "That's just a lie," he mutters at the beginning of part three. "That's why she tells her friends. 'Cause the real song—the real song she won't even admit to herself."

THE REAL SONG, OR I'LL NEVER BE YOUR MIRROR

If the Velvets suggested continuity between art and violence, order and chaos, they posed a radical split between body and spirit. In this way too they were closer to the Who than to any other contemporaries. Like the Velvets the Who were fundamentally ascetic; they too saw the world as hostile—particularly the world as organized by the British class system. Their defiance was cruder than the Velvets', their early music as hard and violent as any to come out of the new wave. But they were not cranks; they were determined to convert the world, and Townshend's guitar smashing expressed his need to break through to his audience as well as his contempt for authority, including the authority of rock-and-roll itself. That need to connect also took another form: even before Townshend discovered Meher Baba, the Who's music had a side that could only be called religious. If it seemed, at first, surprising that the same band could produce music as uncompromising in its bitterness as "Substitute" and as miraculously transcendent as the "You are forgiven!" chorus of "A Quick One," it was no contradiction; on the contrary, it was precisely Townshend's sense of the harshness of life, the implacability of the world, that generated his spiritual hunger.

The same can be said of Lou Reed, except that *spiritual hunger* seems too self-important a phrase to apply to him; the Velvets' brand of spirituality has little in common with the Who's grand bursts of mystical ecstasy or Townshend's self-conscious preoccupation with the quest for enlightenment. It's impossible to imagine Lou Reed taking up with a guru, though he might well write a savagely funny (and maybe chillingly serious) song about one. The aesthete-punk and his fellow demimondaines are not seeking enlightenment, though they stumble on it from time to time; like most of us they are pilgrims in spite of themselves. For Townshend moral sensitivity is a path to spiritual awareness; for Reed awareness and the lack—or refusal—of it have an intrinsically moral dimension. While he is not averse to using the metaphors of illusion and enlightenment—sometimes to brilliant effect, as in "Beginning to See the Light" and "I'll Be Your Mirror"—they are less central to his theology than the concepts of sin and grace, damnation and salvation. Some of his songs ("Heroin," "Jesus," "Pale Blue Eyes") explicitly invoke that Judeo-Christian language; many more imply it.

But *theology* too is an unfairly pretentious word. The Velvets do not deal in abstractions but in states of mind. Their songs are about the feelings the vocabulary of religion was invented to describe—profound and unspeakable feelings of despair, disgust, isolation, confusion, guilt, longing, relief, peace, clarity, freedom, love—and about the ways we (and they) habitually bury those feelings, deny them, sentimentalize them, mock them, inspect them from a safe, sophisticated distance in order to get along in the hostile, corrupt world. For the Velvets the roots of sin are in this ingrained resistance to facing our deepest, most painful, and most sacred emotions; the essence of grace is the comprehension that our sophistication is a sham, that our deepest, most painful, most sacred desire is to recover a childlike innocence we have never, in our heart of hearts, really lost. And the essence of love is sharing that redemptive truth: on the Velvets' first album, which is dominated by images of decadence and death, suddenly, out of nowhere, comes Nico's artless voice singing, "I'll be your mirror / . . . The light on your door to show that you're home. / When you think the night has seen your mind / That inside you're twisted and unkind / . . . Please put down your hands, 'cause I see you."

For a sophisticated rock-and-roll band with a sophisticated audience this vision is, to say the least, risky. The idea of childlike innocence is such an invitation to bathos that making it credible seems scarcely less difficult than getting the camel of the Gospels through the needle's eye. And the Velvets' alienation is also problematic: it's one thing for working-class English kids to decide life is shit, but how bad can things be for Lou Reed? Yet the Velvets bring it off—make us believe/admit that the psychic wounds we inflict on each other are real and terrible, that to scoff at innocence is to indulge in a desperate lie—because they never succumb to self-pity. Life may be a brutal struggle, sin inevitable, innocence elusive and transient, grace a gift, not a reward ("Some people work very hard / But still they never get it right," Lou Reed observes in "Beginning to See the Light"); nevertheless we are responsible for who and what we become. Reed does not attempt to resolve this familiar spiritual paradox, nor does he regard it as unfair. His basic religious assumption (like Baudelaire's) is that like it or not we inhabit a moral universe, that we have free will, that we must choose between good and evil, and that our choices matter absolutely. If we are rarely strong enough to make the right choices, if we can never count on the moments of illumination that make them possible, still it is spiritual death to give up the effort.

That the Velvets are hardly innocents, that they maintain their aesthetic and emotional distance even when describing—and evoking—utter spiritual nakedness, does not undercut what they are saying; if anything, it does the opposite. The Velvets compel belief in part because, given its context, what they are saying is so bold: not only do they implicitly criticize their own aesthetic stance—they risk undermining it altogether, ending up with sincere but embarrassingly banal home truths. The risk is real because the Velvets do not use irony as a net, a way of evading responsibility by keeping everyone guessing about what they really mean. On the contrary, their irony functions as a metaphor for the spiritual paradox, affirming that the need to face one's nakedness and the impulse to cover it up are equally real, equally human. If the Velvets' distancing is self-protective (hence in their terms damning), it is also revelatory (hence redeeming); it makes clear that the feelings being protected are so unbearably intense that if not controlled and contained they would overwhelm both the Velvets and their audience. The Velvets' real song is how hard it is to admit, even to themselves.

That song in its many variations is the substance of *Velvet Underground.* This album can be conceived of—nonlinearly; the cuts are not at all in the right order—as the aesthete-punk's *Pilgrim's Progress,* in four movements. ("Sha la la, man, whyn't you just slip away?" I can hear Lou Reed say to that.)

One: Worldly Seduction and Betrayal

"Sunday Morning," a song about vague and ominous anxiety, sums up the emotional tone of this movement: "Watch out, the world's behind you." "Here She Comes Now" and "Femme Fatale," two songs about beautiful but unfeeling women (in the unlovable tradition of pop—not to mention religious—misogyny, Lou Reed's women are usually demonic or angelic icons, not people), sum up its philosophy: "Aah, it looks so good / Aah, but she's made out of wood." These songs underscore the point by juxtaposing simple, sweet, catchy melodies with bitter lyrics sung in flat, almost affectless voices (in "Sunday Morning," Reed's voice takes on a breathiness that suggests suppressed panic). "White Light/White Heat," a song about shooting speed, starts out by coming as close as any Velvets song does to expressing the euphoria of sheer physical energy; by the end of the trip the music has turned into bludgeoning, deadening noise, the words into a semiarticulate mumble.

Two: The Sin of Despair

"Heroin" is the Velvets' masterpiece—seven minutes of excruciating spiritual extremity. No other work of art I know about has made the junkie's experience so powerful, so horrible, so appealing; listening to "Heroin" I feel simultaneously impelled to somehow save this man and to reach for the needle. The song is built around the tension between the rush and the nod—expressed musically by an accelerating beat giving way to slow, solemn chords that sound like a bell tolling; metaphorically by the addict's vision of smack as a path to transcendence and freedom, alternating with his stark recognition that what it really offers is the numbness of death, that his embrace of the drug ("It's my wife and it's my life") is a total, willful rejection of the corrupt world, other people, feeling. In the beginning he likens shooting up to a spiritual journey: he's gonna try for the Kingdom; when he's rushing on his run he feels like Jesus's son. At the end, with a blasphemous defiance that belies his words, he avows, "Thank your God that I'm not aware / And thank God that I just don't care!" The whole song seems to rush outward and then close in on itself, on the moment of truth when the junkie knowingly and deliberately chooses death over life—chooses damnation. It is the clarity of his consciousness that gives the sin its enormity. Yet the clarity also offers a glimmer of redemption. In the very act of choosing numbness the singer admits the depths of his pain and bitterness, his longing for something better; he is aware of every nuance of his rejection of awareness; he sings a magnificently heartfelt song about how he doesn't care. (A decade later, Johnny Rotten will do the same thing in an entirely different way.) A clear, sustained note runs through the song like a bright thread; it fades out or is drowned out by chaotic, painful distortion and feedback, then comes through again, like the still small voice of the soul. Reed ends each verse with the refrain, "And I guess that I just don't know." His fate is not settled yet.

Three: Paradise Sought, Glimpsed, Recollected

This movement consists of four songs about world-weary sophistication and the yearning for innocence. "Candy Says" defines the problem: "I've come to hate my body and all that it requires in this world / . . . I'd like to know completely what others so discreetly talk about." "Jesus" is a prayer: "Help me in my weakness, for I've fallen out of grace." In "I'm Set Free" the singer has his illumination, but even as he tries to tell about it, to pin it down, it slips away: "I saw my head laughing, rolling on the ground / And now I'm set free to find a new illusion." In "Pale Blue Eyes" the world has gotten in the way of the singer's transcendent love: "If I could make the world as pure and strange as what I see / I'd put you in the mirror I put in front of me."

Musically these songs are of a piece. They are all gentle, reflective. They all make use of the tension between flat, detached voices and sweet melodies. They all have limpid guitar lines that carry the basic emotion, which is bittersweet: it is consoling to know that innocence is possible, inexpressibly painful that it always seems just out of reach. In "Pale Blue Eyes" a tambourine keeps the beat or, rather, is slightly off where the beat ought to be, while a spectacular guitar takes over completely, rolling in on wave after wave of pure feeling.

Four: Salvation and Its Pitfalls

"Beginning to See the Light" is the mirror held up to "Heroin." I've always been convinced that it's about an acid trip, perhaps because I first really heard it during one and found it utterly appropriate. Perhaps also because both the song and the acid made me think of a description of a peyote high by a Beat writer named Jack Green: "A group of us, on peyote, had little to share with a group on marijuana; the marijuana smokers were discussing questions of the utmost profundity and we were sticking our fingers in our navels & giggling." In "Beginning to See the Light" enlightenment (or salvation) is getting out from under the burden of self-seriousness, of egotism, of imagining that one's sufferings fill the universe; childlike innocence means being able to play. There is no lovelier moment in rock-and-roll than when Lou Reed laughs and sings, with amazement, joy, gratitude, "I just wanta tell you, *everything* is all right!"

But "Beginning to See the Light" is also wickedly ironic. Toward the end, carried away by euphoria, Reed cries, "There are problems in these times / But ooh, none of them are mine!" Suddenly we are through the mirror, back to the manifesto of "Heroin": "I just don't care!" Enlightenment has begotten spiritual pride, a sin that like its inverted form, nihilism, cuts the sinner off from the rest of the human race. Especially from those people who, you know, work very hard but never get it right. Finally we are left with yet another version of the spiritual paradox: to experience grace is to be conscious of it; to be conscious of it is to lose it.

CODA: I'D LOVE TO TURN YOU ON

Like all geniuses, Lou Reed is unpredictable. In "Street Hassle" he does as good a job as anyone of showing what was always missing in his and the Velvets' vision. As the song begins, a woman (or transvestite?) in a bar is buying a night with a sexy young boy. This sort of encounter is supposed to be squalid; it turns out to be transcendent. Reed's account of the odd couple's lovemaking is as tender as it is erotic: "And then sha la la la la he entered her slowly and showed her where he was coming from / And then sha la la la la he made love to her gently, it was like she'd never ever come." Of course, in part two he almost takes it all back by linking sex with death. Still.

What it comes down to for me—as a Velvets fan, a lover of rock-and-roll, a New Yorker, an aesthete, a punk, a sinner, a sometime seeker of enlightenment (and love) (and sex)—is this: I believe that we are all, openly or secretly, struggling against one or another kind of nihilism. I believe that body and spirit are not really separate, though it often seems that way. I believe that redemption is never impossible and always equivocal. But I guess that I just don't know.

The Decade in Rock Lyrics
FROM *VILLAGE VOICE*, JANUARY 1980

I ran into a bunch of Martians in Times Square. "Tell me the story of your people," they said. "Listen to rock and roll," I said. They did not comprehend. I took them home with me, grabbed the first record I saw, which happened to be "That'll Be the Day," and stuck it on the turntable. "Well?" I said impatiently. "What do you think?" The Martian next to me nodded appreciatively. "I like your music. It sounds a lot like Buddy Holly."

After that, I decided the only possible way to celebrate the end of the '70s was to compile a history of the decade in rock lyrics. What follows is the barest outline; space limitations have forced me to leave out many crucial subjects, including friendship, family life, teenage pregnancy, the subway, Iran, and the energy crisis (though the discerning reader will note this last as an implicit theme throughout). Rather than use up more space in a futile attempt to figure out what it all means, I'll let the lyrics speak for themselves. I will say, however, that on balance Linda Ronstadt was probably right when she suggested that Standard Oil ought to have more power than the Eagles.

THE PAST

> The dream is over, what can I say?
>
> *—John Lennon*

> We went so far out there, everybody got scared.
>
> *—Roches*

> What a long, strange trip it's been.
>
> *—Grateful Dead*

ROCK AND ROLL

> You know her life was saved by rock and roll.
>
> *—Velvet Underground*

> Rock and roll is here to stay, but who will be left to play?
>
> *—Elliott Murphy*

> I know it's only rock and roll, but I like it.
>
> *—Rolling Stones*

SEX

> Don't say a word, my virgin child
> Just let your inhibitions run wild.
>
> *—Rod Stewart*

> Ali McGraw got mad with you for giving head to
> Steve McQueen.
>
> *—Rolling Stones*

> Hey baby, you want it so fast
> Don't you know that it ain't gonna last?
> Of course, you know it makes no difference to me.
>
> *—Velvet Underground*

> I take the big plunge and oh, she was so good, oh, she was so fine
> And I'm gonna tell the world that I just ah, ah, made her mine.
>
> *—Patti Smith*

LOVE

> You stole my heart, but I love you anyway.
>
> *—Rod Stewart*

> I love you more than madness.
>
> *—Bob Dylan*

> And you, you can be mean
> And I, I'll drink all the time
> 'Cause we're lovers, and that is a fact.
>
> *—David Bowie*

> Once I had a love and it was a gas
> Soon turned out to be a pain in the ass.
>
> *—Blondie*

> I don't love you anymore
> What do you want to talk to me for?
>
> *—Ramones*

THE BATTLE OF THE SEXES

> You're so vain, you prob'ly think this song is about you.
>
> *—Carly Simon*

> You didn't know my name even when I came.
> As I recall, you let me walk home in the rain.
>
> *—Rod Stewart*

> I know you don't like weak women, you get bored so quick
> And you don't like strong women 'cause they're hip to your tricks.
>
> *—Joni Mitchell*

> She was an animal! She was a bloody disgrace!
>
> *—Sex Pistols*

> Oh bondage! Up yours!
>
> *—X-Ray Spex*

DRUGS

Legalize it, don't criticize it.
Legalize it and I will advertise it.

—Peter Tosh

No no no no, I don't smoke it no more
I'm tired of waking up on the floor.

—Ringo Starr

Drivin' that train
High on cocaine
Casey Jones you'd better watch your speed.

—Grateful Dead

If you want to be a junkie, why
Remember, Freddie's dead.

—Curtis Mayfield

THE ME DECADE

Can you cook and sew, make flowers grow
Do you understand my pain?
Are you ready to risk it all, or is your love in vain?

—Bob Dylan

ASPIRATIONS

I wanna be sedated.

—Ramones

I wanna bite the hand that feeds me.

—Elvis Costello

I wish I was your mother, I wish I'd been your father.

—Mott the Hoople

ART

I love the sound of breaking glass.

—Nick Lowe

Pablo Picasso never got called an asshole.

　　　　　　　　　　—Modern Lovers

STYLE

I saw a werewolf drinking a piña colada at Trader Vic's.
His hair was perfect.

　　　　　　　　　　—Warren Zevon

I thought you were being ironic when you ripped your jeans.

　　　　　　　　　　—Nils Lofgren

MASS MEDIA

I need TV, but I got T-Rex.

　　　　　　　　　　—Mott the Hoople

CELEBRITIES

There may be not much difference
Between Raquel Welch and Jerry Rubin
If we hear their heartbeat.

　　　　　　　　　　—Yoko Ono

BRITAIN ON AMERICA

I'm so bored with the U.S.A.

　　　　　　　　　　—Clash

American girls want everything you could possibly imagine.

　　　　　　　　　　—Rolling Stones

AMERICA ON BRITAIN

The king is gone but he's not forgotten.
Is this the story of Johnny Rotten?

　　　　　　　　　　—Neil Young

MORALS AND RELIGION

> Lighten up while you still can
> Don't even try to understand
> Just find a place to make your stand and take it easy.
>
> *—Eagles*

> Jesus died for somebody's sins, but not mine.
>
> *—Patti Smith*

THINGS FALL APART

> Save your neck or save your brother
> Looks like it's one or the other.
>
> *—The Band*

> You can't leave 'cause your heart is there
> But you can't stay, 'cause you been somewhere else.
>
> *—Sly and the Family Stone*

> You're gonna run to the rock for rescue, there will be no rock.
>
> *—Slickers*

> At the age of 37
> She realized she'd never
> Ride through Paris in a sports car with the warm wind in her hair.
>
> *—Marianne Faithfull*

ECONOMICS

> Oh Lord, won't you buy me a Mercedes Benz?
>
> *—Janis Joplin*

> Everybody's desperate, trying to make ends meet.
> Work all day, still can't pay the price of gasoline and meat.
>
> *—Warren Zevon*

POLITICS

> We sat and talked of revolution
> Just like two liberals in the sun.
>
> *—John Lennon*

> Them belly full but we hungry.
> A hungry mob is a angry mob.
>
> *—Bob Marley and the Wailers*

> A woman needs man's love, his love and affection
> But we don't want to live under his subjection.
>
> *—Laura Lee*

> Queer-bashers caught him, kicked in his teeth
> He was only hospitalized for a week.
> Sing if you're glad to be gay, sing if you're happy that way.
>
> *—Tom Robinson Band*

> What's so funny 'bout peace, love, and understanding?
>
> *—Elvis Costello*

HOW MANY OF THE LITTLE FELLERS DOES IT TAKE
TO CHANGE A LIGHTBULB?

> Short people got no reason to live.
>
> *—Randy Newman*

REBELS AND OUTSIDERS

> Tramps like us, baby, we were born to run.
>
> *—Bruce Springsteen*

> I say please don't talk to strangers, baby
> But she always do
> She say I'll talk to strangers if I want to, 'cause I'm a stranger, too.
>
> *—Randy Newman*

Do you think that you could make it with Frankenstein?

—*New York Dolls*

DEATH

When someone turns that blue, well it's a universal truth,
and you just know that bitch'll never fuck again.

—*Lou Reed*

LIFE

Show me your blood, John, I'll show you mine.
They say it's running even when we're asleep.

—*Yoko Ono*

KEEPING THE FAITH

And we'll walk down the avenue and we'll smile
And we'll say baby, ain't it all worthwhile
When the healing has begun.

—*Van Morrison*

Hey babe, I know that all things pass
Let's try to make this last.

—*Neil Young*

Still crazy after all these years.

—*Paul Simon*

THE FUTURE

No future, no future, no future for you!

—*Sex Pistols*

I can see clearly now, the rain is gone.
I can see all obstacles in my way.

—*Johnny Nash*

It's too late to stop now!

—*Van Morrison*

The New Talking World War III Blues
FROM SALON.COM, OCTOBER 2001

Somewhere around the fourth or fifth time I listened to Bob Dylan's new album, *Love and Theft*—after I'd finished being distracted by all the musical influences and had begun paying attention to the voice and hearing some of the words—a thirty-year-old memory surfaced: in the middle of an LSD trip I had begun to worry that my identity was dissolving or flying apart, and as a test I decided to sign my name. I was relieved to see that my signature was exactly the same as usual. And then it occurred to me how silly my worry had been. The truth was, I realized, that my "signature" was so tenacious it would be quite difficult, perhaps impossible, to get rid of even if I wanted to. After all, how many people (I would become one of them not long afterward) spent years in psychotherapy trying to change their signatures just a little bit?

From the earliest years of his career Bob Dylan has had a passionate impulse to obliterate his personal identity. That passion has, at various times, been reflected in his biographical mythmaking, his allergic reaction to his celebrity, his flirtations with religion, his compulsion to confound the expectations of his audience by constantly transforming his persona. (In the process he has often denied that the previous incarnation ever existed: Who, me? Political? A folksinger? A poet? An outlaw?) And ever since *John Wesley Harding*—his dramatic 1967 switch to acoustic "folk songs" that sound more like comments on "the folk song"—much of his work has been defined by an apparent desire to unload the baggage of his own experience and become a vessel, channeling American Music.

Of course, the counterimpulses have also been strong: Dylan has an indelible signature, not to mention an indelible ego. The essential tensions in his music have never been about electric versus acoustic but about personal and idiosyncratic versus collective and generic; topical and profane versus primordial and sacred; transcendence as excess versus transcendence as purgation; *Blonde on Blonde* versus *John Wesley Harding*; *Blood on the Tracks* versus *Time Out of Mind*.

I've always had reservations about Dylan's post-*JWH* attempts to get out of his skin, from the homage to country and western of *Nashville Skyline* to the cult of impersonality in the perversely named *Self Portrait* and his hermetic '90s renditions of old folk songs better left to ethnographers. In *Time Out of Mind*—an album I found virtually unlistenable at the time it came out to near-universal acclaim four years ago and have only now, and grudgingly, come to admire—it struck me that the self-abnegating impulse had doubled back on itself and become a particularly unpalatable form of megalomania, wherein the listener is buttonholed and forced to become a surrogate for the singer's elusive lover or muse.

Love and Theft takes up the quest for anonymity in a quite different way, or so it seems at first. It is mostly pleasant to listen to, yet its self-conscious, let's-give-them-a-tour-of-the-genres shtick is annoying: the first time Dylan did this, in 1970 on *New Morning*, there was arguably a real need to nudge parochial rock and folk fans to stretch themselves and listen to other Americas; here it merely feels like an invitation to critics to parade their musical erudition. Sifting through this album's combinations and permutations of blues, country, honky-tonk, swing, R&B, Tin Pan Alley pop, soul, was that a Chuck Berry riff?, etc., etc.—is certainly a fun game, but the best kind of eclecticism (of which Dylan's corpus is replete with examples) is still the kind that doesn't call attention to itself, that instead creates a whole greater than its parts.

Still, as I said, the game is only temporarily distracting. Soon individual songs begin to break from their generic moorings like Avalon rising out of the mist: the plangent "Mississippi"; the ominous "High Water," punctuated by background rumbles and crashes; "Sugar Baby," with its funereal echoes of "Old Man River" and the traditional "Look Down, Look Down That Lonesome Road." Then Dylan's voice hits me, not pleasant at all. It's beyond raspy, it's laryngitic, maybe consumptive, it sounds some of the time like it's coming from a great distance, through a wind tunnel or something, it's fuzzy. Stuck in the vinyl era, I keep wanting to brush away the lint from an imaginary phonograph needle. It's as impersonal as static or the coughing in a hospital ward, except that every now and then there's an echt-Dylan phrase or inflection to remind us of that signature, scrawled like graffiti into musical concrete.

I take another look at the CD cover: the front has Dylan unadorned, vulnerable, looking hardly different—faint mustache, lined face, bags under the eyes notwithstanding—from his pictures in the '60s; flip the album over and you get some kind of Mexican bandito, whose mustache, along with white hat and quarter-smile, serves as a disguise. Dylan is hardly there at all.

But it's the lyrics, finally, that make *Love and Theft* what it is—an album in which the individual and the generic, the topical and the timeless, merge with maniacal intensity: *New Morning* crossed with *Time Out of Mind*, juiced by turns with opium and speed. Talk about prophetic: "Every moment of existence seems like some dirty trick / Happiness comes suddenly and leaves just as quick / Any minute of the day the bubble could burst." And "I'm stranded in the city that never sleeps. . . . / Some things are too terrible to be true. . . . / The sun in the city leavin' at 9:45 / I'm having a hard time believing some people were ever alive." And "Oh who knows who the bell tolls for, love / It tolls for you and me" (that one rolling with the jaunty beat of the *New Morning*-ish "Moonlight"). And "High water rising, shacks are slidin' down / Folks lose their possessions, folks are leaving town. . . . / Things are breakin' up out there / High water everywhere." And "George Lewes told the Englishman, the Italian, and the Jew / You can't open up your mind, boys, to any conceivable point of view / They got Charles Darwin trapped out there on Highway 5 / Judge says to the high sheriff, I want him dead or alive."

If Dylan manages to predict the next day's news by once again tapping into the language of millennial apocalypse, he also captures contemporary anomie (his own, ours) by inventing a narrator—or narrators, it's hard to tell—who descends into the hell, or purgatory, or limbo, of America's mysterious rural past, which seems to be located mainly in the South. Contemplating the "earth and sky that melts with flesh and bone," "goin' where the wild roses grow," following the southern star, crossing rivers, staying in Mississippi a day too long, staying with his not-real Aunt Sally, dreaming of Rose's bed, proposing to marry his second cousin, our hero (or is it heroes?) (or antihero/heroes?) walks the line between love and battle, not that there's much of a difference. Between "Don't reach out for me, she said / Can't you see I'm drowning too?" and "Sugar baby, get on down the road, you ain't got no brains nohow / You went years without me, might as well keep goin' now" falls a manifesto of sorts: "I'm not sorry for nothing I've done / I'm glad I fight, I only wish we'd won." By the end, the topical is slowly submerged as the timeless closes over our heads.

It's seductive stuff, at moments as compelling as anything Dylan has ever done. And yet I find myself resisting. Something is missing, as it was in *Time Out of Mind*: the irony Dylan once used to undercut his romanticism and his I-am-America self-importance—and not least to befuddle the audience that had taken his latest posture too literally. Since you can't get away from yourself, not really, at some point you have to come to terms with that or become delusional.

In post–September 11 America, the inescapably topical is also enveloped in history and myth. In the gap where the towers used to be rise many ghosts: of our Cold War alliance with the Afghan mujahedin, the Gulf War, the fatwa against Salman Rushdie, the Iranian hostage crisis, Vietnam, the Israeli-Arab War of '67, World War II, Pearl Harbor, Hiroshima, World War I, the Civil War, the American Revolution, and beyond, back before the New World, the New Eden, was envisioned. The American imagination will be taxed with demands for unquestioning unity and generic patriotism, will be burdened or inspired by our sense of loss and defiance, identification and separateness, new tensions between individual and collective. And irony (which in some quarters has been prematurely pronounced dead) will be very, very important. The Dylan line that suits does not appear on this album. Better to go back to the beginning, to "Talking World War III Blues" with its teasing ode to mutual paranoia: "I'll let you be in my dream, if I can be in yours." Like the Woody Guthrie songs that were its inspiration, it shamelessly appropriates traditional form for contemporary purpose, and its coda is "I said that!" with the accent on the "I." You can't get any more mythically American than that.

Chapter 2

THE ADORING FAN

The Big Ones

FEBRUARY 1969

It's my theory that rock and roll happens between fans and stars, rather than between listeners and musicians—that you have to be a screaming teenager, at least in your heart, to know what's going on. Yet I must admit I was never much of a screaming teenager myself. I loved rock and roll, but I felt no emotional identification with the performers. Elvis Presley was my favorite singer, and I bought all his records; just the same, he was a stupid, slicked-up hillbilly, a bit too fat and soft to be really good-looking, and I was a middle-class adolescent snob. Jerry Lee Lewis? More revolting than Elvis. Buddy Holly? I didn't even know what he looked like. Fats Domino? He was *comic*—and black. When I went to rock shows, I screamed, all right, but only so I wouldn't be conspicuous. Actually, I grooved much more easily with records than with concerts, which forced me to recognize the social chasm separating me from the performers (and, for that matter, from much of the audience). The social-distance factor became more acute as I got older; that was one reason I defected to folk music. By the time the Beatles came on the scene, I wasn't paying much attention to rock. Naturally, I was *aware* of them, but I didn't have the slightest inkling of their importance. Their kookiness had the same effect on kids that Elvis's dirtiness had had; as far as I was concerned, the two phenomena were identical, and neither had much to do with me. I didn't realize that Elvis was to the Beatles as a Campbell Soup can is to an Andy Warhol replica. (Of course, the Beatles probably didn't realize it, either.) At first, I reacted to the Stones with equal incomprehension. Mick Jagger had his gimmick: he was a hood. The j.d. image was a familiar one, though Mick played the role with more than the usual élan. He was so aggressively illiterate, his sexual come-on was so exaggerated and tasteless that it never occurred to me he might be smart. (I didn't know then that he'd gone to the London School of Economics.) But his songs, which had all the energetic virtues of rock and roll, also displayed the honesty and clear-headedness I expected only from blues. I loved both rock and blues, but in each case my response was incomplete: rock was too superficial, blues too alien. The Stones' music was the perfect blend. And, I came to realize, so was Mick's personality; he was an outcast, but he was also thoroughly indigenous to mass society. Because he was so unequivocally native, he touched a part of me that black bluesmen and alienated folk singers could never reach. And because I couldn't condescend to him—his "vulgarity" represented a set of social and aesthetic attitudes as sophisticated as mine, if not more so—he shook me in a way Elvis had not. I became a true Stones fan—i.e., an inward screamer—and I've been one ever since.

As a fan, I feel ambivalent about *Beggars Banquet.* It's a good album—the Stones have never put out a bad one—but something of an anticlimax. This is the first Stones LP in a year, and there have been no major performances since 1966. When stars have as little contact with their public as this, everyone's fantasies get so baroque that the eventual reality rarely satisfies. (Bob Dylan has got away with this sort of thing twice; if he tries it again, he'll be pressing his luck.) Besides, *Beggars Banquet* had an unusually long gestation—the rumors of its imminent appearance began back in August. Through the fall, I followed the Stones' hassle with (British) Decca over that men's room-with-graffiti album cover. I took it for granted they'd win. The cover was really pretty innocent, and, anyway, what mere record company could thwart the Rolling Stones? But they lost. For the first time, I had to think of the Stones as losers. So even before I heard the record the reality—that black-and-white jacket designed to look like an engraved invitation—was a letdown from the fantasy.

There's another reason, also having to do with contact, that *Beggars Banquet* doesn't quite make it: I have the feeling that Jagger is responding more to the Beatles than to the world, and that the album gets to us only after bouncing off John Lennon. In a very general way, the Stones' sensibility has always been—at least in part—a revision of and a reaction to the Beatles'. But the symbiosis—or, rather, the competition—has become more pronounced and specific since *Sgt. Pepper* forced them to respond with *Their Satanic Majesties Request.* I'm not putting down *Satanic Majesties* as mere imitation, or parody, or comment. There was nothing mere about that album. The Stones showed they could do the studio thing; they did it with just the right amount of extravagance and wit, and with beautiful songs. Anyway, they could scarcely have ignored an event of *Sgt. Pepper*'s magnitude. But *Satanic Majesties* was a special record for a special time. In practice it was good, in principle very dangerous. While *Satanic Majesties* was still in the works, the Beatles released "All You Need Is Love," and the Stones countered with "We Love You," a better-conceived and more powerful song. Now the best track on *Beggars Banquet* is "Street Fighting Man," which is infinitely more intelligent than "Revolution." I sense an unworthy effort to expose John as callow. (Callowness is part of his charm anyway.) It may be that anything the Beatles can do the Stones can do better, but it never pays to work on someone else's terms. In this case, there is a special risk. What has made the Stones the Stones, more than anything else, is a passionate, thrusting ego. The Beatles' identity is collective, but the Stones are Mick Jagger. The Beatles' magic inheres in their glittering surface, the Stones' in Jagger's genius for visceral communication. Yet in this album, as in *Satanic Majesties,* Mick is—the only word for it is *leashed.* "Parachute Woman" and "Stray Cat Blues" do show traces of the old self-assertion, but in both of them bad production has made the lyrics nearly impossible to catch. In the other songs that have an "I" at all, it is weak, even passive—"Take me to the station, / And put me on a train. / I've got no expectations / To pass through here again," or "But what can a poor boy do / 'Cept to sing for a rock-and-roll band? / Guess in sleepy London town / there's just no place for a street fighting man"—or else, as in "Sympathy for the Devil," it belongs to a stock character. Most of the songs are impersonal artifacts. The "Factory Girl" is just described, not loved or sneered at. "Salt of the Earth" is positively alienating, in the Brechtian sense. What can it mean for Mick Jagger to toast the workers? Is he being sarcastic? Is the song just a musical exercise? Or is he making a sincere, if rather simpleminded, political statement? Like the Beatles, the Stones play with forms: "Prodigal Son," flawless folk blues (another political statement?); "Dear Doctor," a rather overdone parody of country music; "Jig-Saw Puzzle," proof that Jagger (or Richard) can write lyrics exactly like Dylan's. My response to these songs is basically cerebral. "Street Fighting Man" is my favorite, because it really gets down the ambiguous relation of rock and roll to rebellion. It does with politics what early rock did with sex. (Are they deliberately using the tradition, or unconsciously re-creating it?) The lyrics of the old songs had to be bland enough to be played on the radio, but the beat and arrangements that emphasized a phrase out of context here, a double entendre there got the message across. Taken together, the words of "Street Fighting Man" are innocuous, but somehow the only line that comes through loud and clear is "Summer's here, and the time is right for fighting in the streets." Then, there's the heavy beat and all that chaotic noise in the background. So Mick leaves no doubt where his instincts are. (And he didn't fool the censors, either; the single of "Street Fighting Man" was virtually boycotted by AM stations, though "Revolution" was played constantly.) But what can a poor boy do—if he wants to make some bread—'cept to sing for a rock-and-roll band? There it is. Rock is a socially acceptable, lucrative substitute for anarchy; being a rock-and-roll star is a way of beating the system, of being free in the midst of unfreedom. And I know Jagger understands the ironies involved and has no illusions about himself. (Which isn't to say he's cynical—I suspect that his famous cynicism has always been more metaphor than fact.) Still, there was a time when he applied equal energy to having no illusions about other people. It's the direct link between subject and object that I miss.

Apparently, the Stones, too, are worried that all is not right; I hear they're planning an American tour in the spring. Whether that decision stems from a desire for artistic renewal or from nervousness about declining sales doesn't matter—it's wonderful news. The Stones were never meant to be studio recluses. They need to get out and face the people.

The Beatles have also found it necessary to define themselves politically. But unlike the Stones they have little insight into their situation. Instead, they have taken refuge in self-righteousness, facile optimism, and status-mongering (revolution isn't hip, you'll scare away the chicks). Not that I believe the Beatles have any obligation to be political activists, or even political sophisticates. There are many ways to serve mankind, and one is to give pleasure. Who among the Beatles' detractors has so enriched the lives of millions of kids? No, all I ask of the Beatles is a little taste. When Bob Dylan renounced politics, he also renounced preaching. "Revolution," in contrast, reminds me of the man who refuses a panhandler and then can't resist lecturing him on the error of his ways. It takes a lot of chutzpah for a multimillionaire to assure the rest of us, "You know it's gonna be all right." And Lennon's "Change your head" line is just an up-to-date version of "Let them eat cake"; anyone in a position to follow such advice doesn't need it.

We may as well face it. Deep within John Lennon there's a fusty old Tory struggling to get out. Yet I think "Revolution" protests too much. It has been obvious for a while—ever since all the Beatles grew beards and/or mustaches and George announced "We're tired of that kiddie image"—that they're suffering growing pains of the who-am-I-and-where-am-I-going-and-how-do-my-money-and-fame-fit-in variety. When they were four silly kids jumping around on a stage, making tons of money was a rebellious act—they were thumbing their noses at the Protestant ethic. But once Leonard Bernstein had certified them as bona fide artists they began in the eyes of society to *deserve* all that money. They could no longer accept it as just part of the lark. It's no accident that the Maharishi was not only a believer in transcendental meditation but a believer in the virtue of material things. And would John have needed to write "Revolution" if on some level he hadn't felt a little defensive? He can see that all those student revolutionaries are sufficiently well off to do more or less what he's done, if on a less spectacular scale—that is, to find a personal solution within the system—yet they've chosen a far less comfortable route. I notice that in the album version of "Revolution" he has put the ambivalence right into the song: "Don't you know that you can count me out—in?" And he admitted to a *Rolling Stone* reporter that if he were black he might not be so "meek and mild." Good.

Everybody has to grow up, but few people have done it as late or as publicly as Lennon. Though Dylan also went through a protracted adolescence in front of a mass audience, he at least battled the media for every scrap of his private life. John takes us through all the changes—LSD, religion, politics, broken marriage, love affair. In the context of this openness, the nude pictures of him and Yoko are very touching. I'm sure he didn't analyze what he was doing—isn't everyone undressing these days?—but he certainly gets my most-inspired-whim-of-the-year award. What makes the pictures beautiful is that the bodies *aren't* beautiful; by choosing to reveal them John is telling his fans that celebrities aren't gods, that people shouldn't be ashamed of their bodies just because they're imperfect, that even a Beatle can love a woman who isn't a pinup. When I think of both of them looking so vulnerable, I don't resent "Revolution" so much. How can I expect someone to be right all the time?

About the new album. To get it over with, here's what I *don't* like:

(1) Calling the album *The Beatles* and packaging it in a white cover. Everyone's going back to basics, and it's getting boring. The right cover would have been pictures of John and Yoko, clothed.

(2) The slowed-down version of "Revolution." Aside from the lyrics, the song was fine: good, heavy hard rock. You could even dance to it. Why do it at half the speed? So that we can hear the words better?

(3) "Revolution 9." Though I know nothing about electronic music, it sounds to me like the worst kind of pretentious nonsense. Friends who are more knowledgeable than I am concur.

(4) The album is just a bit too in-groupy. It parodies Bob Dylan, Tiny Tim, the Beach Boys, fifties gospel rock, blues, and music-hall songs; a whole song is devoted to discussing the Beatles' previous work; and one of the songs on the record alludes to another. But it's all done so well that this is a minor criticism.

Otherwise, this album is very satisfying. The Beatles have always blended sentimentality with irreverence. Lately, the sentimentality has become fantasy and the irreverence a whimsical disregard of linguistic conventions. Whether or not it has anything to do with their politics, *The Beatles,* even more than *Magical Mystery Tour,* belongs to a private world. And what doesn't work in life works fine in art. By *private* I don't mean exclusive; the Beatle world is one anybody can get into. *The Beatles* is a terrific children's album—much better than Donovan's *For Little Ones*—yet there is nothing prohibitively childish about it. The songs are funny (especially "Piggies" and "Why Don't We Do It in the Road?"), moving ("I'm So Tired" and "Julia"), clever ("Rocky Raccoon"), singable ("Ob-La-Di, Ob-La-Da" and "Back in the U.S.S.R."). For sheer fun with language, none of the lyrics quite comes up to "I Am the Walrus," but the general level is high. A special treat is Ringo Starr's first song, "Don't Pass Me By." It's beautiful, especially the verse that goes, "I'm sorry that I doubted you, / I was so unfair. / You were in a car crash, / And you lost your hair." Ringo, you keep us all sane. The Beatles might still be with the giggling guru if you hadn't turned up your nose at the curry. "Don't Pass Me By" makes up for all of George Harrison's Indian songs, plus "The Fool on the Hill." The screaming teenager in me wants to know how your Beatle museum is coming along and sends her love to Maureen and the kids—and to you.

East versus West
JULY 1971

The Fillmore East has closed, the Fillmore West is scheduled to be torn down, and Bill Graham's imminent withdrawal from the rock-concert business is, in its way, as poignant an ending as the breakup of the Beatles. "The dream is over," said Lennon. "The scene has changed," said Graham in his farewell announcement, citing "the unreasonable and totally destructive inflation of the live-concert scene," and decrying "the music industry of festivals, twenty-thousand-seat halls, miserable production quality, and second-rate promoters," greedy musicians and agents, acquiescent audiences, the scarcity of high-quality artists who were willing to perform regularly, and—a sensitive issue for a thin-skinned egotist like Graham—the constant criticism he received from the freak community and press. I was never very fond of the Fillmore East. Sitting in a confined space for three hours is not my idea of how to relate to a rock band, but, beyond that, there was usually something tense and sullen in the air, as if everyone were getting ready for a bust or a riot; the spirit of San Francisco lost something in the migration. Still, Graham did what no one else had managed—he created a continuing, dependable outlet for live rock in New York—and his detractors have never given him enough credit for that. The fans who accuse him of ripping off "their" music do not appreciate how much hard work, shrewdness, and money are involved in producing a successful rock concert, nor are they willing to face how basically rock is a capitalist art. If it weren't for businessmen, we would not have rock shows at all, and Graham has been a better businessman than most. Though his prices were not low, his customers could at least count on seeing and hearing a well-produced show. Today, that is not something to be taken for granted. All over the country, people are paying five dollars or more (usually more) to sit on floors or in bleachers in enormous arenas with terrible acoustics and obstructed views. One refinement of this scenario is unreserved seating, which means that if you come five hours early you may get to see something besides sound equipment, poles, and the Afro of the kid in front of you. Another is the notorious revolving stage. All in all, it's enough to make me sentimental about the good old Fillmore—which is no easy task.

A week before the fateful closing, which was also two weeks after John Lennon had pepped things up a bit by appearing on the Fillmore stage as a guest of Frank Zappa, I went to say my ambivalent good-byes. B. B. King was the headliner, with a newly reconstituted Moby Grape second on the bill, and Grootna, a lively San Francisco hard-rock band with a strong female lead singer, as a better-than-average filler. The concert was fun. I was almost afraid to see King perform; twice in the past two years, I'd sat through his cornball act for white college students, and I had begun to wonder if he was ruined forever. He isn't. Rock has had an obvious influence on his music, and his style is less cool than it used to be, but the controlling intelligence and dignity that seemed to have lapsed are back and make all the difference between catering to an audience and interacting with it. The Grape also put on a good show. There was considerable pathos and irony in its modest reappearance at this particular time. Moby Grape was an early casualty of the rock revolution; one of the finest of the first-generation San Francisco bands—and I'm not sure the qualification is necessary—it was badly hurt by overpromotion and went through the by now familiar sequence of inflated egos, freak-outs, personnel shifts, bad albums, and, finally, dissolution, leaving behind an enthusiastic Grape cult. Now the five original members are back together, have added a sixth (an electric-viola player), and are making an album for Warner Brothers. That night, they sounded very much like their old selves. They pleased the crowd (a sizable Grape-cult contingent was present) with several favorites from their great first album, including a brilliant performance of "Omaha," and did some new material that was similar in sound and spirit to their early songs. The only real departure was a weird instrumental encore that resembled, and maybe was, a parody of pretentious guitar playing in addition to being an excuse to show that the guitarist Skip Spence, the Grape's house crazy, still is.

Watching the Grape, I wondered if the basic cause of its troubles back in 1968 was that its members weren't true believers. They came on cynical and cocky, and you had the strong feeling that they didn't really take all this revolutionary-culture stuff seriously, whereas rock fans were taking it very seriously indeed. But these days, for the first time in its history, rock is without any unifying myths and metaphors; there seems to be an audience for almost any subgenre that is dreamed up, and the scene has become as absorbent as America itself. The Grape couldn't sell itself as part of the San Francisco renaissance; maybe now it can get people to appreciate its music.

Their Generation
AUGUST 1971

Someone was waving a large pink-and-white sign that read, "Don't Worry. Be Happy." I was trying, and so were at least thirty thousand other bodies waiting, with varying degrees of post-Aquarian patience, to see the Who for the first time in a year. Though the Performing Arts Center in Saratoga Springs is designed for classical concerts and ballet, its schedule includes a series of pop "special events." Above the five-thousand-seat amphitheater is a grassy slope that accommodates an elastic number of general admissions; to get to either, much of the audience has to funnel through several turnstiles on a bridge. This arrangement may be ideal for the Philadelphia Orchestra, but the Who caused a predictably gigantic bottleneck. For two hours or so on a warm Monday evening, we all squeezed toward the gate and debated the merits of sticking to the middle of the mob versus attempting an end run. Though our collective body heat soon became unbearable, the mood remained cool and good-humored. A lot of beer and wine circulated; people were finishing up whatever they had, since no booze was allowed inside. "Where's the Hell's Angels?" someone wanted to know. It was just a typical pack-'em-in, getting-there-is-half-the-trip rock concert; once the Who started to play, everybody would forget about the hassle quicker than you can say Bill Graham.

After most of the reserved seats had been occupied, the general-admissions crowd overflowed into the theater. This set off a mild class conflict between those aristocrats who had paid as much as six dollars for tickets and the two-fifty-a-head proles who now filled the aisles, stood in front of the stage, and wandered through the rows obstructing the view and appropriating latecomers' empty seats. The frustrated aristocrats yelled "Sit down!" until Mylon, the supporting act, drowned them out; after that they threw wadded-up paper torn out of their programs. Mylon's lead singer kept trying to establish himself as a man of the people ("If we seem confused—well, we came here in the same shape you did, heh heh!"). He went into a long stoned rap—something about how if we were sincere enough and smart enough and *together* enough . . . "Just make sure you *sit down* before the Who come on," the kid in back of me warned the kid next to me.

During intermission, the management, with awesome optimism, announced that because of fire regulations the aisles would have to be cleared before the concert could go on. Naturally, nobody moved. After ten minutes of face-saving delay, the Who made their entrance, causing an immediate escalation in the conflict between sitters and standees. Hundreds of programs were sacrificed as the Who began singing "Love Ain't for Keeping," a song from their new album, *Who's Next*. (I had received the record that morning and played it all day long. And to think I'd been wondering what the Who had done for me lately!) Pete Townshend and John Entwistle really had little beards, just like on the album cover, and Roger Daltrey was sporting muttonchops. They were even more manic than usual, kicking dead mikes, stamping on imaginary cockroaches, exaggerating their accents, parodying and teasing each other. Keith Moon was having a hard time maintaining his status as the group's chief clown—Daltrey was having a great time coming on like Screamin' Jay Hawkins, and Townshend kept tantalizing the audience by pretending to go into his old guitar-smashing routine. At one point, a freak in a motorcycle jacket jumped onstage; as he was hauled off by the security people, Townshend pantomimed kicking and punching him, then turned and gave us a coy grin and the V sign. The music reflected this mood; it sounded harder, younger, and more pop than the last time around. The concert included very little of the Who's quieter stuff and none of the flirtation with piano and organ that mellows the overall effect of *Who's Next*. Most of the Who's new material is closer in spirit to their early hits than to *Tommy* or the songs on *Happy Jack* and *The Who Sell Out*. (Even "Behind Blue Eyes," a classic middle-Townshend character sketch, is about a psychopath rather than the usual harmless eccentric.) Apparently, the Who have discovered—or rediscovered—that they, too, are working-class heroes or, rather, working-class saints: one of the most interesting cuts on *Who's*

Next is called "Baba O'Riley." Maybe it's just that they were so much older then; they're younger than that now—introducing "My Generation," Townshend quipped to his college-age audience, "This song could be about *you*." ("Don't cry, don't raise your eye," mourns Baba O' Riley. "It's only teenage wasteland.") At any rate, their performance of "Won't Get Fooled Again," their current hit single and Townshend's answer to "Street Fighting Man," was the high point of the show, as violent and electrifying as "My Generation" used to be before it became so familiar. The synthesizer track—taped for the purposes of live performance—projected alienated energy the way feedback once did. And, oh, yes: Townshend did total his instrument during his last song. It was an anticlimax, after the will-he-or-won't-he tension he had been building all evening, but it said something. Baba O' Riley says some other things, like "Let's get together before we get much older," and "I don't need to fight to prove I'm right, / I don't need to be forgiven." Where this new synthesis leads I'm not sure.

Back at the parking lot, a girl who looked about thirteen asked my friends and me if we knew where she could find the people she had come with. She explained that she was tripping and had been waiting by their car "for hours and hours, since they smashed everything in there." We persuaded her to go on waiting; it had been about twenty minutes. She stared at the crowd that kept coming and asked, "Is this Woodstock?"

"No," I said. "But it's more or less the same thing."

We got into our car, ready to face the traffic jam.

Yesterday's Papers
AUGUST 1972

The hysteria over the Rolling Stones' tour took me by surprise. I did not expect that they would inspire such a rush for tickets that their promoters would find it necessary to hold a lottery to avoid a riot in New York. Nor would I have predicted that *Exile on Main St.*, a double album whose immediate impact was less than compelling, would quickly become a No. 1 record. The 1969 tour had caused plenty of excitement, but not on this high-strung level, and since then there had been a perceptible anti-Stones reaction among erstwhile loyalists. Much of this reaction invoked Altamont, though it had less to do with any genuine moral indignation over the Stones' part in that disaster than with chagrin that they had blown the Woodstock myth. It didn't help that *Sticky Fingers* was not a flashy album (though, like *Exile on Main St.*, it turned out to be a lot better than many of us thought at first). But the main problem was that the Stones were, after all, yesterday's papers. They were the epitome of sixties rock and roll, but the sixties were over. Their swaggering was not only sexist but campy; their lean and hungry cynicism had got fat and well fed. Besides, debunking a legend is almost as much fun as building one. And yet here were all these kids, who had never experienced the world that was re-created for me every time I heard "Satisfaction" on the radio, mailing in their lottery postcards by the dozen, and even by the hundred. All of a sudden, the Stones were a larger-than-life fantasy again. What the fantasy was to be was not exactly clear. I listened intently to "Tumbling Dice," the most enigmatic single the Stones had ever released; no matter how hard I tried, I couldn't make out the words. *Exile on Main St.* was more of the same. It was full of intimations of urban chaos (a white "There's a Riot Goin' On"?), but the hints were obscured by a sound that was both fuller and fuzzier than usual.

Still, there were two obvious factors in the Stones' new ascendancy. One—unfortunate for the sensibilities of moralists (as pop paradoxes usually are)—was the publicity fallout from Altamont, especially the Maysles movie, which, in the way it impressed Mick Jagger's persona on the public, had functioned as the Stones' *A Hard Day's Night.* A lot of people who were rock-and-roll fans only casually, if at all, had become Stones-conscious. "The Stones are just a big social event," sneered a friend of mine, and in one sense, at least, it was true: *everybody* wanted one of those tickets. The other factor, of course, was that the tide of nostalgia had crept up to the early sixties. The Beatles were inaccessible, Dylan virtually so; who knew how long the Stones might be around? Better get it while you can, people reminded themselves, and they sent in their postcards.

Well, their instincts were right. The Stones' opening concert at Madison Square Garden was terrific. In spite of the heroic security—I was checked by no fewer than eight cops, two of whom inspected my handbag—I have never had a friendlier time at the Garden. The crowd was almost too wholesome; I was relieved to see a few freaky costumes and aspiring Alice Coopers. But it was happier than any rock audience I'd been part of in years, and I'd forgotten what a difference that could make. Stevie Wonder's set was weak at the start but soon picked up; that beatific quality of his began to bounce off the audience's warm vibes, and by the time he was through I was feeling very high and not even impatient. At about nine-forty-five, Jagger pranced onstage, followed by the rest of the band, including its temporary extra members—Nicky Hopkins on piano, Bobby Keys and Jim Price on horns. For the rest of the evening, they kept it light. Mick clowned and mugged and leaped and posed. If you wanted to know where he was at, all you had to do was listen to "Midnight Rambler." He began and ended it as a fast, jaunty rocker. In between, a red spotlight switched on and Mick did his old stage-whipping number, flailing his sash and screeching, parodying, exorcising, vomiting up his diabolic side. The only other song that made me feel the weight of all that has been won and lost since "Satisfaction" was "You Can't Always Get What You Want." Mostly, Mick and the band played down personality and played up the sheer excitement of their music. They gave us "Brown Sugar" and "Bitch," "Rocks Off" and "Tumbling Dice," "Jumpin' Jack Flash" and "Street Fighting Man." The audience demanded an encore and got one: Mick and Stevie together, singing "Uptight" and, finally, "Satisfaction." Only then, deaf, hoarse, and ecstatic, were we ready to leave. The message of the concert—and perhaps of *Exile on Main St.* as well—was "Whatever else we may or may not be, *we are rock and roll.* Dig it!" We did. It was a gas, gas, gas.

Several hours later, listening to the radio, I heard Alex Bennett (you remember Alex Bennett, fired by WMCA, martyr of the cultural revolution?) denounce the Stones as decadent, assembly-line performers who were in it only for the money, unlike truly dedicated musicians, blah blah, and imply that anyone who had enjoyed the concert—which Bennett had only reluctantly attended—was a potential Nazi. I reflected that it had been a free concert, a bona fide countercultural scheme, that had killed Meredith Hunter. What can you say about a cultural revolution that died? I unpacked my new Rolling Stones T-shirt—I would wear it tomorrow—and went to bed.

Creedence as Therapy
SEPTEMBER 1972

One day, sometime during Creedence Clearwater Revival's banner year, 1970, I was feeling depressed and confused about music, politics, writing, and almost everything else that was important to me. In an effort to shake off the mood, I stacked all five of my Creedence albums on the stereo and danced to them, one after another. Halfway through the second side of the last album, *Cosmo's Factory*, I was tired and ready to quit. But the next cut was "I Heard It Through the Grapevine," and it wouldn't let me sit still, so I got up again and danced for eleven minutes more, at the end of which I made a discovery: Creedence had edged out the Rolling Stones as my favorite rock-and-roll band. That I wasn't sure exactly when the switch had occurred—it had sneaked into my unconscious without the customary *zap*—says something about the difference between Creedence and the Stones. For all Creedence's immense popularity, John Fogerty has never made it as a media hero, and the group has never crossed the line from best-selling rock band to cultural phenomenon. Of course, nobody really does that anymore; the musicians who have become media personalities, like James Taylor, aren't exciting enough to be phenomena, and rock-and-rollers—with the semi-exception of Rod Stewart and Grand Funk Railroad—haven't been coming across as personalities. But then no recent pop performers have attracted anything like the Creedence audience, which during that peak year included hardcore rock-and-roll fans and hard-core freaks, high-school kids and college students, AM and FM—in short, closely resembled that catholic rock audience whose loss we mourn. Creedence is the only "serious" post-Beatle band to deliver one hit single after another, playing classic rock and roll without ever sounding archival. All of which makes Fogerty's miss the more poignant, for us as well as for him.

Fogerty understands the importance of personality, just as he understands—better than any other American songwriter—what rock-and-roll music is about. Yet he has avoided the obvious image-making ploys—freakiness, messianism, sex, violence. Instead, he projects intelligence and moderation—not the sort of qualities that inflame either journalists or fans. His political lyrics are pithier and more compassionate than Dylan's but so unpretentious and well integrated with the music that they often remain unnoticed. Paradoxically, Fogerty's humanism—for that is what it is—is also one of his strengths and is probably the main reason I have come to prefer him to Mick Jagger. Jagger's male power trip is alienating, and the fact that he obviously doesn't take it all seriously only makes it worse; at some point I discovered in myself an unsuspected frustrated need to know that there was a human being under all those layers of irony.

The fact is, I *like* John Fogerty a lot more than I ever liked Jagger, and, for whatever reason—maybe just because distance gets lonely—that is more important to me than it used to be.

It's possible, even likely, that the golden age of media art is over and that John Lennon is a throwback. Still, Creedence was inevitably disturbed by the celebrity gap. One result was that the group became oversensitive to criticism, which consisted mostly of complaints from the San Francisco–Berkeley art-rock lobby that Creedence was an uncreative "singles band." "We have something to *say*," Stu Cook fumed, as if *that* needed saying; I guess it's hard not to get defensive when you live in the Bay Area, the art-snob capital of the world. In December 1970, Creedence released a new album, *Pendulum*, which added some musical frills to the usual austere hard-rock structure. *Pendulum* made me uneasy, not because I disliked it—I thought it was great, except for a rather point-less flirtation with unaccompanied organ music—but because it seemed to lack John Fogerty's customary authority, that clear sense of where he wanted the band to go. Later, I found out that the rest of the group had been challenging his leadership; they wanted more artistic leeway. In 1971, Tom Fogerty split, and John agreed that Stu Cook and Doug Clifford should play an equal part in writing, arranging, and performing the group's material. Creedence released only two singles that year—"Have You Ever Seen the Rain?" (from *Pendulum*) and "Sweet Hitch-Hiker." And the next album was long in coming, very long by Creedence's previous standards—more than a year.

Mardi Gras is disappointing, though it has its moments. Tom Fogerty's absence is not obtrusive—if the record sounds a bit thin at times, this has to do less with Tom's departure than with the remaining trio's choice of material—but the heralded democratization of the group turns out to have been, from the selfish consumer's point of view, at least, a mistake. Creating a truly collective identity is difficult at best, especially for a band whose aesthetic is as tight as Creedence's, but that may be a fancy way of saying that Cook and Clifford simply do not write or sing as well as John Fogerty. Fogerty has contributed only three songs to *Mardi Gras*; two of those three are by far the best cuts—"Someday Never Comes" and (surprise, surprise) "Sweet Hitch-Hiker." This is not to say that Cook and Clifford are bad—I really like both their collaboration "Need Someone to Hold" and Cook's "Sail Away," and the only song I actively dislike is Cook's

"Take It Like a Friend," which, aside from being uninspired rock, has overtones of that misogynist arrogance Creedence has always spared us. It's just that Fogerty is too good to waste, even in the interests of egalitarianism and self-expression. I listen to John singing "Someday Never Comes," imbuing the typically understated lyrics with the most exquisite pain, yet never for a moment slipping into self-pity, and I find myself losing patience with the rest of the album. Well, given some more time, maybe Stu and Doug will turn out to be geniuses, too. I'm not being facetious, either—such things have happened before.

The other major flaw in *Mardi Gras* has to do with its use of country music. Country rock is the number-one cheapo commodity in pop music; it has long since become boring, and politically obnoxious besides. A few years ago, country rock meant reaffirming roots, discovering the value of simple sentiments; now it has come to mean nothing more noble than escape. So, on first hearing, it struck me as a lapse of taste that *Mardi Gras* should include a country-western song by Fogerty, a good-time number by Clifford, and Gene Pitney's "Hello Mary Lou." On the other hand, Creedence has always had good instincts in such matters, and I decided that some sort of comment must have been intended. My faith was rewarded when I listened to the lyrics of Fogerty's new song, "Lookin' for a Reason: "Every night I ask myself again, / Just what it was that made our dream begin. / Seemed like a good idea way back then, / But I'm wondering now if a daydream took me in. / . . . I'm lookin' for a reason not to go; / When the morning comes I'll be on my way." Heavy! The words are, at the very least, about the counterculture, right? And maybe about Creedence's career as well. It's unclear whether Fogerty is identifying with his persona or mocking it; probably both. The same themes reappear in other songs—escape in "Sail Away," social isolation and the-dream-is-over in "Need Someone to Hold." Very heavy! Still, the country music doesn't work, because in rock the surface is all-important, and on the surface it sounds as if Creedence were trying to do the same sort of thing the Byrds did in 1968. The songs slide down easy, and most people will either dismiss them or batten on them.

Mardi Gras is not the kind of record I can dance to when I'm depressed. This in itself doesn't bother me. (Well, it doesn't bother me a *whole* lot.) What is disturbing is the thought that my favorite rock-and-roll

musicians may be abandoning rock and roll because they feel unappreci-
ated. That would be a real disaster.

Believing Bette Midler, Mostly

On the second night of her engagement at the Palace, I finally caught
up with Bette Midler. Through one of those series of mishaps and mis-
managements that begins to assume a no doubt illusory cosmic importance, I had been missing Midler concerts regularly, starting with her
first, breakthrough performance at the Bitter End, and since I had bought
a new turntable instead of a TV set I couldn't even watch her on Johnny
Carson. I had had to skip her last local extravaganza, the fabled New
Year's show, because of a prior commitment to a friend—a motive commitment to a friend—a motive Bette would appreciate. The result was that
Midler, the sort of figure that is inevitably pronounced a "legend," had
become for me a legend in the ultimate sense—a vivid presence in my
fantasies without ever having been one in the flesh.

It didn't seem to matter. I loved her first album, *The Divine Miss M,*
even though I wasn't supposed to—friends and critics agreed that you
couldn't appreciate the record unless you'd seen the act. But I'd heard
enough about her to grasp what she was trying to do, which was, in essence, to explore the whole idea of theater: what it meant to be a performer, what it meant to be a fan, why all of us were a little of both.
Listening to her versions of "Leader of the Pack" and "Boogie Woogie
Bugle Boy," I would remember how a high-school friend and I had pepped
up a long subway ride by regaling our captive audience with all four parts
of the Quartet from "Rigoletto," or how my cousin and I used to drive
our parents crazy by imitating Jerry Lee Lewis and Gene Vincent and
Elvis for hours on end. My attitude toward my "material" was generally
ambiguous—the same admixture of love, aspiration, and mockery (toward
it and myself) with which I had once dressed up in my mother's clothes.
That kind of ambiguity is characteristic of the sensibility we call camp,
but camp is, I think, only a special case of the general human inclination
to express emotional conflict by adopting roles that are—deliberately or

unconsciously—excessive, awkward, even ridiculous. We all need to pretend, to fool around, in order, paradoxically, to reveal ourselves. By playing roles, we can protect our "real selves" from a hostile society; by playing them with a special flair, individualizing them with small elaborations, undercutting them with irony, choosing whom we care to imitate or make fun of and whom we want for our audience, we can obliquely express our identities.

Women, homosexuals, and other oppressed people have always understood the potency of that compromise. Bette Midler, a Jewish woman whose early fans were gay, seemed to me to embody it. In particular, having fun with roles—and, beyond that, with the idea of role—was her solution to the dilemma of the female performer: how to avoid being suicidally vulnerable (like a long line of victims from Billie Holiday to Janis Joplin) without becoming invulnerably trivial (like the Pointer Sisters) or simply dull (like the ladies a brilliant female songwriter of my acquaintance calls "all those laidback women in long skirts"). Using other people's and other eras' forms, making sure we heard the innocence or the silliness or the melodrama, Midler communicated her need to love and be loved, but without stripping herself naked. My favorite cut on the album was "Chapel of Love." There was something about the way Bette sang "Gee, I really love you and we're gonna get married" that made me want to hug her. On one level, she was indulging her joy in a simpleminded, happy rock-and-roll song. On another, she was saying, "Gee, I really love you." And I believed her; I even believed in marriage.

At the Palace, I realized that all that spiritual stuff was the easy part. The real test of Bette's genius was whether she could make me believe in palm trees and cricket noises, feather-duster fans, the Harlettes in their chorus-girl outfits, and—oh, *God,* as Bette would say—Hawaiian dancing girls. Although I thought I was prepared, the overblown production jolted me into exactly the reaction it was calculated to elicit: What *is* this? Then I remembered that Bette Midler grew up in Honolulu, and I wondered—as I'm sure I was meant to—at how the schlockiest elements of our popular culture always relate in some way to some person's real life. I wondered and began to believe.

I enjoyed the show a lot. I dug Bette's freneticism and her crazy hair and her loud voice and her avidity for every dramatic stance from Joe Cocker's to Lotte Lenya's. I loved what I thought of—probably without her permission—as political touches: her "really *gross* lyric" about ba-a-ad sex with a pickup; the way she changed the words of "I Shall Be Released" to "They say every woman needs protection, / They say every woman's got to fall." I laughed at her cracks about the Harlettes ("This one is so meticulous you can eat off her, she won't mind") and about the audience ("I hope that's not the Quaalude crowd up there, 'cause the orchestra hates it when people fall over on them"); I even laughed at her Nixon jokes and her impression of Betsy Ross. "Chapel of Love" was the high point of the concert, as of the album, stimulating the tenderest audience high since the "You are forgiven!" chorus of the Who's "A Quick One."

And yet I had reservations. It was obvious that the Divine Miss M had not emerged as Bette Midler, Superstar, without strain. As an ambitious artist in every sense, she was facing familiar contradictions: how to remain "the last of the tacky women" and preserve her special relationship with her "real" fans while playing the Palace at fifteen dollars top; how to make the mass audience love her while resisting subtle and not so subtle pressures to pander. Her uneasiness and her need to assure herself of our complicity came through in a running putdown of the celebrity-ridden opening-night crowd. She gasped with mock incredulity at the ticket prices: "Twelve dollars! You could have bought five gallons of gasoline for that." All this embarrassed and offended me. *Bad taste* may seem a weird criticism to make of a performer like Midler, but I can't think of a better phrase. When your artistic rationale is honoring the human content of banal and extravagant forms, it is in bad taste to play them-and-us games; why is "Lullaby of Broadway" worthy of love, and not Dyan Cannon? It is in even worse taste to make disingenuous jokes about the money that you are charging and other people—including those despised first-nighters—are paying. I was also sorry that so little of Midler's new material was rock. Her medley of "Uptown" and "Da Doo Ron Ron" sounded a bit perfunctory, as if she were trying to placate people like me while actually tilting in favor of Middle America.

I have similar doubts about Bette's new album, *Bette Midler*. It is more polished, less funky than the first one, and both the selection of songs and the interpretations tend to be less imaginative. It's still worth getting, if only for a knockout performance of the Denise La Salle masterpiece "Breaking Up Somebody's Home," a lyrical version of "Higher and Higher," and—for the rest of you Brecht-Weill freaks out there— "Surabaya Johnny." I'm sure I'll play it often. I just don't believe it quite as much.

Dylan and Fans: Looking Back, Going On

FEBRUARY 1974

A couple of weeks before Bob Dylan's arrival in New York, I got a letter from my friend, colleague, and fellow Dylan freak Greil Marcus, of *Creem*. He was upset about some lyrics from Dylan's new album, *Planet Waves*, that had been previewed in *Newsweek*—they sounded so complacent—and full of the same ambivalences that had been afflicting me with a queasy stomach ever since the tour was announced. Unreconciled to the happy-family-man posture Dylan had adopted since his motorcycle accident, we hoped and doubted. Did he still have the power to move us—to *matter*—as he once had? If so, did he have any intention of using it? And if not, why was he bothering to tour at all—he certainly didn't need the money. The reports from the first cities on his itinerary were inconclusive, and what little I'd heard about *Planet Waves* was not encouraging—it seemed we were in for more domesticity and low-keyed, moderate angst. But then, Dylan's critics had been obtuse before. Not for nothing was he opening and closing concerts with "Most Likely You'll Go Your Way (And I'll Go Mine)": "Time will tell just who has fell, and who's been left behind."

My theory was that Dylan was consciously working against the grain of his genius in order to communicate honestly about his own strategy for survival. In a way (a classically Dylanesque irony), he was only being consistent: *Blonde on Blonde*, it was worth remembering, was almost entirely about coping. It was the context that had changed. The sixties imperative was to strip away psychic defenses and social hypocrisies: through drugs we were to become Adam and Eve; through a politics of personal encounter and confrontation we were to create, ex nihilo, the postrevolutionary human being. All over the place, people were dismantling their personalities, giving no more thought to the prospect of having to put the fragments back together than the kid who takes a watch apart to see how it works. And at some point in each person's trip there had to come a moment of decision: plunge ahead, with a high probability of ending up dead or insane—or pull back. Dylan was like the rest of us, only more so. He went farther out than most, and his retrenchment was correspondingly dramatic. Since *John Wesley Harding*—which I now think of as the first seventies album, released at a time when it hadn't even crossed my mind that the sixties were going to end—he had been increasingly preoccupied with putting himself back together and making some sort of peace with the world as it existed. I couldn't fault him for that; in my own way, I was trying to do the same thing. Nor could I justify demanding that Bob Dylan get my kicks for me—or take my risks for me. The only sixties figure that had meant anywhere near as much to me as Dylan was Janis Joplin, and I didn't need a weatherman to know which way *that* wind blew.

The other part of the irony was that Dylan's new direction posed its own risk. Rock in the sixties had a redemptive quality; it put us in touch with our potential. The Beatles brought out our joy, the Stones our sensuality. Dylan's great contribution was to enlarge our capacity for freedom, help us break out of mental and emotional, musical and lyrical boxes. To decide that there was no freedom like chaos, and chaos was no freedom at all, was to relinquish his special gift and become just another—well, not quite *just* another—intelligent and talented songwriter, struggling with the problem of how to make maturity interesting. The risk was not that Dylan would destroy his myth, which was exactly what he intended to do, but that in the process he would lose his old audience without gaining a new one. It occurred to me that Dylan's return to the stage might very well have been calculated to forestall that possibility. If so, it was a characteristically brilliant move. The emergence of the sixties' chief culture hero—possibly for the last time—was bound to attract enormous crowds and maximum publicity. Dylan's performances were giving him a chance to reestablish his ties with old fans and reach thousands of new ones. Perhaps most important in the long run, excitement over the tour had stimulated a huge advance sale for *Planet Waves,* which appeared certain to become Dylan's first No. 1 LP.

Ultimately, it was this evidence of Dylan's continuing preeminence as a media artist that convinced me that his concerts at Madison Square Garden would be momentous. I was right. The two evening performances were masterpieces of controlled intensity. The first show, in particular, was a catharsis I hadn't even known I needed—a celebration of the past and a going beyond. Dylan performed his old songs almost exclusively, but if he was looking back, it was not to invite but to reject nostalgia. Nostalgia implied revival, which implied death, and it was obvious from the moment the concert began that even Dylan's earliest songs were not only still alive but resonant with new meanings. When the crowd cheered a line like "Even the President of the United States sometimes must have to stand naked," it was reacting less to a fortuitous political reference than to the uncanny adaptability of Dylan's vision. The songs themselves were enough to make the point, but Dylan underscored it with new arrangements—a country-rock "It Ain't Me, Babe," an upbeat "Ballad of a Thin Man," an acoustic "Just Like a Woman." During his acoustic set—the part of the concert I liked least—he did a lot of fooling around with his voice, which occasionally worked but more often strangled songs with excessive volume and heavy-handed, arbitrary phrasing. What he seemed to be saying (at least to me—God knows what all the eighteen-year-olds were thinking!) was that we had been through some very special years. They had shaped us, marked us. They would always be part of us, something that we shared; they still had meaning for our lives. Yet we had to move on. That evening, anyway, Dylan wasn't about to tell us how—it was tact, as well as showmanship, that dictated his repertoire. We would go our way, he would go his, but that didn't mean we couldn't be friends.

Toward the end, after the Band's second set, Dylan did two songs from *Planet Waves.* "Forever Young" was supposedly addressed to his children, but its advice (Dylan never could resist being didactic, even when he was proclaiming that messages were a drag) was obviously meant for us as well: "May you always know the truth and see the light surrounding you. . . . / May you have a strong foundation when the winds of changes shift," and, finally, a child-of-the-sixties blessing (or curse) if there ever was one, "May you stay forever young." "Something There Is About You," a love song to his wife, made the only direct comment of the night on Dylan's current state of mind: "I was in a whirlwind, / Now I'm in some better place." And then came the big one—"Like a Rolling Stone." It crept up on us—Dylan had changed the intro, of course—and exploded.

"How does it feel?" we screamed.

"How does it feel—to be on your own—no direction home—"

It felt as I would have expected: wonderful. The lights went out; flickering matches transformed the Garden into a giant planetarium. Dylan and the Band came back for a reprise of "Most Likely You'll Go Your Way," left, came back again, and ended with a rousing electric version of "Blowin' in the Wind." I went home as high on Dylan as I'd ever been.

I'm still feeling that way, and in my present mood I can almost psych myself into thinking that *Planet Waves* is a great album. It isn't, but neither is it as inconsequential as those *Newsweek* quotes portended. By now, we ought to know better than to judge Dylan's words on paper; it is his singing that makes the difference. And the singing on *Planet Waves* is fine. The polish of *Nashville Skyline* and *New Morning* has been abandoned in favor of a crude expressiveness that undercuts the lyrical banalities— which on closer inspection often turn out to be not so banal after all. Take "Wedding Song," for instance. "Your love cuts like a knife"? "I love you more than blood"? Not exactly your conventional images of marital bliss. As he often does, Dylan is using clichés, or apparent clichés, to camou- flage innovation. Though nobody seems to have noticed, *Planet Waves* is unlike all other Dylan albums: it is openly personal. It could be argued that Dylan's mask has simply become subtler, but I don't believe it. I think the subject of *Planet Waves* is what it appears to be—Dylan's aesthetic and practical dilemma ("I been walkin' on the road, / I been livin' on the edge, / Now I just got to go / before I get to the ledge") and his immense emotional debt to Sara. The album is dominated by tributes to her. But there is also an antilove song called "Dirge," whose antiheroine (suc- cess? the audience? Joan Baez? Albert Grossman? Sara's alter ego?) is "a painted face on a trip down suicide road." This kind of symbolism can be embarrassing. Dylan has always tended to get sticky about women—to classify them as goddesses to be idolized or bitches to be mercilessly trashed. Yet his conviction that he has been saved by love is so poignant and so obviously genuine that it transcends the stereotype. Which is, in a sense, what popular culture is all about.

Chapter 3

THE SIXTIES CHILD

Pop Ecumenicism
MAY 1968

Van Dyke Parks's first album, *Song Cycle*, has become a cult record. Not that it has been kept a secret; on the contrary, since it came out, last winter, critics and arbiters of hip have been plugging it everywhere from the *Times* to *Crawdaddy!* Only, nobody seems to be listening, or buying. The salesmen for Warner Brothers don't know what to make of it, so they don't push it. The distributors have never heard of Parks, so they don't try to sell him to record stores. The result is that *Song Cycle* has sold only seven thousand copies. This information confirms the suspicion aroused by my own informal survey. (Q: "How do you like Van Dyke Parks's album?" A: "Whose?") I suppose this is not surprising. After all, *Song Cycle* is a serious experimental work that does a lot of esoteric things with sound. It's not rock; it's not traditional pop; it feels a bit like folk music, but it's almost complex enough to be classical. So you can't blame Warner Brothers for not promoting Parks as if he were the Monkees, or the reviewers for making him seem forbiddingly avant-garde. Still, it's too bad, because

Song Cycle does have a potential appeal for a large audience, and it has come along at exactly the right time. Given a proper chance, it could capitalize very nicely on the growing trend toward ecumenical pop—music that reaches both the kids and their elders.

In general, this trend has not been salutary. What it demands is *pleasant* music—nothing too noisy, or too raunchy, or too angry, or too anything—that still manages to be, or to seem, youthful. And though these criteria do not rule out excellence—the post-*Rubber Soul* Beatles qualify most of the time—the usual formula is pap in a hippie package. *Song Cycle,* however, subsumes generational tastes without compromising. Older people will find that, for all its subtlety, it goes down easily; the melodies are both prominent and singable, and both the music and the lyrics owe much to the Broadway theater. Furthermore, the theme that unites these loosely related songs—the American frontier, past and present ("I came West unto Hollywood"), personal and historical ("Widows face the future. / Factories face the poor")—could scarcely be more traditional. But Parks's own generation will appreciate his treatment of this theme, which is totally contemporary. Although many of his songs are set in Los Angeles, the great pop city, the frontiers that concern him most are not geographical but technological (*Song Cycle* makes fuller use of recording-studio techniques than any previous pop record) and psychedelic (in fact, marijuana is to *Song Cycle* what Polaroid glasses were to 3-D movies).

Studio-oriented musicians like the Beatles and Brian Wilson showed Parks how to manipulate sound, and now he has gone beyond them. The experience he offers is aural supersaturation limited, apparently, only by the quality of the listener's stereo set and/or grass. At the same time, he has worked hard to avoid a cluttered sound. Like Charles Ives, another major influence, he crams allusions into his music—Beethoven's Ninth, "The Battle Hymn of the Republic," "Nearer, My God, to Thee," the drumroll from John Kennedy's funeral—without any sense of strain. His most nearly perfect triumph is "Donovan's Colours," an exquisite three-and-a-half-minute instrumental track that sounds like a nice, simple piano piece played by someone with six hands.

In contrast to the richness of the instrumentation, Parks's voice is weak and lacking in range—a mediocre-to-fair folk singer's voice. The result—undoubtedly deliberate—is to strengthen the impression of simplicity: Aw, shucks, fellers, all that engineering don't mean a thing. The secret of Parks's ecumenicism is that he understands how potent sophistication can be when it is dressed in naïveté.

The first pop performers to straddle the generation gap were Simon and Garfunkel. They shared the basic prerequisites—a soft sound, only peripherally related to rock, and a somewhat attenuated sensibility. But their special gimmick was their ideas. Starting out as folk singers, they broke into pop during the first big folk-rock boom. Bob Dylan, so we kept hearing, had banished the infamous Tin Pan Alley cliché. Accordingly, Paul Simon (he writes the songs; Art Garfunkel arranges them) became a "rock poet," dealing with such noncliché subjects as the soullessness of commercial society and man's inability to communicate. This appealed to kids who hadn't read much modern poetry but knew what it was supposed to be about, or were overimpressed with their own nascent weltschmerz, or both. As for parents, they could feel at ease because the catchwords were familiar; they had read "Dover Beach" and "Richard Cory," and maybe even "The Waste Land," in school. And it was reassuring that two bona fide alienated young rock poets wanted most of all to *communicate,* not to spit in their eye. Besides, Simon and Garfunkel were so nice- looking—so *collegiate.* Certainly an improvement over that skinny runt with the wild hair who kept warning, "Something is happening here, / but you don't know what it is, / *do* you, Mr. Jones?"

S & G's first hit single, "The Sounds of Silence," was a re-release, with a superimposed rock beat, of a song originally included in their folk album *Wednesday Morning, 3 A.M.* ("The author," explained Art Garfunkel's album notes, "sees the extent of communication as it is on only its most superficial and 'commercial' level [of which the 'neon sign' is representative]. . . . The words tell us that when meaningful communication fails, the only sound is silence.") I liked that record in spite of its ersatz protest, which it—well, *communicated,* even though the dubbed-in drums happily obscured most of the lyrics. Perhaps it was this unintended irony that saved the song; perhaps it was the melody. In any case, the overall effect was mysterious and moving. But the songs that followed were just arty bores. The plebeian beat disappeared in favor of lush, gutless arrangements that ruined Simon's better-than-average melodies and emphasized his increasingly pretentious academic verse. This process reached some sort of apotheosis in "The Dangling Conversation," a failure-of-communication extravaganza featured on their third LP, *Parsley,*

Sage, Rosemary and Thyme. Parsley was so much overpraised that a critical reaction began to set in. Had the next Simon and Garfunkel album arrived on schedule, it would likely have been badly panned. But it was delayed—the rumor spread that Simon had a writing block—and the three songs he did write, all of which were released as singles, showed clearly that he was trying to move in a new direction. One of them, "Fakin' It," was truly impressive; it had strong, direct, colloquial lyrics, an excellent melody, and a *beat.* Now the long-awaited album, *Bookends,* is out. It includes the three singles, and it is certainly S & G's best collection of work so far. On the front cover is a disheartening picture of those two grave, sensitive faces, but turn to the back, where the lyrics are printed, and you can see that something has happened. Item: references to Mrs. Wagner's Pies, Greyhound, the New Jersey Turnpike, the New York *Times,* Kellogg's Corn Flakes, and Joe DiMaggio. Item: a track of old people's voices, recorded by Art Garfunkel "in various locations in New York and Los Angeles." Item: only one really corny image ("We're just a habit / Like saccharin"). It seems that our boys have discovered pop. Of course, they hedge—one song, "America," is really about how the pop vision isn't good enough—and they are still obsessed with loneliness. But at least they talk about it in the language of the sixties; always intelligent imitators, they have finally begun to imitate their contemporaries. As for the music, it turns out to be simple and lively. In fact, some of it is almost like—what was that again?—rock and roll.

Randy Newman
AUGUST 1971

Randy Newman composes melodies that sound like forties jazz tunes, writes lyrics that combine the cynicism of the fifties with the pop insouciance of the sixties, and is one of the few artists I feel confident can survive the Nixon/midi/post-Altamont seventies with equanimity. Newman has immense talent; he is one of the cleverest lyricists in the business and plays fine jazz piano (he usually accompanies himself on his records). He is also a weirdo—the straight man for a black-comedy team that consists of him and his subconscious and expresses itself in a voice that makes me think of wet sand being eased out of a bottle. Although he is only twenty-six, his place in a militantly youthful culture is ambiguous. His sensibility owes as much to George Gershwin and Bruce Jay Friedman as to Lennon-McCartney or Dylan. Often he seems to be acting out a favorite myth of the Silent Generation—that beneath each button-down shirt beat the heart of an individualist who knew that his society and life in general were absurd, who believed that rebellion was useless but enjoyed ironically contemplating the disparity between his conformist façade and the anarchist within. At the same time, Newman is very much a contemporary figure. In the first place, he is an Angeleno, which immediately separates him from the Silents: in the culture of the fifties, America consisted of Madison Avenue and the Ivy League universities, and maybe Chicago. He has also made the essential pop affirmation: I am a white, middle-class American, and I'm not ashamed of it. Newman is a cheerful, short-haired, slightly paunchy suburbanite who lives in a comfortable, not especially luxurious house. He has a wife and baby, and relatives who are big shots in the movie-music business. The difference between Newman and that fifties cynic is that although Newman is quite conscious of the absurdities and cruelties of straight America, he refuses to be a snob about them—to pretend he is merely the surface without the substance. What, after all, is straight America but people like him? How can you pose as something without becoming it?

The songs on Newman's first album, *Randy Newman,* show an intimate familiarity with, and affection for, all the nuances of American life—the settings and characters, the family relationships, the romantic fantasies, the euphemisms—as well as an unsparing awareness of our oppression of old people, fat people, and other nonmainstream types. Newman sees himself as both a perpetrator of the culture and its victim and is philosophical about it all—one of the traits shared by the Silent and pop generations is cool. In "Love Story," the narrator is telling his girl his vision of their future. They will marry, breed, watch the late show, and ultimately, when their children are grown, "They'll send us away / To a little home in Florida / We'll play checkers all day / Until we pass away." The indictment in that ending is real and biting, but, on the other hand—what's really so terrible about a little home in Florida? ("Will you still need me, will you still feed me / When I'm sixty-four?") If you asked Andy Warhol, he would probably say it was groovy; it's certainly better than being thrown off a cliff. In many of these songs, Newman seems to be saying that yes, the best of all possible worlds can get pretty hairy, but that doesn't mean it isn't the best.

Newman's second album, *12 Songs,* is a logical outgrowth of the first, although it is very different in spirit. In a low-keyed, almost subliminal way, it is political. Again, Newman is insistent about telling us who he is. A black-and-white photograph on the album jacket features a lawn with a television set, a rocking chair, and a child-sized chair in the foreground, and a house and wooden fence in the background; enclosed, on the back of a lyric sheet, is a color picture of Randy carrying some groceries and his wife holding their kid. The record itself is full of chaos, absurdity, and loneliness. Rebellion is no longer unthinkable: on one of the cuts, Newman sings slowly, painfully, at times almost inaudibly, "Let's burn down the cornfield / And I'll make love to you while it's burning." Other songs are about a wild party, a girl who gets run over by a beach-cleaning truck, men hungry for women or strung out on dope and booze ("I been up so long / That it looks like down to me"). A pervasive theme is racism. The music on this album is much blacker than usual for Newman; for the first time, he plays around with several different kinds of rock and blues—more successfully than I would have anticipated. (Especially good is "Have You Seen My Baby?") The last cut on the first side is "Underneath the Harlem Moon," by Mack Gordon and Harry Revel, the only song not written by Newman himself. The first cut on the second side, the most typically Newmanesque-eccentric of the songs, is called "Yellow Man." It's a deadpan account, sung in an upbeat, jazzy style, of a yellow man who lives with a yellow woman in a foreign land, "believes / In the family / Just like you and me," eats rice, and "keeps his money tight in his hand." Newman has also counterposed to the general bluesy feeling of the album an excellent country song. The intention would be clear—country music is the product of the white South—even if Newman hadn't called it "My Old Kentucky Home." The album, then, is basically a warning that we may get our cornfield burned down. Where does that leave Newman, with his TV and rocking chair? He doesn't say—he is still cool. He is also, as usual, very funny. There is a grin in every song. When I think about it, I don't understand why he should be grinning, but when I listen to the songs it seems perfectly appropriate. Which is why I say Newman will survive. "Let's Burn Down the Cornfield" might cause a few frowns, but what could Spiro Agnew say about "Yellow Man"?

George and John

FEBRUARY 1971

All things must pass—even the most spectacular mass-cultural phenomenon in history. I think the Beatles as an idea began to erode when George Harrison discovered India. Eastern mysticism was antithetical to the Beatle tradition of cheerful Western pragmatism, and the group's attempt to assimilate it, besides producing some wonderful music and some platitudinous philosophy, seemed to put a strain on the collective psyche that might have been irremediable even if John had never married Yoko or hired Allen Klein. George, of course, has had some assimilating of his own to do, the composer of "Love You To" and "Within You Without You" being, after all, none other than the composer of "Taxman." *All Things Must Pass* is Harrison's attempt to bring it all together—to weld good old rock and roll to religion, and the Eastern concept of enlightenment to the Christian ideals of peace and love. Phil Spector has coproduced the album with Harrison, and its overall sound is beautiful. The sense of grandeur Spector evokes is rock at its most religious; the unity miraculously wrought out of so much busyness might be said to be rock at its most Eastern. The cut that best fulfills these ecumenical aspirations is "My Sweet Lord." It is, first of all, rock that has proved itself the way rock is supposed to; as a single, it topped the charts. The beat reinforces the words and Harrison's vocal conviction to give the feeling of a revival meeting. In the beginning, the background chorus's response to Harrison's prayer is "Hallelujah"; soon it switches to "Hare Krishna"; by the end its invocations to various Hindu deities have become the focus of the song. Similar in spirit but less successful is "Awaiting on You All," an abortive mixture of nervous rock and lyrics that I suppose were meant to be funny: "You don't need no passport, you don't need no visas, / You don't need to designate or to emigrate before you can see Jesus."

The theme that most naturally links rock and religion is love. Many bands, notably Jefferson Airplane, have used the conventions of the pop love song to suggest more communal or sacred emotions; Harrison does this effectively in songs like "Let It Down" and "I Dig Love." In its emphasis on love, Harrison's spirituality has a lot in common with Bob Dylan's new-found tranquility, and Dylan is much in evidence on this album. It includes one Dylan song ("If Not for You"), one collaboration with Dylan ("I'd Have

You Anytime," a kind of secular version of "My Sweet Lord," without the beat), and two songs that are obviously tributes to Dylan ("Apple Scruffs," an ode to that legendary group of fans featuring an exuberant harmonica, and "Behind That Locked Door," a sentimental Nashville-type song that doesn't make it—Dylan has already written too many of them, and his are better).

Considering that *All Things Must Pass* consists almost entirely of moral and spiritual propaganda, it is remarkably (though by no means totally) free of the pretensions that have detracted from some of Harrison's recent work. For one thing, the music is unassumingly Western—the Indian influence has been integrated quietly. Occasionally, Harrison uses Dylan's technique of reclaiming clichés—which Dylan probably picked up in the first place from Lennon—to mitigate his sermonizing: "Sunrise doesn't last all morning, / A cloudburst doesn't last all day. / . . . All things must pass, / all things must pass away." But mostly the songs work because Harrison is using his words—along with his music and his tone of voice— less to convey a message in the intellectual sense than to instruct us in states of mind. The best example is "Beware of Darkness," the most mind-blowing musical evocation of the bad trip or the Valley of the Shadow of Death, or whatever your favorite metaphor is for that sad and fearful mental place, that I've ever heard: "Watch out now, take care beware of / falling swingers, dropping all around you / . . . The thoughts that linger / winding up inside your head, / The hopelessness around you in the dead of night."

All Things Must Pass is a double album. Included in the package is a bonus LP, *Apple Jam,* on which Harrison, Eric Clapton, and assorted other musicians jam away. Like most records of rock musicians jamming away (compare *Grape Jam*), it's a harmless, if superfluous, ego trip.

Lennon's new album, *John Lennon/Plastic Ono Band,* is on one level the metaphysical opposite of Harrison's. It's a collection of songs about Lennon's feelings—personal rather than cosmic, emotional rather than meditative, cathartic rather than persuasive, and disillusioned with a catalogue of snares ranging from religion ("Keep you occupied with pie in the sky. / There ain't no guru who can see through your eyes") to class climbing ("There's room at the top they are telling you still, / But first you must learn how to smile as you kill"). Unlike single-minded George, John is always looking for a new and better revelation; having been through acid, the Maharishi, and peace, he is now into Arthur Janov's *(The Primal*

Scream) psychotherapy, which the introspection on this album reflects. But the two ex-Beatles do have one thing in common: they both believe in love. For John, love is no lofty agape; it's longing, deprivation, protectiveness, and has-this-really-happened-to-me awe. Harrison digs love. Lennon tries to define it: "Love is real, real is love. / Love is feeling, feeling love. / Love is wanting to be loved." Yet his conviction that love is truth and hope in a hostile world borders on the mystical—Yoko Ono is the most durable of his revelations. And Lennon's album, like Harrison's, is about being saved. Salvation—from childhood hurts, from false panaceas for those hurts, from the oppression of the middle class and the dogmatism of radicals and the treachery of supposed friends—lies in facing one's feelings, acknowledging the pain, and, above all, loving: "I just believe in me, / Yoko and me, / And that's reality."

The music on this record is artfully simple, some of it (particularly "Look at Me") of a piece with the music on the white *Beatles* album. The lyrics are mostly spare, sometimes biting, sometimes self-indulgent. I especially like "Mother," Lennon's protest to the parents who walked out on him, and "Isolation," a soft, almost timid song that refers obliquely to the putdowns Yoko received from Paul, George, and the Apple staff (related in John's notorious and wonderful interview in *Rolling Stone*). "Working Class Hero" is a surprisingly trenchant political song, and so, in a more convoluted way, is "Well Well Well." "God," "I Found Out," and "Mummy's Dead" are more interesting as autobiography than as music or poetry ("God is a concept / By which we measure / Our pain" may be the most awkward lines Lennon has ever written), but that's OK, too.

Yoko has put out a companion album, *Yoko Ono/Plastic Ono Band.* Those who liked *Wedding Album* and *Live Peace in Toronto 1969*—I didn't—should enjoy this one.

Consumer Revolt

SEPTEMBER 1971

Here it was Thursday, the Band was to appear at Monticello Raceway Sunday night, and not only were stores around town still selling tickets but they seemed glad to get rid of them. Besides the Band (not the Stones or Grand Funk but still, these boys started the Woodstock myth, after all), the bill included Kris Kristofferson, the first out-front early-sixties-type folkie to become a star in five years or so; Joan Baez's awful version of "The Night They Drove Old Dixie Down" was ubiquitous on AM radio. And yet how long is it since you tried to get tickets to a big-name concert at the last minute and the guy you asked said, "You bet!" so heartily you could see his teeth over the phone? The admission charge was an absurd seven dollars for unreserved seating at the track; the show was advertised as a benefit for a local hospital, but the fine print disclosed that only one dollar out of the seven was being donated. The whole deal was even more of an insult to the public's intelligence than usual. "If I had the seven bucks, I'd spend it on dope," said a hitchhiker I picked up on my way to Monticello. Along with a girlfriend and another pair of hitchhikers, he was going out to the Raceway to try to get in free.

The small turnout—five thousand at the most—left huge empty spaces; the scene was as depressing as a half-filled ballpark after the pennant has been lost. A fair-sized crowd of kids without tickets began to collect outside. Some climbed over the fence, with the audience cheering them on, and a group of bikers threatened to crash; halfway through Kristofferson's act the promoters and the track management, eager to avoid trouble, opened the gates. At least, nobody had any problem seeing. I found a great place to sit, on the few feet of overhang in front of the upstairs boxes, unobstructed by either standees or poles. Hearing was something else again. The sound system was one of the worst I've ever been subjected to. Voices came out thin and instruments tinny; soft singing was inaudible, and loud singing made the mikes screech. Incredibly, some genius kept interrupting songs in the middle to page track employees over the PA system.

The concert dragged badly. Kristofferson was on for two hours, the last hour and a half of which was superfluous. I had been curious to see him. For the past few months, he had been generating a lot of excitement, including numerous comparisons to early Dylan. From records, I couldn't figure out why. His singing was nothing special, and, except for "Me and Bobby McGee," I couldn't really get into his songs, which all seemed to be about drug addicts dying of overdoses, rebels dropping out, and singers resisting the Devil to keep faith with their vision; there was a certain Berkeley-in-1963 smugness about them. His performance at Monticello left me equally apathetic. He had no presence or vitality, and, as if to make up for his lack of rapport with the audience, kept apologizing for everything—his material, the mikes, the price of tickets, the fact that the Band was late. Under better circumstances—in a small club, say—I might enjoy listening to him, but Dylan, early or otherwise, he's not.

Happy and Artie Traum came on next and played some tangy country rock. Their music was fun, and they were having fun. Unfortunately, the logistics of the evening were against them. Time was passing; people were getting impatient. The Band finally showed up at eleven-thirty, and made the wait almost worth it. My interest in the Band tends to go in cycles. The group has given me great pleasure; I think the second Band album, in particular, is one of the classic rock records of the sixties. But it's an unspectacular, middle-energy kind of pleasure—*solid* is the word that comes to mind—that's easy to forget about for a while. The rediscovery is always a high, and Monticello was no exception, in spite of the miserable sound. The set included several songs from each of the Band's three albums—with a slight bias in favor of *Stage Fright*—and two Motown oldies. There was a lot of good instrumental stuff, especially Garth Hudson's long organ introduction to "Chest Fever." (The Band is also about the only rock group whose musicianship I enjoy for its own sake.) The one major disappointment was the omission of any new songs—an inexplicable lapse, considering that a fourth album is imminent. I mean, for seven dollars we at least deserved a preview—right, fellas?

My Grand Funk Problem—and Ours
FEBRUARY 1972

Although Grand Funk Railroad achieved its current preeminence with little help from the media and none from the "serious" rock press, it has been enjoying—or, it may yet turn out, suffering—a critical frontlash. I wasn't a Grand Funk fan to begin with and I'm not now, but I've gone through pretty much the same changes as the frontlashers, most of whom aren't Grand Funk fans, either. I first heard Grand Funk at a G.I. coffeehouse in Colorado about two years ago. An acidhead soldier told me he dug the group's first album, so I listened to it. My reaction was oh, well, another son-of-heavy-white-blues band. But some hunch made me hold on to the album, and to the next one. While Grand Funk was becoming the most popular son-of-heavy-white-blues band in the world, I listened some more, on the usually reliable theory that a band beloved of teenagers must be doing something right. The music still didn't do much for me; I caught myself thinking of it as abunchanoise, and I knew what *that* meant, all right—creeping senility. Hadn't my parents reacted the same way to Little Richard? (Little Richard was the supreme test: my mother liked Elvis, but she couldn't stand Little Richard.) I had been nursing this private worry for some time when I picked up an issue of *Creem,* a Detroit-based rock magazine, read Greil Marcus on Grand Funk ("Rock and roll critics and their peers . . . when they put it down . . . are acting out the roles once played by archetypal rock and roll parents when, fifteen years ago, they threw Little Richard 45s in the trash can"), and realized once again that in rock, as in politics, there are no private worries. Since then, *Creem's* editor, Dave Marsh, has defended Grand Funk as *the* teen music of the seventies, which if we don't hear it we are moldy, toothless, crippled, craven, and anti–malted milk.

The message is more complicated than it sounds. *Creem,* after all, is not put out by fresh kids who have never heard of Little Richard and could care less but by—and largely for—fifties and sixties rockheads. Unlike *Rolling Stone,* which is a bastion of San Francisco countercultural "rock-as-art" orthodoxy, *Creem* is committed to a pop aesthetic; it speaks to fans who consciously value rock as an expression of urban teenage culture and identify with a tradition whose first law is novelty. Marsh's taunts are meant to provoke us by hitting us right in the ideology, at the same time that they appeal to our weakness for irony (another ingredient of the pop aesthetic): the analogy to our parents is unflattering, but its poetry is irresistible. Behind the provocation is the hope that the enormous success of bands like Grand Funk and its English counterpart Black Sabbath can re-create a cohesive rock community by polarizing what has become an amorphous, fragmented audience. We all know there can be no "us" without "them"; once the Beatles belonged to everybody, there was no centripetal force to keep them from splitting four ways, each with his own group of loyalists, and their situation says a lot about the present state of rock. (John and Yoko have their own us-and-them thing going, and I'm on their side against Paul—or, for that matter, George—but I can't really be *part* of them; three's a crowd.) Every rock fan I know has been wishing that something would happen to reverse the energy drain. Is Grand Funk it? Here is where the Little Richard metaphor breaks down: Would our parents ever ask such a question? My answer to it has to be no, if only because my survival instincts are against letting myself be trapped by a myth, even when it's one I helped invent. I have no quarrel with Mark, Mel, and Don because they are crude city kids who "can't play" and "can't sing." I'm glad they're around as an antidote to James Taylor and the other upper-class brats; their adrenaline is bound to do us all good in one way or another. But their records (I've never seen them perform) don't get me off. And though this has something—maybe everything—to do with my being fifteen years older than the average Grand Funk enthusiast, anyone who tries to define me as "them" on that basis will have to drag me away from my jukebox kicking and screaming.

To first-generation rock fans, growing up meant being like your parents, which meant, among other things, no rock and roll. The sixties were our triumph: rock and roll had lasted, in spite of some bad times; it had come back stronger than ever, and we had not grown out of it. Having lived through adolescence, we were now reliving it with musicians who were our peers, whose music reflected our common past. At this point, the distance between us and high-school kids may have less to do with the aging process per se than with the spectacular success of our revolt against it. We are still self-centered, involved with our own history, and—despite the inevitable loss of momentum, the undertow of art snobbery, the plethora of music that soothes instead of goading, the coming of age of Bob Dylan, and even our confusion about who "we" are—we still have a lot going for us. Even Grand Funk is an extension of our music, whereas early rock was (for white kids, at least) a rebellion against a vacuum. Mark Farner's political clichés are fallout from counterculture fantasies that were once exciting because taboo and later embarrassing because naive. To the kids, his exhortations are simply conventional, no more to be taken literally than the love lyrics that cemented our solidarity; and that's fine. But for me to hear them that way would require a cultural lobotomy. Ironically, the whole thrust of the frontlash is to squeeze Grand Funk into our context. Age is *our* obsession; it is shared by *our* superstars (just listen to *New Morning* or *Who's Next* one of these days). To hand Grand Funk our hope-I-die-before-I-get-old banner is to strip the boys of their most potent claim to the status of rebel barbarians—the fact that the critics have ignored them. Worse yet, critics have ignored them. Worse yet, they may notice that they are being "taken seriously" and try to live up to it.

The fragmentation of the rock audience is just one symptom of social and political developments that cut pretty deep; I doubt whether one person or one band, no matter how potent, can put it back together—not now, anyway. And when we're ready for the next cultural upheaval, the catalyst may not be teenagers—or even music.

Into the Seventies, for Real
DECEMBER 1972

It's a few long weeks after Nixon's landslide and I'm sitting home listening to albums by Five Dollar Shoes, a local product, and the Hoodoo Rhythm Devils, a bunch of rock-and-roll crazies from Berkeley. If the sixties as a cultural unit can be said to have ended with Altamont, the deaths of Hendrix and Joplin, or the collapse of the peace movement (choose one), I think the seventies can be said to have begun with this election. Rock-and-roll fans are already beginning to launch an antisixties backlash that parallels (or parodies) the Nixon victory. It incorporates the standard grievances about musical-poetical-political pretension's crowding out fun and noise, but goes further. As Rockin' Ron Weiser puts it in a fanzine called *Flash,* "Then we got the Beatles . . . look at these phony jerks wearing TIES and SUITS and really clean-cut looking . . . and singing songs about 'Wanting to Hold Your Hand'!!!" He also accuses the Stones of ripping off Chuck Berry. The rest of the magazine is less extreme but still abounds in withering references to "doped-out dullards," tea-drinking, crumpet-eating Britishers, and peace-loving hippies. Nor is this mood confined to cultists. Turn to *Rolling Stone* and there's Nick Tosches agreeing "that eating . . . is more fun than spiritual introspection; that sex and violence and stuff like that are more vital than cosmic awareness."

You get the idea. We're supposed to get back to the mythic crudity and crassness reputed to be at the heart of rock and roll before it was corrupted by meaning, sensitivity, taste, and the like. The aestheticians of the backlash may overlap with the fifties-R&B nuts we've always had with us, but in general they take the spirit rather than the sound of fifties rock as their inspiration—particularly the Dionysiac illiteracy of Jerry Lee Lewis and Little Richard. *Punk-rock* has become the favored term of endearment. I have mixed feelings about all this. For one thing, the blood-'n'-raunch-forever approach to rock tends to degenerate into a virility cult. Besides, having lived through the fifties, I find it impossible to romanticize them. In spite of rock and roll, they were dull, mean years—at least for middle-class high-school girls. For all the absurdities of the counter-culture, it was better than what we had before; there's something to be said for a little cosmic awareness, provided it doesn't get out of hand. And if it hadn't been for the Beatles (I wonder, did Rockin' Ron despise Buddy Holly for wearing suits and glasses and looking like a schoolteacher?) we might never have developed the kind of consciousness about our shared past that allows a rag like *Flash* to exist. Still, I do have a weakness for dedicated crudity and crassness, and so I've been digging these two back-lashy bands, Five Dollar Shoes and the Hoodoo Rhythm Devils.

On Thanksgiving weekend, I saw Five Dollar Shoes at the Mercer Arts Center's Oscar Wilde Room—which may yet become New York's revenge on San Francisco—and was impressed. The group combines an unmistakably neopunk sensibility and what-am-I-doing-here humor with a sound that comes out of sixties-mainstream-hip rock. Its first album, *Five Dollar Shoes*, owes much to the Stones, Dylan (especially the Dylan of *Blonde on Blonde*), and the Velvet Underground (whose pervasive in-fluence is becoming more and more apparent).

The Hoodoo Rhythm Devils have released two albums—*Rack Jobbers Rule* and *The Barbecue of Deville*. Their stuff is a mash of rock-and-roll styles from honky-tonk to post-white-blues and a mish of lyrical modes from unintelligible doubletalk to innuendo, all overlaid with California good-timey zaniness. The resident genius of the group is Joe Crane, who provides vocals, piano, guitar, and élan. Of the two albums, I prefer *Barbecue*, a piece of monomaniacally (or maybe just maniacally) one-dimensional slop that includes such gems as "Eating in Kansas City," which is about eating in Kansas City; "Lotta Fine Mama," which is about lotta fine mama; "Suite 16," which is about a long, lean hotel room; "Sign Your Life Away," which is about inflation; and "All Tore Down," which is about existential despair.

Another album I've been listening to a lot lately is *Black Sabbath Volume 4*. Black Sabbath isn't really a seventies band. It belongs to the transi-tion period of the past couple of years, a time of romantic, self-indulgent pessimism, when people were acknowledging that the dream was dead but weren't quite ready to spit on its grave. Black Sabbath's first three albums are mostly awful, but this one moves me. In particular, I love two songs. "Wheels of Confusion" is the definitive postpsychedelic teenager's dirge: "Long ago I wandered through my mind. . . . / Lost in happiness I knew no fears, / Innocence and love was all I knew. / Was an illusion!" The logic of the song is kind of murky. In the last verse, our disillusioned one warns, "Life is just a game. / Don't you know there's never been a winner? / Try your hardest you'll still be a loser," which suggests that he hasn't so much said good-bye to all that as merely switched from a good trip to a bad one. But logic isn't as important here as Ozzy Osbourne's voice, which expresses teenage angst in all its essential purity and dumbness, and the music, which has resonances of "Gimme Shelter" and "Tomorrow Never Knows." The other song, "Changes," is a contemporary version, with feminist overtones, of the old fragility-of-young-love-in-an-alienating-world riff. It has the kind of radiantly naive lyrics that sixties heavies from Bob Dylan on down have been imitating for years—lines like "I feel unhappy, I feel so sad, / I've lost the best friend that I ever had," and "But soon the world had its evil way. / My heart was blinded, love went astray." And Ozzy *means* them.

The genius of these songs is that they convert the residue of a decade's aborted visions into the timeless melancholy of adolescence. They remind me that the antisixties backlash is an anachronism even before it begins. Pretty soon, there's going to be a new crop of kids, who, whatever they may inherit from the sixties, won't know where it came from, or care—until, of course, they grow up and get self-conscious, like everybody else.

Roseland Nation
OCTOBER 1973

A lot of people are excited about the Pointer Sisters. A lot of excited people recently crowded into Roseland Dance City (did anybody except me have the impression that Roseland had closed up a long time ago?) to see the group's New York debut while less fortunate aficionados milled around on the sidewalk outside. A lot of people are buying the Pointer Sisters' album *The Pointer Sisters* and watching them on television and, I suppose, reading all about their rags-to-rags career in *Newsweek*. Me, I sit so patiently, waiting to find out what price I have to pay to get out of going through all these things twice. Seriously, even I have to admit that the Pointer Sisters are very good at what they do; in fact, they do it with enough style and energy to make me feel like something of a sorehead for not letting them make me happy. But the truth is that the Pointer phenomenon provokes in me the alienating sensation that I am stuck in a peculiarly inhospitable time warp.

For those who haven't been following the publicity blitz, the Pointer Sisters, four exuberant black singers from Oakland, California, are being hailed as the seventies' answer to the Boswell Sisters, the Andrews Sisters, the McGuire Sisters, and the Supremes. Their slick nouveau forties sound—a blend of rock, jazz, and traditional pop that emphasizes scatting, complicated rhythms, and close harmonies—comes packaged with an ebullient, not to say manic, stage act and flamboyant threads: forties dresses, huge earrings, butterfly hair ornaments, and other accoutrements of haut-thrift-shop, post-Midler chic. Their sources range from Lambert, Hendricks, and Ross ("Cloudburst") to Willie Dixon ("Wang Dang Doodle"), and they've written songs of their own as well.

The Pointers (they really are sisters; both their parents are preachers, and they learned to sing in church) have already acquired a legend. The beginning of the saga has them unemployed and down-and-out in the South, where they spend their last dime or so to wire producer David Rubinson, who doesn't know them from Lambert, Hendricks, and Ross but agrees nevertheless to help them out. After some modest success as a backup group (notably for Taj Mahal) and some modest failure as rhythm-and-blues singers, they get their big chance: an act cancels out of the Troubadour in Los Angeles. They substitute and are an instant sensation. On to Johnny Carson, Helen Reddy, and national acclaim.

Admittedly, I don't know Lambert, Hendricks, and Ross from Wynken, Blynken, and Nod, and the only cultural event of the forties that ever meant much to me was the bubble-gum shortage. But it wasn't sheer narrow-mindedness that made me feel so out of it at the Pointers' Roseland performance. Sitting on the fabled dance floor in the midst of thirtyish Lance Louds, married couples from Brooklyn, black college kids, gold lamé loincloths, and urgent rumors that "Cicely Tyson is here! In the front row!," I felt as if I were crashing some weird parody of Woodstock—as if the crowd were not just an audience but a community that had come to celebrate an antirock festival. What these people wanted, and what the Pointer Sisters were ready to give them, was fantasy that didn't risk getting too real; entertainment that could be relied on not to overstep conventional bounds; above all, cheery sexiness and relentless good humor, free from embarrassing undercurrents of pain, anger, or love. As David Rubinson puts it, "We're bringing show business to people who haven't seen anything but rock and roll." Needless to say, I am less convinced than he that that's a good thing. What bothered me most about Roseland, I think, was that so much of the audience was my own age. It's been apparent for some time that there are several generation subgaps in the rock audience, but it felt freaky to look across one at my putative peers.

The Pointer Sisters are bound to be compared to Bette Midler—she is certainly responsible for them in the same sense that Bob Dylan can be said to be responsible for James Taylor—but I think the similarities are less crucial than the differences. Miss M plays her role in order to transcend it; she knows that masks can reveal as well as hide, that blatant artifice can, in the right circumstances, be poignantly honest, and she expresses the tension between image and inner self that all of us—but especially women—experience. But for the Pointer Sisters the role, the mask, the artifice are the whole point. Their purpose is to ensure a safe distance between performers and audience, so that, whatever the enthusiasm on both sides, emotional law and order will be maintained. In an introduction to one song, the Pointers announce, "Ladies and gentlemen, children, too, these brown babies gonna boogie for you." Laughs, cheers. Can you imagine any sixties audience feeling comfortable with that greeting? Is this the decadence everybody's been warning me about?

Slade is my second-favorite seventies British rock band (next to Mott the Hoople), but I was pretty thoroughly turned off by the group's October 6th performance at the Academy of Music. The problem was not the concert itself but Noddy Holder's idiotic attempts to get the audience to sing along. His haranguing, which ranged from the merely irritating to the positively fascistic ("Anybody who doesn't sing is going to get his ass kicked"), reached some sort of apotheosis in a competition between the "fellows" and the "ladies" to see who could sing the loudest. (The fellows won.) All the pump-priming not only inhibited whatever response I might have had to the music but made me want to curl up like an embryo under my seat. I don't know if Holder does this in England or if he just thinks it's what American fans want, but I hope next time he'll have the sense to shut up and sing.

Sympathy for the Stones
JULY 1975

I love watching the Rolling Stones perform. Yet if some visitors from Mars were to request a sample of the Stones at their best, I'd get them a bunch of records rather than take them to a concert. In part, I suppose, this preference reflects the bias of the obsessive listener, aware of and addicted to musical—particularly vocal—and spiritual subtleties that tend to get lost in the effort to project to the last row of an arena like Madison Square Garden. But even from a sheerly orgiastic point of view the choice holds, for ultimately it has less to do with subtleties than with the baldly obvious: sex. Mick Jagger's preeminence as a singer depends to a large extent on his incredible erotic power. Whatever else they may be, his recorded performances are nearly always seductions, sometimes blunt and blatant, sometimes overlaid with anger, pain, tenderness, or—in recent years—weary confusion (*not* the same thing as decadence). But for some reason (a reaction to Altamont? a desire to shake his macho reputation? the conviction that being a sex symbol is kid stuff?) Jagger seems to have decided to play down his sexuality onstage. On the Stones' current tour, as in 1972, Mick has chosen, rather, to embody some abstract principle of rock and roll: Jumpin' Jack Flash is an imp, not a man—a lightning rod for an impersonal, asexual, superhuman energy. The result is uniquely exciting, but it has a certain one-dimensional quality. It is as if Jagger's sexual being were so tied in with the rest of his emotions that to submerge it was to submerge himself. Some songs—mainly pure rockers, like "Brown Sugar" and "It's Only Rock & Roll"—are perfect vehicles for this sort of minimalist intensity. But when Jagger moves on to "Gimme Shelter" or "Wild Horses," or even "Rip This Joint," one has an uneasy sense of something missing. As if to distract from that lack, Mick clowns a lot. His humor—undoubtedly influenced by Ron Wood, who has replaced Mick Taylor's solemn musicianship with the Faces' brand of working-class zaniness as well as an earthier guitar style—is uncharacteristically silly. Mick plays that masterpiece of lubricity "Star Star" for yuks, sparring with an inflated phallic prop that looks like Casper the Friendly Ghost; he dumps buckets of water on the audience and on himself. Usually, the trouble with rock stars is that they take themselves too seriously; Jagger seems at times to be denying his seriousness altogether. I find the denial disingenuous, and it makes me uncomfortable.

These reservations intruded sporadically on my enjoyment of the Stones' opening night in New York, on Sunday, June 22nd. There were other problems too: bugs in the sound system; dull patches—particularly an interminable version of "Fingerprint File." Still, I spent most of the evening dancing in my seat—and in my seat merely because the people behind me insisted. I arrived at the Garden early; like most of the audience, I was already stoned on anticipation. Shortly after eight, the buildup began. Bands of steel drummers, situated in strategic parts of the hall, slowly converged in front of the Stones' collapsible six-pointed stage, which was folded up like a huge silver tulip. The drummers played; strings of tiny blue lights flashed, faster and faster; projections of the Stones' eagle logo circled the walls. At nine-twenty-five, when the crowd could no longer be denied, the stage opened to reveal Mick Jagger clinging to one of its points, dressed in what looked like magenta lounging pajamas. The concert began with "Honky Tonk Women"; it concluded with "Jumpin' Jack Flash." In between, for nineteen songs and more than two hours, Jagger kept up an amazing pace, dashing, dancing, tumbling, miming all around that pretentious stage, and finally swinging out over the audience on a trapeze-like contraption, as if only flying could satisfy his urge to move.

As an encore, the Stones did "Sympathy for the Devil," for the first time in America since Altamont. It was a daring idea, and the moment when they played the first notes of the introduction—when I realized, without quite believing it, what was going on—was mythic. But, as it turned out, the idea was more daring than the reality. The performance—except for a surprise guest solo by Eric Clapton—was perfunctory; the Stones shared it with a horde of steel drummers, who regrouped onstage for the purpose; and instead of an affirmation of their (and our?) ability to survive and face down trauma, it became an admission that they couldn't quite—which didn't invalidate the effort but did make it less than mythic. Afterward, another writer remarked, "The reason he had so many people on the stage with him is so he wouldn't get shot."

Because several friends compared Sunday's concert unfavorably with others they'd been to, earlier on the tour, I went back for the Thursday show. But whatever hopes I may have had of seeing the ultimate Stones concert soon dissipated. There were still problems with the sound, and the general energy level was perceptibly lower. The crowd was unaccountably hostile. All night, people kept throwing things onto the stage, and though the objects were relatively benign—flowers, Frisbees, toys of various sorts—the feeling was not. Once, I thought about Jagger's being shot; at the exact moment that the fantasy flashed into my mind, some rockets went off in the audience, and Mick flinched. At the end, the lights went out and the crowd waited tensely for the encore. Suddenly, a cherry bomb exploded four rows in front of me. A woman was led out, her hands over her face; I couldn't tell whether she was hurt or just stunned. The lights went up immediately, and the loudspeakers broadcast a firm good night. I was angry and upset. And yet with my critic's head I had to acknowledge that although the opening concert had been more fun, in a way this one had been better. The challenge of a difficult, capricious audience had forced Jagger to be harder, more serious, more real. It was an irony I might have appreciated more if that cherry bomb had not hit quite so close.

Creedence Clearwater Revival

FROM *ROLLING STONE ILLUSTRATED HISTORY OF ROCK 'N' ROLL,* 1980

For two years, 1969 and 1970, Creedence Clearwater Revival—John Fogerty (composer, singer, lead guitarist, arranger, manager, spiritual center), Tom Fogerty (guitarist), Stu Cook (bassist), Doug Clifford (drummer)—was the most popular rock band in America. During those years the group released five of its seven albums and seven (mostly two-sided) hit singles. At a time when the rock audience had already divided into antagonistic subgroups—hard-core rock-and-roll fans versus hard-core freaks, high school kids versus college students, AM versus FM—Creedence kept us all, dominating Top Forty radio while continuing to be acknowledged as "serious" by the industry-media-fan cabal that arbitrates such matters. Yet for all this ecumenical appeal, Creedence was always somewhat estranged from its generational and musical peers. Its image was of a group stubbornly loyal to unfashionable values. The geographical metaphor will do as well as

Originally published in *The Rolling Stone Illustrated History of Rock 'n' Roll,* edited by Jim Miller. New York: Rolling Stone Press, 1980.

any. Though Creedence shared turf with the acid-rock bands, its roots were not in psychedelic San Francisco or political Berkeley but in El Cerrito, an East Bay suburb with even less cachet, if possible, than Oakland. Its members were not former folkies converted to electric music by Bob Dylan; they had been a rock-and-roll band ever since high school in El Cerrito, surviving five years of touring as the Blue Velvets, three as the Golliwogs, and one more as Creedence before their first gold single, "Proud Mary," put them over the top in January 1969. They were not "underground" or "avantgarde" or into drugs or given to revolutionary rhetoric. They were at home with the short, tight, hit-single aesthetic that most "serious" rock musicians scorned in favor of the feckless, improvisatory aesthetic of the jam.

Despite these divergences, and the reservations about the counterculture that they implied, John Fogerty and his cohorts were very much a part of that culture, iconoclastic freaks, but freaks nonetheless. As often as not, their songs addressed the issues—political, cultural, musical— that moved the hip community. In response to the spoiled-rich-kid aspect of cultural-revolutionary politics, songs like "Fortunate Son" and "Don't Look Now" insisted on the touchy subject of class—of privilege and the lack of it. "Proud Mary," with the Huck-and-Jim-on-the-Mississippi echoes that lent its lyrics about dropping out a historical dimension, was an implicit critique of the idea that radicals had nothing to learn from American tradition. "Lookin' Out My Back Door" was at once a sillyserious celebration of tripping (with or without chemicals, as you prefer) and a send-up of pretentious visionaries. The band's eleven-minute version of "I Heard It Through the Grapevine" was a brilliant synthesis of opposing musical ideas; it was effective improvisation and effective rock and roll. The tension between identification and skepticism that informed Creedence's relation to its own subculture had a lot to do with why the group was great—and also with why it eventually fell apart.

John Fogerty's dedication to the formula of rock and roll—energy rigidly structured by what were originally commercial constraints—was, in a looser, freer era, as much an aesthetic choice, dictated by temperament, as other musicians' revolt against it. At bottom the choice was a function of Fogerty's populist instincts. Practically it meant that Creedence could reach the mass radio audience. Formally it meant loyalty to rock's plebian roots, and to its most basic pleasures (Creedence was *the* white American dance band; no one else came close). Fogerty's musical choice had its verbal analogue in his commonsense politics. But here an ambiguity arose.

For if Fogerty's sensitivity to the realities of class made him reject the elitist romanticism of sixties revolutionaries, it often led him into the opposite trap, a fatalism best expressed in his repeated use of rain as a metaphor for social ills. Weather, after all, is something you can't do anything about. Fortunately, Fogerty's lyrics were both compassionate enough and angry enough to take the curse off their pessimism; his persona in songs like "Who'll Stop the Rain" and "Wrote a Song for Everyone" was not the smug liberal secretly happy that he won't have to give up his two cars, but you and me on a bad day. And "Saw the people standing a thousand years in chains /Somebody said it's different now, but look it's just the same" was undeniably truer to most people's reality than "We want the world and we want it NOW!" But it was also undeniably less exciting. If this was not necessarily disastrous in itself, it was nevertheless symptomatic of a serious limitation.

Fogerty's populism and the counterculture's utopianism converged on one important point: being a best-selling rock band was not enough. A serious rock star aspired not only to entertain the public but to alter its consciousness and so in some sense affect history. By the end of the sixties the fragmentation of the audience that had coalesced around the Beatles, the Stones, and Dylan had made that aspiration increasingly unrealistic. Creedence remained the one band capable of uniting that audience and therefore of penetrating—and transforming—its fantasies. But it didn't happen. Creedence never crossed the line from best-selling rock band to cultural icon. And that failure seemed directly attributable to Fogerty's peculiar virtues.

The great sixties superstars did not make the pantheon on the strength of their music alone; they or, rather, their public images, were also aesthetic objects. Though Fogerty understood this, there was not much he could do about it without being false to himself. He had no affinity for the obvious image-making ploys: flamboyant freakery, messianism, sex, violence. Nor was he a flash ironist. Instead he projected intelligence, integrity, and moderation—not the sort of qualities that inflame either fans or journalists. In certain respects he resembled the solid, sustaining husband who is forever being betrayed for the dashing, undependable lover.

It was no accident that my interest in Creedence progressed from warm to obsessive at a time when I was in a state of emotional upheaval brought on by politics, drugs, writing blocks, and problematic personal

relationships. It was also a time when I was feeling alienated from my erstwhile favorite rock band, the Rolling Stones, partly because of Altamont,
partly because of feminism, but mostly because I was tired of chasing
Mick Jagger's mysterious soul through the mazes of fun house mirrors he
had built to protect it. Maybe it was all the politics and all the drugs, but
I craved a simpler, more direct, more human connection to rock and roll
and I connected with John Fogerty in a way I never could with Jagger. Yet
my realization that Creedence had edged out the Stones on my personal
rock chart came long after the fact. The switch happened gradually, eas-
ing into my subconscious without the customary *zap*—which says something about the difference between Creedence and the Stones.

It could be, of course, that none of this really mattered, that the
Warholian age of the media artists was irrevocably over, and that Creedence
never had a chance. But that was not the way the boys perceived it; they
were profoundly demoralized by the celebrity gap. One result was that they
became oversensitive to criticism, which consisted mostly of complaints
from the diehards of the Bay Area art-rock lobby that Creedence was an
uncreative "singles band." They began making defensive comments like
"We have something to *say.*" Their sixth album, *Pendulum,* released in
December 1970, included what Creedence watchers took to be some tentative concessions to Art—stuff like improvised organ music. I liked the
album, but it made me uneasy; it seemed to lack Fogerty's usual authority. Later I found out that the rest of the group had been challenging his
leadership; they wanted more artistic leeway. In 1971 Tom left the band,
and John agreed that Stu and Doug should play an equal part in writing,
arranging, and performing Creedence's material. Creedence put out only
two singles that year. The next album was long in coming, very long by
Creedence's previous standards—over a year. When it did come, in the
spring of 1972, it was disappointing.

Mardi Gras wasn't bad, just mediocre. Its rock was softened and
countrified. More important, Stu Cook and Doug Clifford simply did not
write or sing as well as John Fogerty, who contributed only three of the
album's songs. Perhaps, given enough time, they would have grown into
their new responsibilities. But in October Creedence Clearwater Revival
disbanded. Their situation was hardly unique. It had become a commonplace among political and cultural radicals that leadership was inherently oppressive, and all over the country groups of people who tried to
live by an ideology of leaderlessness were disintegrating in bitterness

Reading early feminist literature, 1970.

At a friend's country house in 1970. Willis occasionally retreated upstate or to Long Island to read or to write her *New Yorker* columns.

With journalist Karen Durbin in the *Village Voice*'s University Place offices, ca. 1977. Durbin and Willis met at *The New Yorker* in 1968. Durbin was a copy editor, and Willis would perch on her desk to talk about Vietnam and feminism.

From left, Ronnie Eldridge, Anna Quindlen, and Ellen Willis at a Barnard talk, "Objectivity in the Media: Women Reporting on Women," 1978. Willis graduated from Barnard College in 1962 and often said that, despite its reputation, feminists at Barnard reunions were few and far between.

In her Greenwich Village apartment, ca. 1980. This was often how she tested out albums: dancing by herself in front of a mirror.

In 1982, after another long meeting with her women's group. The group met in each other's apartments—here, at Ann Snitow's.

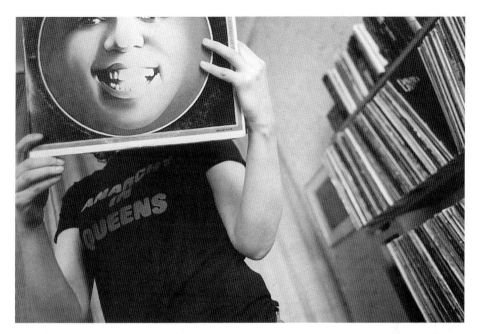

In her apartment with Bessie Smith's *Any Woman's Blues* record, ca. 1982.
Willis had the Anarchy in Queens T-shirt made for a punk costume for
a Halloween party, but she always said that she would have liked to have
just found it somewhere.

Taking notes on her newest record, ca. 1982.

The unnamed women's group that Willis was a part of for decades; this photograph was on the cover of the *New York Times Magazine* in 1984. My mother was pregnant with me at the time. Back row, from left: Ann Snitow, Brett Harvey, Karen Durbin, M Mark; middle row: Bonnie Bellows, Cindy Carr, Ellen Willis; front row: Alix Kates Shulman, Shelagh Doyle. Photograph by Dorothy Handelman.

and confusion. In the circumstances of its dissolution Creedence was, for once, utterly typical of the dissident community to which it so uneasily belonged.

Janis Joplin
FROM *ROLLING STONE ILLUSTRATED HISTORY OF ROCK 'N' ROLL*, 1980

Janis Joplin was born in 1943 and grew up in Port Arthur, Texas. She began singing in bars and coffeehouses, first locally, then in Austin, where she spent most of a year at the University of Texas. In 1966 she went to San Francisco and got together with a rock band in search of a singer, Big Brother and the Holding Company. The following summer Big Brother performed at the Monterey Pop Festival; Janis got raves from the fans and the critics and from then on she was a star. *Cheap Thrills*, Big Brother's first major album (there had been an early record on a small-time label), came out in July 1968. By then there were tensions between Janis and the group, and she left soon afterward.

With her new backup band she made another album, *I Got Dem Ol' Kozmic Blues Again Mama!* But the band never quite gelled, and in the spring of 1970 Janis formed another, Full-Tilt Boogie. They spent most of the summer touring, then went to Los Angeles to record an album, *Pearl*. It was Janis's last. On October 4th, 1970, she died of an overdose of heroin.

The hippie rock stars of the late sixties merged two versions of that hardy American myth, the free individual. They were stars, which meant achieving liberation by becoming rich and famous *on their own terms;* and they were, or purported to be, apostles of cultural revolution, a considerably more ambitious and romantic vision of freedom that nevertheless had a similar economic foundation. Young Americans were in a sense the stars of the world, drawing on an overblown prosperity that could afford to indulge all manner of rebellious and experimental behavior. The combination was

---

Originally published in *The Rolling Stone Illustrated History of Rock 'n' Roll*, edited by Jim Miller. New York: Rolling Stone Press, 1980.

inherently unstable—Whitman's open road is not, finally, the Hollywood Freeway, and in any case neither stardom nor prosperity could deliver what they seemed to promise. For a fragile historical moment rock transcended those contradictions; in its aftermath our pop heroes found themselves grappling, like the rest of us, with what are probably enduring changes in the white American consciousness—changes that have to do with something very like an awareness of tragedy. It is in this context that Janis Joplin developed as an artist, a celebrity, a rebel, a woman, and it is in this context that she died.

Joplin belonged to that select group of pop figures who mattered as much for themselves as for their music; among American rock performers she was second only to Bob Dylan in importance as a creator/recorder/ embodiment of her generation's history and mythology. She was also the only woman to achieve that kind of stature in what was basically a male club, the only sixties culture hero to make visible and public women's experience of the quest for individual liberation, which was very different from men's. If Janis's favorite metaphors—singing as fucking (a first principle of rock and roll) and fucking as liberation (a first principle of the cultural revolution)—were equally approved by her male peers, the congruence was only on the surface. Underneath—just barely—lurked a feminist (or prefeminist) paradox.

The male-dominated counterculture defined freedom for women almost exclusively in sexual terms. As a result, women endowed the idea of sexual liberation with immense symbolic importance; it became charged with all the secret energy of an as yet suppressed larger rebellion. Yet to express one's rebellion in that limited way was a painfully literal form of submission. Whether or not Janis understood that, her dual persona— lusty hedonist and suffering victim—suggested that she felt it. Dope, another term in her metaphorical equation (getting high as singing as fucking as liberation) was, in its more sinister aspect, a painkiller and finally a killer. Which is not to say that the good times weren't real, as far as they went. Whatever the limitations of hippie rock star life, it was better than being a provincial matron—or a lonely weirdo.

For Janis, as for others of us who suffered the worst fate that can befall an adolescent girl in America—*unpopularity*—a crucial aspect of the cultural revolution was its assault on the rigid sexual styles of the fifties. Joplin's metamorphosis from the ugly duckling of Port Arthur to the peacock of Haight-Ashbury meant, among other things, that a woman who was not conventionally pretty, who had acne and an intermittent weight problem and hair that stuck out, could not only invent her own beauty (just as she invented her wonderful sleazofreak costumes) out of sheer energy, soul, sweetness, arrogance, and a sense of humor, but have that beauty appreciated. Not that Janis merely took advantage of changes in our notions of attractiveness; she herself changed them. It was seeing Janis Joplin that made me resolve, once and for all, not to get my hair straightened. And there was a direct line from that sort of response to those apocryphal burned bras and all that followed.

Direct, but not simple. Janis once crowed, "They're paying me $50,000 a year to be like me." But the truth was that they were paying her to be a personality, and the relation of public personality to private self—something every popular artist has to work out—is especially problematic for a woman. Men are used to playing roles and projecting images in order to compete and succeed. Male celebrities tend to identify with their mask making, to see it as creative and—more or less—to control it. In contrast, women need images simply to survive. A woman is usually aware, on some level, that men do not allow her to be her "real self," and worse, that the acceptable masks represent men's fantasies, not her own. She can choose the most interesting image available, present it dramatically, individualize it with small elaborations, undercut it with irony. But ultimately she must serve some male fantasy to be loved—and then it will be only the fantasy that is loved anyway. The female celebrity is confronted with this dilemma in its starkest form. Joplin's revolt against conventional femininity was brave and imaginative, but it also dovetailed with a stereotype—the ballsy, one-of-the-guys chick who is a needy, vulnerable cream puff underneath—cherished by her legions of hip male fans. It may be that she could have pushed beyond it and taken the audience with her; that was one of the possibilities that made her death an artistic as well as human calamity. There is, for instance, the question of her bisexuality. People who knew Janis differ on whether sexual relationships with women were an important part of her life, and I don't know the facts. In any case, a public acknowledgment of bisexual proclivities would not necessarily have contradicted her image; it could easily have been passed off as more pull-out-the-stops hedonism or another manifestation of her all-encompassing need for love. On the other hand, she could have used it to say something new about women and liberation. What makes me wonder is something I always noticed and liked about Janis: unlike most female performers whose act is intensely erotic, she never made me feel as if I were crashing an orgy that consisted of her and the men in the audience. When she got it on at a concert, she got it on with everybody.

Still, the songs she sang assumed heterosexual romance; it was men who made her hurt, who took another little piece of her heart. Watching men groove on Janis, I began to appreciate the resentment many black people feel toward whites who are blues freaks. Janis sang out of her pain as a woman, and men dug it. Yet it was men who caused the pain, and if they stopped causing it they would not have her to dig. In a way, their adulation was the cruelest insult of all. And Janis's response—to sing harder, get higher, be worshiped more—was rebellious, acquiescent, bewildered all at once. When she said, "Onstage I make love to 25,000 people, then I go home alone," she was not merely repeating the cliché of the sad clown or the poor little rich girl. She was noting that the more she gave the less she got and that, honey, it ain't fair.

Like most women singers, Joplin did not write many songs; she mostly interpreted other people's. But she made them her own in a way few singers dare to do. She did not sing them so much as struggle with them, assault them. Some critics complained, not always unfairly, that she strangled them to death, but at her best she whipped them to new life. She had an analogous adversary relationship with the musical form that dominated her imagination, the blues. Blues represented another external structure, one with its own contradictory tradition of sexual affirmation and sexist conservatism. But Janis used blues conventions to reject blues sensibility. To sing the blues is a way of transcending pain by confronting it with dignity, but Janis wanted nothing less than to scream it out of existence. Big Mama Thornton's classic rendition of "Ball and Chain" carefully balances defiance and resignation, toughness and vulnerability. She almost pities her oppressor. Her singing conveys, above all, her determination to survive abuse. Janis makes the song into one long frenzied, despairing protest. Why, why, *why*, she asks over and over, like a child unable to comprehend injustice. The pain is overwhelming her. There are similar differences between her recording of "Piece of My Heart" and Erma Franklin's. When Franklin sings it, it is a challenge: no matter what you do to me, I will not let you destroy my ability to be human, to love. Joplin seems rather to be saying, surely if I keep taking this, if I keep setting an example of love and forgiveness, surely he has to understand, change, give me back what I have given.

Her pursuit of pleasure had the same driven quality; what it amounted to was refusal to admit of any limits that would not finally yield to the virtue of persistence—*try just a little bit harder*—and the magic of extremes. This war against limits was largely responsible for the electrifying power of Joplin's early performances; it was what made *Cheap Thrills* a classic, in spite of unevenness and the impossibility of duplicating on a record the excitement of her concerts. After the split with Big Brother, Janis retrenched considerably, perhaps because she simply couldn't maintain that level of intensity, perhaps for other reasons that would have become clear if she had lived. My uncertainty on this point makes me hesitate to be too dogmatic about my conviction that leaving Big Brother was a mistake.

I was a Big Brother fan. I thought they were better musicians than their detractors claimed, but more to the point, technical accomplishment in itself was not something I cared about. I thought it was an ominous sign that so many people did care, including Janis. It was, in fact, a sign that the tenuous alliance between mass culture and bohemianism—or, in my original formulation, the fantasy of stardom and the fantasy of cultural revolution—was breaking down. But the breakdown was not as neat as it might appear. For the elitist concept of "good musicianship" was as alien to the holistic, egalitarian spirit of rock and roll as the act of leaving one's group the better to pursue one's individual ambition was alien to the holistic, egalitarian pretensions of the cultural revolutionaries. If Joplin's decision to go it alone was influenced by all the obvious professional/commercial pressures, it also reflected a conflict of values within the counterculture itself—a conflict that foreshadowed its imminent disintegration. And again, Janis's femaleness complicated the issues, raised the stakes. She had less room to maneuver than a man in her position, fewer alternatives to fall back on if she blew it. If she had to choose between fantasies, it made sense for her to go with stardom as far as it would take her.

But I wonder if she really had to choose, if her choice was not in some sense a failure of nerve and therefore of greatness. Janis was afraid Big Brother would hold her back, but if she had thought it was important enough, she might have been able to carry them along, make them transcend their limitations. There is more than a semantic difference between a group and a backup band. Janis had to relate to the members of Big Brother as spiritual (not to mention financial) equals even though she had more talent than they, and I can't help suspecting that that was good for her not only emotionally and socially but aesthetically. Committed to the hippie ethic of music-for-the-hell-of-it—if only because there was no possibility of their becoming stars on their own—Big Brother helped Janis sustain the amateur quality that was an integral part of her effect. Their zaniness was a salutary reminder that good times meant silly fun— remember "Caterpillar"?—as well as Dionysiac abandon; it was a relief from Janis's extremism and at the same time a foil for it. At their best moments Big Brother made me think of the Beatles, who weren't (at least in the beginning) such terrific musicians either. Though I'm not quite soft-headed enough to imagine that by keeping her group intact Janis Joplin could somehow have prevented or delayed the end of an era, or even saved her own life, it would have been an impressive act of faith. And acts of faith by public figures always have reverberations, one way or another.

Such speculation is of course complicated by the fact that Janis died before she really had a chance to define her post–San Francisco, post–Big Brother self. Her last two albums, like her performances with the ill-fated Kozmic Blues Band, had a tentative, transitional feel. She was obviously going through important changes; the best evidence of that was "Me and Bobby McGee," which could be considered her "Dear Landlord." Both formally—as a low-keyed, soft, folkie tune—and substantively—as a lyric that spoke of choices made, regretted, and survived, with the distinct implication that compromise could be a positive act—what it expressed would have been heresy to the Janis Joplin of *Cheap Thrills*. "Freedom's just another word for nothing left to lose" is as good an epitaph for the counterculture as any; we'll never know how—or if—Janis meant to go on from there.

Janis Joplin's death, like that of a fighter in the ring, was not exactly an accident. Yet it's too easy to label it either suicide or murder, though it involved elements of both. Call it rather an inherent risk of the game she was playing, a game whose often frivolous rules both hid and revealed a deadly serious struggle. The form that struggle took was incomplete, shortsighted, egotistical, self-destructive. But survivors who give in to the temptation to feel superior to all that are in the end no better than those who romanticize it. Janis was not so much a victim as a casualty. The difference matters.

Selections from
"Don't Turn Your Back on Love"
LINER NOTES TO *JANIS*, A JANIS JOPLIN BOX SET, 1993

In 1969 I wrote a review of that echt-'60s road movie, *Easy Rider*, that contemplated with some anguish the coming crack-up of my generation's culture. I ended the piece with an imagined conversation in which a former hippie reminisced fondly, "Remember Janis Joplin?" A year later Janis Joplin died of an overdose of heroin in a Los Angeles hotel room. An ending far more brutal than the obscurity I'd glumly anticipated, it mirrored the violent climax of *Easy Rider*—and foreshadowed the abrupt shift in the social atmosphere that was at that very moment taking shape.

I had thought I was prepared for the change, but I wasn't. In particular, I hadn't understood that memory under such circumstances isn't fond or nostalgic; it's disorienting. Overnight, it seemed, the values that Joplin and her music had embodied—the commitment to excess, the insistence on raw, intense feeling, the utopian vision of ecstasy as a way of life—were consigned to some weird and unreal collective psychodrama labeled "the '60s." "The '60s," as they began to be defined, were not a period of history but a fantasy, probably drug induced. Except, of course, for the deaths. Joplin, Hendrix, and before them the Kennedys, Martin Luther King Jr., Malcolm X: their brutal endings were real enough. Indeed, the very reality of those deaths was said to prove the consummate unreality of all the other stuff.

The theme of the '70s was austerity, material and moral. "The days of wine and roses are over," the arbiters of the Zeitgeist kept telling us, even as they denied that the wine was ever as heady, the roses as fragrant, as we thought. Efforts to confront the meaning of the recent past, to find continuities between past and present, or even to insist on the palpable existence of a decade's worth of experience were derided as symptoms of a dread disease called "getting stuck in the '60s." Apparently, we were simply supposed to wake up from our pasts as if from a dream and carry on as if the cultural upheaval that had shaped our lives had never happened. This attempt at historical lobotomy was also, in effect, an attack on a certain kind of artist. There was no denying that Janis Joplin had happened: her voice was on record, her performance on film, her face at its most transcendent captured in photographs. But to grasp the full measure of Joplin's accomplishment, you had to understand that she was part of a vibrant, complex, and contradictory culture—one that she had also helped create.

It's likely, though, that she would have been somewhat bemused by the trajectory of rock and roll rebellion—and sexual rebellion—over the next two decades. In the age of punk, the lingua franca of cultural opposition was rage. Not only was utopian optimism out of the question: love was sentimental, pain to be hidden at all cost. With the emergence of feminism, which had its own all too brief utopian moment, women too were furious, and they reserved a special vehemence for the hypocrisies of romance, for sexual powerlessness and the betrayed promises of the sexual revolution. Sometime in the '80s, a new generation of female rebels and rock and rollers began developing sexual sensibilities that crossed punk with feminism, added a dollop of sexual ambiguity, and often dressed it all up, with high irony, in the enduring cultural symbols of the bad girl—scarlet lipstick, black lace, spike heels. They demystified sex: what's love (or utopia) got to do with it? They did not aspire to connect with some deeper cosmic reality but to play with the ubiquitous virtual reality of mass-mediated eroticism. Pleasure was still the name of the game, but the fantasy they played out was not excess and abandon; it was autonomy, distance, power, control. While Janis had rejected ladyhood by drinking and swearing and acting like one of the guys, these women flung femininity back in the face of the culture. If the counterpoint to Janis's lust was anguish, the undercurrent in the new bad girls' sexuality was always that postpunk, feminist-inspired anger.

JANIS JOPLIN, MEET MADONNA CICCONE

Equally committed to flamboyance, refusal of nice-girl respectability, getting it while she can, and outfitting herself in playful cultural collages, Madonna is the triumphant sequel to Janis's cautionary tale. The sexual contradictions that trapped Janis, and arguably killed her, are the ironies Madonna has thrived on and turned to her own uses, appropriating the image of the whore, melding it with androgyny and deviance, flaunting it without a plea for anyone's approval, and so achieving an artistic control of her public persona unprecedented for a woman. In all her perilous vulnerability, Janis Joplin opened up the sexual territory on which postpunkfems from Madonna to the riot grrrls have drawn their line in the sand. History did not, in fact, end and then begin again in 1970. The pressure to obliterate the '60s was, if anything, a tribute to their power: music, pop culture, sex, women would never be the same. And if Janis could have used some of her successors' hard-edged, self-protective pragmatism, they too have something to learn from her aching sense of possibility—and the emotional risks it entailed.

As for my generation, those of us who were inspired by Janis, who saw in her an emblem of our own struggle for freedom, have had to live with a kind of survivor's guilt, rooted in the question of whether we somehow collaborated in, or benefited from, her self-destruction. Like any other war, the '60s assault on the culture exacted a price that real people paid: this must never be denied. Yet finally, to invoke Janis Joplin's death as an excuse for closing down, playing it safe, would be to trivialize both her life and her art. For the truth is that antiutopianism also has its price, which is the inability to feel our deepest longings and ultimately to feel much of anything at all. Even anger can be a kind of numbness.

During the years after Janis died, there were long stretches when I couldn't bear to listen to her music; there was nowhere I could go with the feelings she aroused. But as the millennium winds down, I hear a few sounds of armor cracking. I think, for instance, of two movie heroines, born again desperadoes, who smash one limit after another, uncover the hidden places where anger and despair, defiance and love converge, and finally leap into the Grand Canyon because freedom's just another word for nothing left to lose. It occurs to me that perhaps *Thelma and Louise* is the memorial Janis deserves. And with that thought, I grab my *Joplin in Concert* album off the shelf—the one with the cover picture of Janis wearing funny round glasses and feathers in her hair and an immortal smile—and play "Get It While You Can" at top volume. This above all is Janis's message to the world: Don't you turn your back on love.

Chapter 4

THE FEMINIST

But Now I'm Gonna Move

OCTOBER 1971

The women's movement has inspired a lot of talk about male supremacy
and misogyny in rock, but most people seem to have missed a crucial
point: that there is an alarming difference between the naive sexism that
disfigured rock before, say, 1967 and the much more calculated, almost
ideological sexism that has flourished since. What happened in between
was that rock got integrated into the so-called counterculture and what
had been a music of oppression became in many respects a music of
pseudoliberation. Early rock was sexist in all the obvious ways. The industry was controlled by men; most singers and virtually all instrumentalists were men; song lyrics assumed traditional sex roles and performers
embodied them. (Although the Beatles made important changes in the
masculine style, the substance remained pretty much the same.) Yet insofar as the music expressed the revolt of black against white, working class
against middle class, youth against parental domination and sexual puritanism, it spoke for both sexes; insofar as it pitted teenage girls' inchoate

energies against all their conscious and unconscious frustrations, it spoke implicitly for female liberation. The Big Bear was a universal code that meant "Free our bodies." Since most of the traditional themes of rock and roll had to do with sex and rebellion, they were in one way or another bogged down in the contradiction between male-supremacist prejudice and revolutionary impulse. Male performers perpetuated the mythology that made woman the symbol of middle-class respectability and kicked over the pedestal without asking who had invented it in the first place. The British groups, in particular, tended to make women scapegoats for their disenchantment with the class system: Mick Jagger, the Stanley Kowalski of rock, brought down rich playgirls with crude exhibitions of virility; the Who condemned the romantic illusions and self-protective hypocrisies of wives and girlfriends. Female singers, for their part, often expressed their own rebellion vicariously by identifying with a (usually lower-class) male outlaw, as in "Leader of the Pack." Female fans made an analogous identification with male rock stars—a relationship that all too often found us digging them while they put us down. This was not masochism but expendiency. For all its limitations, rock was the best thing going, and if we had to filter out certain indignities—well, we had been doing that all our lives, and there was no feminist movement to suggest that things might be different.

When rock was taken over by upper-middle-class bohemians, it inherited a whole new set of contradictions between protest and privilege. The new musicians are elite dropouts and, as such, tend to feel superior not only to women but to just about everyone. Their sexism is smugger and cooler, less a product of misdirected frustration, more a simple assumption of power consistent with the rest of their self-image. It is less overtly hostile to women but more condescending. A crude but often revealing method of assessing male bias in lyrics is to take a song written by a man about a woman and reverse the sexes. By this test, a diatribe like "Under My Thumb" is not nearly so sexist in its implications as, for example, Cat Stevens's gentle, sympathetic "Wild World"; Jagger's fantasy of sweet revenge could easily be female—in fact, it has a female counterpart, Nancy Sinatra's "Boots"—but it's hard to imagine a woman sadly warning her ex-lover that he's too innocent for the big bad world out there. The new sexism is also less honest. The rock culture has not merely assimilated male supremacy but, with its own Orwellian logic, tried to pass it off as liberation. Reverence for such neglected "feminine" values as gentleness and nurturance becomes an excuse to bad-mouth women who display "masculine" characteristics like self-assertion or who don't want to preside as goddess of the organic kitchen. Freedom for women is defined solely as sexual freedom, which in practice means availability on men's terms. The rock community is a male monopoly, with women typically functioning as more or less invisible accessories; around male musicians I've often felt as out of place as a female sportswriter in a locker room. The classic statement of the rock attitude toward women appeared in a *Rolling Stone* supplement on groupies. It seems that rock bands prefer San Francisco groupies to New York groupies: the latter, being coldhearted Easterners, are only out for conquests; Bay Area chicks really dig the musicians as people, not just bodies, and stay afterward to do their housework. This sort of disingenuous moralism offends me much more than the old brutal directness. At least, the Stones never posed as apostles of a revolutionary lifestyle.

Like the educated middle class that produced them, the new rock musicians are art snobs, and one facet of their snobbery is a tedious worship of technical proficiency. The cult of the Musician has reinforced the locker-room aspect of the rock scene. There, as elsewhere, musicianship, like most technical skills, is considered a male prerogative, and female instrumentalists—those few who have managed to resist pervasive cultural intimidation well enough to learn to play *and* take themselves seriously—have been patronized and excluded. Besides, the pretension, competitiveness, and abstraction from feeling that go along with an emphasis on technique are alienating to most women. (This may be why there are relatively few female jazz fans.) In an overwhelmingly male atmosphere, female performers have served mainly as catalysts for male cultural-revolutionary fantasies of tough chicks, beautiful bitches, and super-yin old ladies. Janis Joplin half-transcended this function by confronting it, screaming out the misery and confusion of being what others wanted her to be. But she was a genius.

Of course, contradictions have a way of resolving themselves, as a nineteenth-century revolutionist pointed out. The same social events that produced a sexist "cultural revolution" produced a sexist radical left, which, in turn, gave rise to the women's liberation movement. Rock has been particularly resistant to the inroads of a resurgent feminism, but it is not impervious. A year ago, there were probably fewer female rock performers of stature than at any other time in the past decade; today there is a noticeable influx of female singers and composers, and they are finding a receptive audience. More important, women are beginning to break away from the hip stereotypes. Carole King is scarcely a counterculture heroine, and Joni Mitchell's latest album, *Blue,* makes me wonder what ever happened to the sweet folksinger who used to talk about baking cookies to the crowd at the Bitter End. For a long time, I didn't listen to Alice Stuart's album, because its title, *Full Time Woman,* turned me off; when I did, I discovered that the title song starts out "I hear you've got a full-time woman now, / Does she love you like I never could?" and ends "You gotta set me free. / I'd do it for you, baby; now do it for me." Deliberate or not, the reversal of expectations was in itself a statement: things are seldom what they seem.

Women musicians are also starting to emerge. A number of all-female rock bands have formed, some actively feminist, but as yet this remains almost entirely a local, "underground" phenomenon; the main exception is Fanny, which has put out two disappointing albums. The most exciting female musicians to surface so far belong to a mixed group. They are Toni Brown and Terry Garthwaite, the leaders of a Berkeley quintet called Joy of Cooking. Toni writes most of the group's material, plays a conspicuous electric piano, and sings; Terry sings lead and plays guitar; they are backed up by three men, including a conga drummer. Joy has made two excellent albums—*Joy of Cooking,* which came out last January, and a new release, *Closer to the Ground*—and is a popular performing band on the West Coast. Now that it is making a major tour of the East and the Midwest, its audience should begin to expand.

Toni and Terry are not propagandists, except by implication; even in "Only Time Will Tell Me," Toni's one overtly feminist song, we are warned that "Everybody wants some power in this land of liberty, / But having lots of power never made anybody free." Still, they are, among other things, propaganda. Besides being intelligent and inventive musicians, they have flouted the convention that women in rock must be either passive or bitchy or desperate. Toni's voice is sweet, Terry's rougher and funkier; both seem to be controlling strong feelings in a way that suggests a desire to keep some of their resources for themselves rather than give body and soul to the audience. Terry, in particular, communicates a female sensibility that is strong, straightforward, independent, exuberant. So do the songs themselves. Although Toni has written some moving portraits of women dumped on by men, particularly "Too Late, but Not Forgotten" and "Red

Wine at Noon" (the only cuts from the first album on which she sings lead; ballads are more her style than Terry's), the mood of "Only Time Will Tell Me" (also included in the first album) is more typical: "Been standing on a corner, trying to get across the street, / So many years now I've been staring at my feet, / But now I'm gonna move. . . . / I'm gonna stretch out and find my wings and fly away." Toni's lyrics, some of them quasi-political intimations that the world and people are in a mess and what are we gonna do about it, reflect a cautious, tough-minded optimism. The music, an original, unclassifiable mixture of rock, country, and gospel, with a lot of upbeat vocal improvisation and irresistible rhythms, is—not joyful, exactly; zestful is closer. It is also very polished—occasionally too much so. Fortunately, the group's reserve generally comes across as dignity—not the kind that excludes a good time, either—rather than stinginess. The new album is very much an extension of the first. As its title suggests, the country influence is stronger; the lyrics are somewhat more contemplative and romantic, although there is also plenty of dry comment on the sexual revolution, as in "First Time, Last Time": "If you make it with a stranger you better really know the score, / because no matter what he tells you there's bound to be a whole lot more." Terry has contributed two of the songs, and she holds her own with Toni; the lyrics to "Humpty Dumpty," a rocker about the futility of waiting for the king's men to put you together, are especially good.

Joy of Cooking has been around for four years. That the group should begin to make it at this particular time suggests some questions, the most obvious being: would Toni and Terry have been overlooked if it weren't for all the women's-liberation publicity of the past year or two? Take that one step further: if record companies were benignly neglecting them because they were women, did the lack of pressure help them develop as beautifully as they did? More cynically: is it easier for them now that the prominence of solo singer-songwriters has made the mystique of groups and musicianship less central? Perhaps all this is irrelevant. Joy of Cooking is not just a good band but an exceptional band, and it's more than possible that the public would have had to recognize that fact, women's liberation or no. It just may be that, unlike a lot of less exceptional bands, Joy had the sense to wait to make an album until it was ready. On the other hand, chances are that if it were any less exceptional it would never have survived at all.

Joni Mitchell: Still Traveling
MARCH 1973

Joni Mitchell's fourth album, *Blue*, converted me from a well-wisher to a fan. I had always liked her, but we had never really connected. Her image tended to stand between me and her music. I saw the gentle, soft-spoken, fair-haired folk singer, the classic old lady, the Muse to numerous folk-rock *machers* who had to encourage her to overcome her shyness and record—the compleat hippie chick, in short—and I was looking for other models. Besides, I thought of her voice as a curiosity, a freak of nature that ought to be of some use but was really more of a distraction than anything else. Several of her songs—"Both Sides Now" and "Big Yellow Taxi," in particular—were among my favorites, but I preferred other people's versions.

Then came *Blue*. What hit me first was that the freaky voice had found its purpose. Before, it had just been *there*; now Joni was controlling it, using it to express an exploratory urgency that her lyrics confirmed. *Blue* was less a collection of songs than a piece of music divided into sections. Its central theme was travel, literal and spiritual—a familiar folk metaphor, except that instead of a man on the road the traveler was a woman pursuing her female identity through the byways of the pop world. The sensibility that emerged (it had been lurking inconspicuously in Mitchell's previous albums, particularly *Ladies of the Canyon*) was a blend of romanticism and stoicism that illuminated the pop milieu in a new way—a feat I wouldn't have thought possible. Although Joni never forced the analogy, the men she loved-hated with such forgiving irony obviously embodied that milieu; from one angle, *Blue* was a neat reversal of the world-as-bitch-goddess fantasy. But neat did not mean simple. There were more resonances in lines like "You're my holy wine, / You taste so bitter and so sweet, / Oh, I could drink a case of you, darling, / And I would still be on my feet" than most performers put on an entire album.

Blue established Joni Mitchell as a better singer-songwriter than Crosby, Stills, Nash and Taylor combined. Her fifth album, *For the Roses*, is an elaboration of *Blue*—both technically and thematically—and is in some ways even finer. Unfortunately, it is also less accessible. Joni's melodies and lyrics and rhythms are so rich and complicated and un-pop-song-like, her voice such a subtle instrument, her artistic pretensions so overt that if the record were any less brilliant it would be a disaster. As it is, I'm not sure how I would have reacted if I hadn't heard "You Turn Me On, I'm a Radio" first—on the radio. "You Turn Me On" is an irresistible tour de force, a metaphysical poem (I mean the kind dispensed by Donne, not Rod McKuen) based on the crucial technological metaphor for rock and roll. Witty, playful, gently self-mocking, it explores the lighthearted surface that half covers, half exposes Mitchell's passionate fatalism (or fatalistic passion). But the album also has its dark side. In "Banquet" and "Cold Blue Steel and Sweet Fire," the surface is stripped away. Other songs just display the cracks: "I heard it in the wind last night, / It sounded like applause. Chilly now, / End of summer." Like *Blue*, *For the Roses* is full of acerbic comment about men and the difficulties and ambiguities of love. But where *Blue* emphasized the adventures of new emotional terrain, *For the Roses* is more preoccupied with dead ends, limitations, final failures. At the same time, recurrent images of electricity and fire speak of a new kind of gathering energy, abstract and awesome—can it be anger? "You've got to roar like forest fire. . . . / They're going to aim the hoses on you. / Show them you won't expire," Joni cries in "Judgment of the Moon and Stars." But that's material for another album.

Even before Carly Simon married James Taylor, she wasn't exactly one of my favorite people. Her wide-eyed lyrics inevitably aroused my class antagonism. Maybe that's the way *she* always heard it should be, I was wont to grumble, but us funky types from the streets of Queens knew better before we were ten. Which is to say that I would never have predicted that one of my favorite singles of the past year would be a Carly Simon song. But I love "You're So Vain." It's great rock and roll; the inspired sloppiness of its language is positively Dylanesque; and it has a lot more feminist verve than Helen Reddy's manifesto. It's not so much the words that carry the message—although "You're so vain, you prob'ly think this song is about you" is one of the all-time great lines—as the good-humored nastiness in Carly's voice.

   "You're So Vain" inspired me to pay more attention than I normally would have to Simon's latest LP, *No Secrets*. I'm not sure whether I'm sorry or relieved that I can't report any great breakthrough. I'm moderately fond of a few of the songs—notably "We Have No Secrets," which is about how openness and honesty can be a pain. (Yeah, I know, words like "In the name of honesty, in the name of what is fair, / You always answer my questions, but they don't always answer my prayers" sound silly when you repeat them. So do a lot of Dylan's.) But Carly's father fixation is still much in evidence, and her melodies are too often muddy, her phrasing amorphous, her voice self-important. Oh, well. I guess "You're So Vain" is one of those happy tributes to the democratic promise of rock and roll—that each of us, even a rich little rich girl, has something worthwhile to communicate over AM radio.

Women's Music
JUNE 1974

Last fall, a singer-songwriter-guitarist named Kristin Lems enrolled as a graduate student at the University of Illinois in Champaign-Urbana. Eager to get in touch with other women musicians, she put an ad in the local paper, and eight women answered. They began getting together, playing and singing, helping each other develop. When a campus coffeehouse sponsored a folk-music festival that included not a single female performer, Lems and her friends organized a folk festival for women. It drew an enthusiastic crowd, and the women began to think bigger. Why not a national festival, where women involved in all areas of music—not just folk—could come together and perform for each other, exchange experiences, discuss how to combat discrimination against female musicians? A festival committee coalesced and began making plans for the first National Women's Music Festival, to be held on campus from May 28th to June 2nd.

The scope of the project was soon narrowed to nonclassical music, but in other respects it became more and more ambitious. The committee announced that a number of name performers—including Fanny, Yoko Ono, Labelle, and Janis Ian—had agreed to appear without pay except for expenses. I heard that CBS-TV was going to send a camera crew, and that *Time* was doing a picture story. When I first learned about the festival, it occurred to me to wonder if the organizers, most of whom were undergraduates, knew what they were getting into. As it turned out, my doubts were neither unfounded nor particularly relevant. It would be frivolously hyperbolic to call the festival a women's Woodstock, but there were certain parallels: just about everything that could go wrong did, and almost everybody had a good time anyway.

The festival committee's first big headache was the university, which seemed unaccountably hostile. The administration was stingy with space for concerts, workshops, and jams, refused the committee permission to sell tickets to individual events (registration for the entire festival cost ten dollars), and at the last minute almost called the whole thing off, apparently on the rather laughable ground that it was a commercial enterprise. It didn't help that the festival was held a week after most students had left the campus for the summer. But the most conspicuous foul-up arose from the defection of the festival's one paid employee, a Chicago booking agent. It was this woman who had got, or claimed to have got, commitments from the celebrities advertised in the festival's publicity. When she disappeared, on the second night of the festival, the organizers, who, in their naïveté, had not even bothered to keep a list of the heavies' phone numbers, had no way of reaching them. None of them showed up.

Under most circumstances I can think of, such a blunder would have created a major crisis. But feminists tend to disdain star worship, and the main response to the drastic change of program was "Who needs them, anyway?" By the time everyone realized what was happening, the festival had gelled. There was no shortage of talent—many of the performers, who had been recruited from both coasts as well as the Midwest, had solid hometown reputations, especially in women's-movement circles— and people were excited by what they were hearing. The workshops were generating a lot of discussion about the prospects for women's music and, beyond that, for a revolutionary female culture. New friendships and musical alliances were being formed. In short, the festival was a grass-roots success, and in view of the modest attendance—and correspondingly modest revenue—it was probably just as well that the committee did not have to cope with huge transportation bills and demanding egos.

My own reaction was mixed. I didn't especially miss Fanny, but I did miss rock and roll. Rock is, among other things, a potent means of expressing the active emotions—anger, aggression, lust, the joy of physical exertion—that feed all freedom movements, and it is no accident that women musicians have been denied access to this powerful musical language. I think it's crucially important for female performers to break that barrier and force rock to reflect their experience and aspirations. But though the burgeoning of local female rock bands has been one of the more interesting developments in women's music, there was virtually no electric music at the festival. The only rock act actually to perform onstage was Carla Peyton, an excellent black R&B singer from Champaign, and her lackluster white male band, the Coal Kitchen. After a wearying hassle over space and equipment, there was a rock jam, organized by Susan Abod, of the defunct Chicago Women's Liberation Rock Band, and her sister Jennifer, who is in the process of re-forming the New Haven Women's Liberation Rock Band. (It needs a bass player.) Artemis, a newly formed electric group from Ann Arbor, led another jam. Individual rock and jazz musicians wandered around seeking each other out. But the vast majority of performers were working in the two forms traditionally available to women: folk music and straight pop.

On the whole, I felt that the folk music was more effective, if only because folk is a natural medium for a communal gathering—simple enough to encourage participation, informal enough to blur the distinction between amateurs and professionals, and, of course, the traditional vehicle for political sentiments. Many of the folk performers contributed topical songs about women's experiences, old folk ballads about women workers, songs that explicitly or implicitly linked the women's movement with other radical struggles. Though the propaganda occasionally got heavy-handed, I was happy to note that folksingers have learned a lot since 1963: most of the political songs were graphic and personal, and some were very funny. My favorite in the latter category was "The Bloods," a song about menstruation that has got to become a feminist classic. The band that performed it, the Clinch Mountain Back-Steppers (the music they played sounded exactly like their name), was the best folk act at the festival, largely because of the zany warmth of lead singer Woody Simmons and the spirited fiddle playing of Robin Flower. I also enjoyed Redwing, a radical band from Milwaukee; Jo Mapes, a veteran Chicago folksinger, who performed witty, original songs about her work and her sexuality (as well as one awful saga-of-suburbia that hit every cliché, including the bored wife seducing the delivery boy); and Kristin Lems, a charmer in the most literal and least artificial sense of the word, who livened up the down-homey proceedings by wearing a shiny multicolored gown, delivered some nice feminist lyrics, and (with her sister Karen) did a moving version of "George Jackson." Barbara Dane, the best-known folkie on the program, displayed an unfortunate tropism for ideological anthems ("The masses, the masses only, are the makers of our history") devoid of redeeming aesthetic value, but she did sing one song I really liked—a foot-stomper called "Insubordination." I couldn't help thinking it would have been even better with a rock band behind it.

The pop singers were at once more sophisticated and less interesting. I was impressed by their skill but disturbed by what I saw as their essential conservatism: in spite of their jeans and rock-influenced rhythms, their music was basically nightclub stuff—romantic, "feminine," non-threatening, a cross between Laura Nyro and Melissa Manchester, with maybe a little Joni Mitchell for spice. The best of them, a Los Angeles–based singer, composer, and pianist named Margie Adam, was as talented an exponent of the genre as I've seen anywhere. Her songs were well crafted; her voice was expressive, her piano original, her personality appealing. The festival participants loved her. And yet her music didn't turn me on; on the contrary, it left me with a traitorous itch to sneak off and listen to "Satisfaction."

This year's festival was only a beginning; Lems and her cohorts are planning to make it an annual event. The idea is a good one, and with time and practice the reality should become more various, less insular. I hope the rock bands come next year, and I hope the stars do, too—not because they are necessary to justify the festival's existence but because I think that women who have chosen to deal with the aesthetic and commercial pressures of the mass media have a valuable perspective to offer. Before we can even begin to create a new culture, we need to understand the one we've got.

After the Flood
APRIL 1975

I receive my copy of *Blood on the Tracks* on a day when I've been worrying more than usual about the economic crisis. I put it on the turntable and start reading Pete Hamill's liner notes, a florid rave that pushes all the old Dylan-myth buttons. Its implicit message is that if we don't consider *Blood on the Tracks* the divine poet's most glorious masterpiece yet, we are certainly creeps and possibly CIA agents. Something is happening here. For years, Dylan has been trying to bury the successor-to-Blake-Rimbaud-Yeats stuff. Why is he letting Hamill revive it now?

What is Dylan saying about his relation to his past? The songs themselves prompt the same questions. I hear simple major-key melodies, a Dave Van Ronkish guitar, inimitable harmonica and organ passages, Biblical images, blasts of anger, flashes of humor, on-the-road restlessness. One side of the record is dominated by a tale of romance, robbery, and murder called "Lily, Rosemary, and the Jack of Hearts"; its lyrics belong on *John Wesley Harding*, its sound on *Highway 61 Revisited*. The other side has "Idiot Wind," which sounds—at first—like a classic Dylan hate song: "One day you'll be in the ditch, / flies buzzin' around your eyes. . . . / You're an idiot, babe, / it's a wonder that you still know how to breathe." Yet it's clear that this album is not just a seductive throwback. A new kind of naked grief—the inverse of the joy on *Planet Waves*—haunts the quiet, ethereal beauty of songs like "If You See Her, Say Hello" and "Simple Twist of Fate"; demolishes the sarcasm of lines like "You're a big girl now"; blows through the rage of "Idiot Wind" ("I'll never know . . . your holiness or your kind of love, / And it makes me feel so sorry. . . . / We are idiots, babe"). Dylan sings in half a dozen different voices, all of them familiar but not quite placeable. From one phrase to the next, they evoke all his periods, all his changes. What unifies them is pain.

You could say that *Blood on the Tracks* is about Bob Dylan's estrangement—physical or spiritual, literal or symbolic; permanent or temporary—from a woman, or from women. I would say that it's pretty obviously about his own marital troubles, except that, as is usual with Dylan, the publicity has been confusing. Have Bob and Sara broken up? Are they back together? The facts aren't really important; what matters is that on this record the relationship between Dylan's self and his persona seems richer, scarier, and more intense than it has in years. The role I take him to be playing—and my sense of it has as much to do with his former happy-husband posture as with his present agonies—is embarrassingly ordinary; it comes from a stock postfeminist drama that appears to be settling in for a long run. A man is married to a woman who has made him a home, in every sense of the word. He assumes that she is as content as he is. Suddenly, she declares that their marriage is intolerable. She reveals needs, expectations, bitter resentments that he never suspected; makes demands that he doesn't know how to meet. He reacts with love and hate, guilt and self-pity, fear and despair. He is angry that she has disrupted not only his comfort but his sense of reality, that she is not what she represented herself to be; and at the same time he is deeply wounded that she has guarded her secret self from him. Eventually, the marriage ends or survives, and he learns something about himself and women or doesn't. In assuming this role, Dylan risks seeming pathetic, even ridiculous. Instead, he makes us see in his dilemma our own unreasonable yearnings, punctured illusions, furious defenses, painful accommodations.

The song that says it best is "Shelter from the Storm." Dylan is adrift in the terrifying, chaotic world of his early prophetic poems: "Well, the deputy walks on hard nails and the preacher rides a mount, / But nothing really matters much; it's doom alone that counts." At the end of each verse, respite seems to beckon: " 'Come in,' she said, 'I'll give you shelter from the storm.' " But he finds out that nothing is as it seems. His apocalyptic vocabulary abruptly gives way to language that is flat, stark, as if it represented unadorned reality emerging from fantasy and confusion: "I took too much for granted. I got my signals crossed." The refrain begins to sound more and more sinister: is it an invitation to safety or to destruction? In the end, Dylan howls, "I bargained for salvation and she gimme a lethal dose." But it is really his own past and present illusions that he is trashing, the quest for easy answers, for political and psychedelic and domestic utopias. In a sense, "Shelter from the Storm" is a "My Back Pages" for the seventies, and the album as a whole a statement about learning old lessons in new ways. Dylan is miserable not only because he has lost his woman but because he has been forced to admit that what he thought was his innocence was only his ignorance. Even if he is reconciled with his lover, or finds a new one, certain kinds of thoughtless, pleasurable assumptions are no longer possible for him. He knows too much, knows that there is no shelter from the storm anywhere—there is only life. In the last verse of the last song on side two, he concludes, with just the faintest touch of self-mockery, "Life is sad, life is a bust. / All ya can do is do what you must."

Still, it would be wrong to call *Blood on the Tracks* a pessimistic album. For all their failures, Dylan's happy-husband years taught him something precious: vulnerability. He is able, in a way he rarely was before, to express love, hurt, need without hiding behind a protective irony. And that ability has enabled him to integrate the "old" and "new" Dylans, the sixties and the seventies—an accomplishment that poses a challenge to all of us. As Dylan puts it in "You're a Big Girl Now," "I can change, I swear. Oh, see what you can do."

Beginning to See the Light

FROM *VILLAGE VOICE*, 1977

On November 7, I admitted I was turned on by the Sex Pistols. That morning I had gone from my shrink to my office and found that a friend who takes an interest in my musical welfare had sent me a package of British punk singles and albums. He had been urging me to listen to the stuff, and I had been resisting; I was skeptical about punk, in both its British and American versions. The revolt against musical and social pretension, the attempts to pare rock to its essentials, the New York bands' Velvetesque ironic distance had a certain déjà vu quality: wasn't all that happening five years ago? When I had first heard "God Save the Queen" on the radio, my main reaction had been, "They sound like Mott the Hoople—what's the big deal?" And the Ramones bored me; I felt they were not only distanced but distant, apologists for coldness as a worldview. I had dutifully gone to see them at CBGB's and bought their first album, hoping to be interested in what they were trying to do, but duty goes only so far. I was also put off by the heavy overlay of misogyny in the punk stance.

In October I had gone to an art show opening in Queens and had run into another punk evangelist, Bob Christgau. He argued that people who put down the punk bands as "fascist" were really objecting to their lack of gentility. The English bands, he said, were overtly antifascist, and after all it was in England that fascism was a serious threat, not here. I wasn't so sure, I said, either that fascism wasn't a threat here or that the punk rockers were incapable of flirting with it.

I wasn't referring to the swastikas or sadomasochistic regalia that some punk bands affected to prove they were shocking, though I felt that to use Nazi symbolism for any purpose was both stupid and vicious. I meant that sexism combined with anger was always potentially fascistic, for when you stripped the gentility from the relations between the sexes, what too often remained was male power in its most brutal form. And given the present political atmosphere, that potential was worrisome. The American right was on the move; the backlash against feminism was particularly ominous. Jimmy Carter, with his opposition to abortion, his fundamentalist religion, and his glorification of the traditional (i.e., male-dominated) family, was encouraging cultural reaction in a way that was all the more difficult to combat because he was a Democrat and supposedly a populist. Closer to home, I found it deeply disturbing that so many liberal and leftist men I knew considered Mario Cuomo[1] some sort of working-class hero—that they were at best willing to ignore, at worst secretly attracted to, Cuomo's antifeminist attitudes. The punk rockers were scarcely defenders of the family, or of tradition, but like pseudo-populist politicians they tended to equate championing the common man with promoting the oppression of women. That the equation was as inherently contradictory as "national socialist" was unlikely to deter men from embracing it.

The following week I went hiking in the Blue Ridge Mountains. At the inn where I was staying I took a lot of more or less friendly kidding about being from New York, to which I responded with more or less friendly defensiveness; no, there had been no looting in my neighborhood during the blackout, and yes, I walked around at night by myself. Back in the city, in the early morning, my clock radio clicked on to wake me up. I lay in bed drifting. The deejay delivered a commercial about a *Voice* article on punk rock: "A cult explodes and a movement is born!" Then came the news: the West German commandos had made their triumphant raid on the terrorists at Mogadishu. I lay in bed confused. Were the punk rockers the terrorists or the raiders?

Some friends of mine were giving a Halloween costume party. I decided to go as a punk. I wore a black T-shirt that read in yellow letters "Anarchy in Queens" (I would love to be able to say I found it somewhere, but in fact I had it made up), a huge safety-pin earring, pasty white makeup, green food coloring on my teeth, and fake vomit that I had bought in a magicians' supply store.

Around the same time I was beginning to emerge from a confusing and depressing period in my life. I had a problem I needed to face, a painful and scary choice to make, and I had been refusing to think about it. In such circumstances, music was my enemy. It had a way of foiling my attempts at evasion; when I was least prepared, some line or riff or vocal nuance would invariably confront me with whatever I was struggling to repress. And so I had simply stopped listening. I told myself that the trouble was I was tired of old music, and there was no new music that excited me.

1. A candidate for mayor of New York in 1977.

I wondered if I were coming to the end of an era—was rock and roll no longer going to be important in my life?

Then I gave up trying to censor my thoughts. Immediately there were plenty of records I needed to hear: *Blood on the Tracks*; *Loaded*; *Heat Treatment* and *Howlin' Wind*; *Astral Weeks*; *Exile on Main St.*; *The Bessie Smith Story, Volume 4,* which includes "Send Me to the 'Lectric Chair" and "Empty Bed Blues." I realized with a shock that although I'd listened to "Send Me to the 'Lectric Chair" hundreds of times over the years, I had never really heard it before. It was a fierce, frightening song: a woman described how she had killed her lover, reeling off the brutally graphic details with almost casual defiance, saying in effect, "I lost my temper and I blew it and I'm sorry now but it's too late so fuck it." Bessie had concentrated more intensity in that one song than Janis Joplin had achieved in her whole career. I played it over and over.

And now I had all these punk-rock records, by the Sex Pistols, the Clash, Slaughter and the Dogs, the Unwanted, Wire, the Adverts, Johnny Moped, Eater, X-Ray Spex, the Buzzcocks, Chelsea, the Rezillos. I liked them; they made most of what passed for rock these days sound not only genteel but out of focus. And I was knocked out by the Sex Pistols. How could I have denied that they had a distinctive sound? I knew I might react differently if I saw them live, or if I could hear more than about 1 percent of their lyrics, but for the moment—as had so often happened in the past—my conceptual reservations were overwhelmed by the immediate, angry force of the music. WE DON'T CARE!—but they cared about not caring.

Later I listened to my Ramones album and found that it moved me more than it had before. It seemed that the British had done it again—beamed my culture back at me in a way that gave it new resonances. The last time (when "swinging London" was prosperous and euphoric) they had done this by achieving an aesthetic distance—based on their detachment from America's racial history—that was also a kind of innocence. This time (when England was in deep economic and political trouble) they were doing it by ignoring—or more precisely smashing—the distance the American punk bands had taken uninnocent pains to achieve. It was not that groups like the Sex Pistols and the Clash had no irony of their own, that their punk persona was not a calculated creation. But the passion with which they acted out that persona reflected England's unambiguously awful situation; the Ramones were stuck with the American dilemma, which is that the system is bad enough to piss us off, and not bad enough so that we can make up our minds what to do about it.

Months before my capitulation to the Sex Pistols I was talking to an editor and we got on the subject of pop music. I said that I still felt involved with the increasingly distinct subgenre of contemporary rock and roll, but there wasn't that much of it around, and what there was was often disappointing. The editor asked what sort of music I was talking about. "Well, the bands that play CBGB's . . . Graham Parker . . . Springsteen . . ." "Patti Smith?" "Yes." The editor shook her head. "All these people," she said, "are still caught up in the past, in the myth of the sixties." "I disagree," I said, feeling a bit prickly because I'd had this argument before. "It's just that they *acknowledge* the sixties, instead of trying to pretend all that stuff never happened."

The argument bothered me. Talk about irony: the worst insult you could throw at those of us who had been formed by the sixties was to imply that we were living in the past; not to be totally wired into the immediate moment meant getting old, which we hoped we would die before. The thing was, I really felt not guilty. In the past couple of years, especially, the sixties had seemed very distant to me. When I thought of the person I had been in 1967, or even 1970, she was almost as much of a stranger as my college-student self. I rarely played music that had been popular in the sixties; most of it lacked a certain dour edge that felt necessary in this crabbed decade. It was nevertheless true that many of my favorite records had been made by veterans of the sixties, just as it was true that I was still interested in my past, felt a continuing need to understand and absorb it. Was this need regressive?

I had once raised the question in a letter to Greil Marcus, and he had replied:

Well, we're caught in our own trap. We promoted and got across a myth of the '60s and now we're paying for it—having it thrown back on us as some sort of strange aberration that we all caught a disease from—i.e., it wasn't a real era, wherein real things happened, it was some giant anomaly. Well, it can seem like that, because so much of such intensity happened so fast. . . . more happened in rock and roll in six months of '65 than in all of the '70s. . . . More happened politically in 1968—in terms of stuff

we will live with and think about all our lives with great emotion
and puzzlement—than since. Etc.

That was part of the problem—too much had happened to assimilate
all at once. Culturally and politically, the seventies had been at best dull,
at worst grim, yet for me the retreat into work and introspection had its
positive side; it was a chance to consolidate what I'd learned, live down
some of the egregious silliness I'd been party to. How else was I to figure
out where I was heading? Feminism, drugs, Vietnam, the flowering of pop
culture had changed me. They were no longer "the sixties"; they were part
of my luggage.

Yet what was finally most insidious about the whole "You're caught in
the myth of the sixties" business was not its denial that the sixties were
real—and therefore consequential—as well as mythical, but its use of *the
sixties* as a dismissive label with which to quarantine certain ideas and
attitudes. What, for instance, did it really mean to relegate Patti Smith or
the Ramones to the sixties? True, seventies rock and roll had roots in the
sixties, but then so did disco, which editors and other cultural arbiters
agreed was quintessential seventies music: the original disco audience—
middle-class blacks who retained a black cultural identity rather than imitating whites—had been created by the civil rights movement and black
nationalism. The difference was that rock and roll, as a musical language,
was always on some level about rebellion, freedom, and the expression of
emotion, while disco was about cooling out as you move up, about styl-
izing and containing emotion.[2] I knew I was supposed to consider the
first set of concerns as outdated as the miniskirt. Yet owing to the par-
lous state of New York's economy, I was, for the first time ever, somewhat

---

2. While this is all true as far as it goes, it is a bit beside the point. Despite its base
in minority subcultures (black and gay), disco is a mass cultural phenomenon and so
inevitably embodies the spirit of the times in a more immediate and central way than
rock and roll, which has become a somewhat abstracted comment on itself and (like
jazz in the fifties) an essentially bohemian taste. In any case, seventies rock and roll is
obsessed with its formal tradition, a concern that links it to the past in a special way.
Finally, there are distinctions to be made: Bruce Springsteen is far more tied into the
sixties than the punk and new wave bands. (For elucidation of these last two points, see
my essay from *Stranded* on the Velvet Underground.)

downwardly mobile; I aspired to have less control over my feelings, not more; liberation was still a potent idea for me, not because I was clinging to the utopian sixties but because I was still oppressed as a woman—and still angry about it—in the conservative seventies. In short, though I had nothing against disco, rock and roll had a lot more to do with my life. And I couldn't help suspecting that "You're still living in the sixties" was often nothing more than code for "You refuse to admit that what really matters to you is to stake out a comfortable position in the upper middle class." Well, not only did I refuse to admit that: I didn't even think it was true.

I was grappling with my uncensored thoughts, finding them no less scary and painful, the night I went to see Ms. Clawdy at the Women's Coffee House. Ms. Clawdy is a singer-songwriter from Oakland. In the early seventies she managed and wrote songs for an all-female rock-and-roll band called Eyes; later she sang with another women's band, Rosie and the Riveters; now she performs alone, accompanying herself on the piano. She has a local following, particularly though not exclusively in the San Francisco Bay Area's lesbian/feminist/alternative-women's-culture community, but she is unknown outside California. I've rooted for Ms. Clawdy for years, not only because she is good but because of what she is good at. Her music successfully combines two of my main passions: feminism and rock and roll. The Women's Coffee House gig was her first performance in New York, and to see it I had passed up Graham Parker at the Palladium.

For those of us who crave music by women who will break out of traditional molds, write and sing honestly about their (and our) experience, and create art so powerful that men and the society in general will have to come to terms with it whether they want to or not, the seventies have offered scant comfort. Though many women performers give me pleasure, few have touched those specifically feminist yearnings. There is the Joy of Cooking, whose music endures but whose lyrics seem dated and sentimental now; Joni Mitchell's *Blue,* ditto; some of Yoko Ono's stuff; great songs here and there like Helen Reddy's "Summer of '71," Carly Simon's "You're So Vain," Patti Smith's "Redondo Beach" . . . give me an hour and I'll think of a dozen more examples, but that only proves my point.

As a woman who has made a significant contribution to what I've called contemporary rock and roll, Patti Smith stands alone. Her best songs are as good as any in rock and roll, and she is capable of an electrifying live performance. But she is erratic; in concerts she has a habit of generating enormous energy, then diffusing it with rambling, pointless raps. I've always wondered if she were afraid of her considerable power. I'm also uncomfortable with her androgynous, one-of-the-guys image; its rebelliousness is seductive, but it plays into a kind of misogyny—endemic to bohemian circles and, no doubt, to the punk-rock scene—that consents to distinguish a woman who acts like one of the guys (and is also sexy and conspicuously "liberated") from the general run of stupid girls.

So Patti Smith may be a rock-and-roll hero, but she is not quite a feminist heroine. Ms. Clawdy, on the other hand . . . I watched her with an avidity that came from discovering someone who was distinctively herself yet fit my generic fantasy. Her style was at once functional and matter-of-factly sensual; her plump, womanly body was encased in red mechanic's overalls. She was funny, ironic, passionate, self-deprecating without being masochistic, vulnerable without being pathetic, and political in the best sense—that is, willing to tell the truth about the conditions of her life. I enjoyed her funny songs—especially a discourse on compulsive eating called "Ice Cream Cone"—but I liked her best at her most serious. Of her newest songs the one that most compelled me was "The Dark Side," which she introduced by noting that Chairman Mao had urged revolutionary artists to emphasize the bright side of life and that she hadn't followed his advice. But my favorite was still her signature song, "Night Blindness." Whenever she sang it I heard something new. This time, the lines that got to me were "We all need love, it's worth any price you pay / That's what my mother said, and she lives alone today."

I had gone to the show with a woman friend, and afterward we were so high that we ran down the street, shouted, and hugged. Some weeks later, I had dinner with Ms. Clawdy, aka Ella Hirst, and we talked about the possibilities for an alternative women's culture. I had once been attracted to the idea but had long since become convinced that it was unworkable and even reactionary. It was, I believed, inseparable both in theory and in practice from political ideas I had rejected: that sexual and cultural separatism were a solution to the oppression of women or an effective strategy for ending that oppression. For me feminism meant confronting men and male power and demanding that women be free to be themselves everywhere, not just in a voluntary ghetto. Separatists argued that a consistent feminist had to break all sexual and emotional ties with men, yet it seemed to me that not to need men for sex or love could as easily blunt one's rage and pain and therefore one's militance; I also had the feeling that there was a lot of denial floating around the separatist community—denial that breaking with men did not solve everything, that even between women love had its inescapable problems. I suspected that a culture based on separatist assumptions was unlikely to be angry enough, or truthful enough, to be revolutionary.

I had arrived at these conclusions not by thinking about the issue abstractly, but by trying to answer a specific question: why did I like so little of the women's-culture music I had heard? The feminist music scene had two main tendencies. One was a women's version of political folk music, which replicated all the virtues (simplicity, intimacy, community) and all the faults (sentimentality, insularity, heavy rhetoric) of the genre. Some of it was fun to listen to, but the idiom was too well worn to promise anything exciting or original. The other tendency actively turned me off: it was a slick, technically accomplished, rock-influenced but basically conventional pop. I believed that this music could be a commercial success; supposedly the product of a dissident culture, it struck me as altogether compatible with the MOR blandness of most white pop music.

What disturbed me most about both brands of women's-culture music was that so much of it was so conventionally feminine. Years ago Ella Hirst had told me that she thought most female performers did not have a direct line to their emotions, the way men did—they were too busy trying to please. It seemed to me that too many of the women's-culture people had merely switched from trying to please men to trying to please other women.

A couple of years ago I had gone to see the feminist folk-rock group the Deadly Nightshade at a lesbian bar in Boston. They sang "Honky Tonk Women" with rewritten, nonsexist lyrics. Someone in the audience sent them an outraged note, attacking them for singing an antiwoman song. The lead singer read the note aloud and nervously and defensively complained that the writer hadn't been listening. The incident had helped me understand why I wasn't enthusiastic about the group. They did not have the confidence, or the arrogance, to say or feel "If you don't like it, tough shit." It was not that I thought performers should be indifferent to the response of their audience. I just thought that the question they ought to ask was not "How can I make them like me?" but "How can I make them hear me?"

Ella protested that I was harder on these women, who were at least trying to create an alternative system of values, than on traditional female performers. She had a point. Why did the Deadly Nightshade's wimpiness bother me more than Linda Ronstadt's sex-kitten routine? For the same reason, probably, that the radical left's offenses against women always incensed me more than everyone else's.

But rock and roll, as always, posed a more troublesome paradox. Listening to the Sex Pistols, trying to figure out if "Bodies" was really an antiabortion song, I discovered that it was something even worse. It was an outburst of loathing for human physicality, a loathing projected onto women because they have babies and abortions and are "a fucking bloody mess," but finally recoiling against the singer himself: "I'm not an animal!" he bellowed in useless protest, his own animal sounds giving him the lie. It was an outrageous song, yet I could not simply dismiss it with outrage. The extremity of its disgust forced me to admit that I was no stranger to such feelings—though unlike Johnny Rotten I recognized that the disgust, not the body, was the enemy. And there lay the paradox: music that boldly and aggressively laid out what the singer wanted, loved, hated—as good rock and roll did—challenged me to do the same, and so, even when the content was antiwoman, antisexual, in a sense anti-human, the form encouraged my struggle for liberation. Similarly, timid music made me feel timid, whatever its ostensible politics. What I loved most about Ms. Clawdy was that I could have liberating form and content both; I could respond as a whole person. Listening to most rock and roll was like walking down the street at night, automatically checking out the men in my vicinity: this one's okay; that one could be trouble, watch out. Listening to most feminist music was like taking a warm bath. Ms. Clawdy did not make me wary—but that didn't mean she let me relax.

The other day, I was sitting on a bench in front of the laundromat on my corner. While I waited for my wash, I thought about the choice I still had to make. For some reason I happened to glance upward, and my eyes hit a stop sign. I laughed; if my life had to be a series of metaphors, I ought to pick some better ones. Like, say, the last verse of "Night Blindness": "I never thought that anyone would know me like you do. / If I let you make me happy you could make me unhappy too. / I told my friend, she said she knows just how I feel / But I have to take a chance and find out if it's real."

The Abyss
FROM *VILLAGE VOICE*, JUNE 1979

Sunday midnight: I have a late drink with my friend the artist and long-time feminist activist. We talk about women and art. With a mixture of affection, rueful self-recognition, and deflating parody, my friend para-phrases Simone de Beauvoir lecturing the Independent Woman: "It's all very well not to be fooled; it's all very well to know you're oppressed. But to create art, you must look into the abyss!" When I get home, I look up the relevant section of *The Second Sex*. Beauvoir does have this inimi-tably cavalier way of nailing the objects of her ruminations to the wall: "Lucidity of mind . . . is a conquest of which they are justly proud but with which alone they would be a little too quickly satisfied." Yet I find myself making little noises of protest at her insistence that only "the caste of the privileged" can feel in command of the universe and so entitled to re-create it as the greatest art requires. True, when you're at the bottom of the abyss it's hard to look out, but you do get to see some very weird sights just by keeping your eyes open.

Tuesday: I am working on the last section of a long essay. It is refus-ing to come together; there is a structural problem whose solution eludes me. I arrange and rearrange with growing desperation. The abyss yawns just inside the range of my peripheral vision, but right now lucidity of mind is essential. It is not, evidently, a conquest I can take for granted.

The phone rings; it is another Independent Woman of my acquain-tance. I bitch about my work for a while; then the conversation drifts to another problematic area of our lives. Love, of course. Subtopic: What do these men want, anyway? (Lucidity of mind is no great help here.) Subtopic: What do we want, anyway? (Ditto.)

Wednesday: Two female colleagues and I make plans to see a Lou Reed concert. We joke about how best to mau-mau Reed for his surly at-titude toward girls. Perhaps we should wear giant masks of vaginas, with or without teeth? "How about masks of Judy Chicago dinner plates?"

someone suggests. There is an edge to these jokes, but a paucity of serious anger. The truth is that none of us takes Reed's woman-baiting outbursts too seriously; he pisses us off, but on the level of kids making faces at each other in the sandbox. Which response has everything to do with what Reed's songs say about the urgency and destructiveness of posturing. Much as he would detest such hippy-dippy rhetoric, Lou Reed's message to the world is that underneath our hard-earned defenses, we are all one: "I'll be your mirror / Reflect what you are in case you don't know." But Reed never underestimates the power of the surface and neither do I. I've tried fantasizing conversations in which we transcend our sandbox personae; they always come out something like this: "Look, Lou, I know you probably think I'm an uptight media person but really, I'm more complicated than that, I mean I have *my* façade just like you have *your* façade, but—" "Shut up, cunt!"

Thursday: My essay has begun laughing and baring its teeth. Time for a break. I pick up a book I started a while ago and didn't finish— *Motherlines,* by Suzy McKee Charnas, the second in what will eventually be a trilogy of science fiction novels. The first, *Walk to the End of the World,* is set in a bleak postholocaust society where women are brutally enslaved. It is a compelling book; one image in particular keeps coming back to me: women working in a rendering factory, recycling their corpses. *Motherlines,* in which the protagonist escapes "civilization" and finds her way into two different all-female cultures, is not nearly so interesting. As often happens, the author writes much more powerfully about oppression than about freedom: *Walk* in its small way re-creates the universe, *Motherlines* does not.

Saturday: Having wrestled my piece to the mat, more or less, I am spending the day sorting through a year's worth of magazines, papers, and other detritus. Clippings on abortion, pornography, the Middle East, Iran, the new wave, trekking in the Himalayas. Antifeminist clippings: Margaret Drabble thinks rape is not so terrible, R. Emmett Tyrrell thinks feminists can't tell the difference between a nut and a bolt. Angry unsent letters to the editor. Angry unsent personal letters. Transcriptions of dreams: "Driving on a crowded highway I keep losing control of the car. Veering over to the other side of the road, changing lanes right in front of a truck etc. I realize the problem is I have forgotten my glasses and can't see anything."

Sunday night: As Lou Reed walks onstage I feel tense; the Bottom Line is a small sandbox. I have always found Reed's concerts a letdown. Faced with an audience, he can't seem to sustain the emotional complexity of his records, instead of playing off his postures—affectlessness, belligerence—he gets trapped in them. But about ten seconds into this show I realize tonight is different. Reed is all there—defiance, humor, sharp edges, sweet center. He is, no mistaking it, in a genial mood— "Maybe he's beginning to see the light," one of my friends quips—but there is nothing genial about his set, which includes "Heroin" and several of the grimmer songs from *Berlin*.

It is a transcendent performance. Afterward we plot how to get into the sold-out late show. Enter another friend, an English rock musician, with tickets—it is that kind of night. Euphoric, we sit and drink and gossip. We get on the subject of birthdays and ages; our English friend says that all the women he knows who are in their midthirties have nesting urges. I think he is saying "nasty urges"; I nod enthusiastically.

At first it seems that this set will be a repeat of the last, but suddenly the genial mood is gone. Reed crackles, rides his sharp edges. He manhandles the mikes, commits electronic mayhem. It dawns on me that this performance may be even better than the other; it may also be a disaster. Something was missing from the first show after all: danger. The tension builds to a version of "Heroin" that blows away every shred of everyone's defenses. In the middle of it Reed bursts out, "When I say it's my life and it's my wife—you think I don't *mean* it? *My life*—do you *know*? Do you have *any idea*? How weird it is, man, to get *paid* for singing about it?" Yes, I know, I have an idea, there are other addictions besides junk. No, I don't know, that's one line I've never crossed. Yes, I have an idea, because you get paid for singing about it. "Of course," Lou says, grinning genially, "You know I'm not serious." A little while later, singing "All Through the Night," he forges a pop cliché into an epic about loneliness, sexual craving, endurance, seeing in the dark.

The last song over, the crowd claps and waits for the encore. And claps. And waits. Finally the clappers begin to chant *"Bull-shit! Bull-shit!"* As if on cue Reed appears. He looks relaxed. He sings five more songs. One of them is "I'll Be Your Mirror."

Monday, 3 A.M.: I am hungry. In a few hours I have an appointment with my shrink. Feeling very lucid of soul, I slip away.

Preface to Barbara O'Dair's Trouble Girls: The Rolling Stone Book of Women in Rock

1997

As I read the essays in this book, I imagined my female students digging in and enjoying. I should be used to it by now, but it still thrills me that so many young women I know are feminists and pop music freaks without a second thought. I was formed by a time when feminist rock and roll fans were exotic characters, at least to the mainstream media. Assuming that these loyalties were inconsistent required a simpleminded view of both art and politics and was in consequence a highly popular mode of thought. During my rock critic days—and for years afterward, since reporters only clean out their Rolodexes once a decade or so—I must have been asked several hundred times some version of the question posed by sister rock-and-roll feminist Karen Durbin, writing about the Rolling Stones in *Ms.* magazine in 1974: "Can a Feminist Love the World's Greatest Rock & Roll Band?"

I used to try to explain that love didn't preclude tension and conflict. Once I cracked that my subject was "the bloody crossroads where rock and feminism meet." As I saw it, the confrontation was good for women because rock and roll liberated aggression: not only anger, though that was of course part of it, but a sense of entitlement to seize the world, uninhibited by the feminine commandment, thou shalt not offend. In a *Village Voice* piece written near the tail end of the seventies, shortly after the emergence of punk, I defended the Sex Pistols and their antiabortion song "Bodies" on feminist grounds: the song, I wrote, was

> an outburst of loathing for human physicality . . . an outrageous song, yet I could not simply dismiss it with outrage. The extremity of its disgust forced me to admit that I was no stranger to such feelings—though unlike Johnny Rotten I recognized that the disgust, not the body, was the enemy. And there lay the paradox: music

Originally published in *Trouble Girls: The Rolling Stone Book of Women in Rock*, edited by Barbara O'Dair. New York: Random House, 1997.

that boldly and aggressively laid out what the singer wanted, loved, hated—as good rock and roll did—challenged me to do the same, and so, even when the content was antiwoman, antisexual, in a sense antihuman, the form encouraged my struggle for liberation.

I was speaking as a fan, but also as a critic of women performers who, in my view, were failing to seize the world. Had I pursued my paradox to its logical conclusion, I might have predicted what actually happened: that punk would inspire a whole new genre of female rock star, who rather than deferring to the canons of femininity would use them as material—for parody, reclamation, scathing critique, or all of the above.

But there's another theme in that piece—another place where women's liberation and musical liberation could be said to intersect—that went underground in the eighties and is still largely unspeakable: rock and roll as a catalyst for the moment of utopian inspiration, that out-of-time moment when you not only imagine but live the self you would be in the world that could be. Whenever I listened to music during the sixties and seventies I was listening for the voice of that utopian moment, through the filters of pop conventions and clichés, the performer's defenses and cover-ups: it was the spiritual equivalent of listening for the "pure music" through an old scratchy recording. But feminism made me lust for the voice without the filters, and so I longed for a female rock and roller who would be my mirror. She would make music I loved as much as *Blonde on Blonde* or the Velvet Underground's third album. And she would be a stone feminist, a radical intellectual, a New York Jew with curly hair— yes, I'm joking, but just barely.

The closest I ever came to realizing that fantasy was discovering, in the early seventies, a singer-songwriter known as Ms. Clawdy. An East Coast lefty and feminist, she had migrated to the Bay Area and achieved some local celebrity, first as the manager and auteur of a women's rock-and-roll band and then as a solo performer. A feminist friend of a friend, in New York promoting Ms. Clawdy's songs to record companies, played me a tape and gained an instant convert. As far as I know, Ms. C. never did make a record, but I still have and still play a couple of her tapes, homemade tapes that are gradually wearing out—sounds of the bloody crossroads where Bob Dylan and Bessie Smith meet, with lyrics to match.

I can imagine some of this music being adopted by postpunk female rockers. I think, for instance, of a song whose first verse recounts a rape:

"I must have been expecting him, I was so collected and calm / I even found myself thinking of you as he pinned back my arms." Yet even such postpunky lines would lose something in the translation; for Ms. Clawdy, bitterness, defiance, deadly irony, scarifying humor—even art!—were so much underbrush on the trail of that elusive moment of wholeness. In my *Voice* piece, playing her off against the Sex Pistols (it so happened that she was performing in New York right around the time I became a punk fan), I implicitly gave her credit for inspiring me to make a particularly fraught choice of love over sexual-political common sense—to seize the utopian moment of connection even as everything I knew about the world and male-female relations was putting me on red alert. The message was that a Johnny Rotten could help me figure out what I wanted, but only my female alter ego could help me embrace it.

As Lou Reed put it, those were different times (though to those who would proclaim that utopia, like God, is dead, I say not so fast). Or maybe it's just that the longer I live, the less I need some other larger-than-life woman to reveal me to myself. Or that in truth my daughter (an Alanis Morissette fan) does this better than any singer could. Anyway, it's been a long time since I asked, of each new rock-and-roll woman to come to my attention, is she the one?

A few years back I found myself transfixed as I watched Thelma and Louise drive across the desert and listened to Marianne Faithfull on the sound track, singing "The Ballad of Lucy Jordan." The protagonist of this song is the oldest feminist cliché on record—the rich suburban housewife, bored literally out of her mind by a pointless existence, who has a breakdown, losing herself finally in the fantasy she could never make real, the one about riding through Paris in a sports car with the warm wind in her hair. For that matter, she's an outdated cliché—how many bored suburban housewives are there in the nineties? Never mind. I had always loved Faithfull's magnificently grim rendition of this song; in the context of the movie it came across as a harrowing cry of thwarting and foreclosure and bone-deep loss, foreshadowing the heroines' no-exit plunge into the Grand Canyon. But as I thought about it, I realized for the first time that "Lucy" moved me to the core not in spite of the trite words but in large part because of them.

This is an old story in pop music: the flip side of searching for the pure utopian moment through those obscuring filters is embracing the poignancy of the filters themselves, representing as they do the condensed stories of human joy, tragedy, and resignation inadequately but insistently expressed. And it occurred to me that one measure of the advance of women's liberation in rock and roll is the increasing variety of filters available to female performers, from new variations on the old staples of sex and romance to ironic deconstructions of same to sheer brattiness to the pop feminist clichés that are now an integral part of our culture's canned fantasy life. Women—performers, fans, critics—have also achieved more power to construct their own filters out of the cultural detritus and fool around with them, as men have always done.

This book is, among other things, a riveting document of how the process works. And in the end, inevitably, it trains the reader's critical eye on the most universal filter of them all: the male-female polarity itself. In her essay "True Confessions: Alternative Sounds," Jancee Dunn remarks drily, "The question of gender might just become universally annoying." Perhaps. I'd certainly be curious to hear *that* music—and read that book.

Chapter 5

THE NAVIGATOR

Newport: You Can't Go Down Home Again
AUGUST 1968

It was a hot, bright Saturday afternoon, and some nine thousand sun-burned fans roamed through Newport's Festival Field sampling the folk-music workshops. Although there was a semblance of a schedule (the staff had mimeographed a map of offerings ranging from Folk Dance to Banjo, from Bluegrass to Blues Jam Session Open to All), groups formed and dissolved and regrouped pretty much as they pleased. Some people tried to guess where the celebrities would go—the workshops provided informal contact with performers, and everyone wanted informal contact with B. B. King, Taj Mahal, and Janis Joplin—but most took potluck. Over at Area 17 (Contemporary), Tim Buckley sang to fifty people; down behind the food tent, Pete Seeger admired a Yugoslavian fan's homemade guitar and told someone from WBAI if he ever needed free records to write to him. The ticket-buying crowd was on the straight side. Most of the grungier types—the ones who made Newport cabdrivers slow down and say "Willyalookit that!"—were nonpaying fellow-travelers who gathered in the hills behind the fairgrounds, like Hitchcock's birds, waiting for the evening concert. Inside, the norm was hair above shoulders, work shirts rather than beads, McCarthy and Peace and We Cry Harder Schlitz Beer buttons. Near the main gate, next to tents displaying guitars, Times Square–psychedelic jewelry, and Joan Baez's autobiography, stood a VISTA recruiting booth emblazoned with a poster of Dustin Hoffman captioned "What'll You Do When You Graduate?"

Then into this pastoral carnival crashed the sound of—electric blues. The workshops were not supposed to use amplification, but, for obvious reasons, this rule could not apply to City Blues, so a minimum of sound equipment had been set up on the amphitheater stage. Behind the amps, the stage filled up with kids; others gravitated to the seats below. They were hoping for B. B. King or Big Brother and the Holding Company but were happy to get Junior Wells and Buddy Guy. Wells and Guy are much closer to pop than to folk. Their blues are hard, almost R&B, with drumming that could pass at Motown; their act—dancing, hugging each other, exhorting the audience, jumping off the stage—resembles a soul show. And they are loud. Within minutes, they had attracted a concert-sized crowd (nearly as large, in fact, as the audience the previous night). Finally, George Wein, the festival's rotund director, clambered onstage and suggested turning down the sound a bit.

The spectators groaned.

"But it's too loud, it's interfering with the other workshops."

"Kill the others!"

"Stop the other workshops!"

Supporting shouts and applause.

"Suppose we turn these mikes off and turn them on when somebody's singing—"

The crowd booed and hissed.

Wein capitulated, and Buddy Guy announced, "This is my first year at Newport, and now you people have to come to Chicago. We play *loud*! I'd like this mike even louder!"

Everybody cheered.

As soon as Wells and Guy had finished, the audience began yelling "B. B.!" and "Big Brother!" and "Jan-niss!"

"We had something unique set up here," Wein announced sadly.

"Twenty-two workshops . . . no amplification . . . so each little group could . . ."

"BIG BROTHER!"

They settled for the Jim Kweskin Jug Band and, a little less graciously, for Doc Watson ("This was supposed to be *blues*," someone grumbled), but the excitement was gone. Watson, an excellent country guitarist, did a fine set, which got an appreciative but reserved reaction, and everyone filed out. A blonde girl in a floppy hat raced backstage to join some friends. "Hello, you freaks!" she squealed. "I shook hands with Buddy Guy!"

That same afternoon, Richard Goldstein, pop-music columnist for the *Village Voice*, entered the press tent to make a phone call. Goldstein, who is twenty-four but looks eighteen and has long, straggly hair, a mustache, and muttonchops, was wearing a white jacket trimmed with embroidered flowers. A festival official, Charles Bourgeois *(sic)*, stopped him at the door;[1] when he showed his press pass and stood his ground, Bourgeois called him "just another one of those young punks" and confiscated the pass, because, he said later, he assumed it was stolen.

That was the way it went at Newport this year. Perhaps it is presumptuous to call the Folk Festival a failure; it did draw seventy thousand people, and most of the concerts were worth hearing. But it failed as a *festival*. Instead of camaraderie, there was tension; instead of participation, consumership. All weekend, the management was busy trying to manipulate a sullen audience and a bunch of equally hostile, if more reticent, performers. As usual, the trouble can be traced less to individuals than to the system. The Newport Folk Festival and its many imitators were conceived according to a simple and (at the time) brilliant formula: popular folk stars, performing for almost no money, would attract a huge audience and subsidize the appearance of noncommercial, traditional musicians, thus exposing the kids who came to see Baez and Dylan to authentic ethnic music. During the peak years of the folk revival, the formula worked beautifully. Folk festivals were, above all, exercises in community. There

---

1. I interpreted this *sic* as Willis's mischievous wink to the readers—sort of like, "No, I'm not a hippie giving this guy a clever nickname. This is actually what his name was." Of course, I can't be sure, but I'm leaving the word in with the hope that some people get the joke.—Ed.

was a continuity of values, style, and musical goals between urban and ethnic musicians; the former regarded the latter as their mentors and were eager to meet them. Similarly, the audience approached the traditional performers receptively and reverently, even making heroes—new stars— out of the Doc Watsons and the John Hurts. There was real respect for amateur creation; thousands of kids brought their own instruments and spent their time learning from performers and from each other. The producers, the fans, and many of the musicians shared the urban folk ethos, which combined rejection of mass culture with an amorphous, sentimental, pro–civil rights, pro-peace leftism. But now the folk revival has been eclipsed by the excitement over pop music, and an entirely different spirit prevails. Most pop stars, including those whose roots are in folk music, have little in common with rural, ethnic types. They are pros, very much involved in commerce, in show business, in pleasing an audience, and not at all apologetic about it; they are also personalities, incapable of effacing themselves in the we-are-all-equals-here folk manner even if they should want to. Nor is the rock audience especially interested in traditional musicians and the values they represent. As a result, the strategy that was so successful in 1963—pack 'em in to see the stars and hit 'em with Mountain Sam—was a fiasco in 1968. The stars brought the crowd, all right, but their glow failed to illuminate the less commercial acts, which were received with restless apathy. So were attempts to appeal to political emotions. One performer invoked Fannie Lou Hamer, another compared a Serbian peasant uprising to the Vietnamese revolution, another sang songs about burning cities and indifferent middle-class Negroes. No one seemed to hear. Only Joan Baez, reminiscing about the time she spent in jail for civil disobedience, revived some of the old feeling, but then she was Joan Baez.

Most of those seventy thousand people had apparently come not as true believers but as businesslike consumers, determined to get their money's worth. I saw few offstage guitars and banjos, or groups of kids getting together to play and sing. The audience wanted to participate in its own way—to be allowed to respond to the idols it had come to hear. But orgiastic hero worship was exactly what the festival staff was trying to avoid. The focus of the tension here was amplification. Every year since 1965, when a purist crowd booed Bob Dylan for playing his electric guitar, Wein has cautiously increased the festival's quota of electric musicians. But he can go just so far. The town, which has always been dubious about the festival and the assorted bohemians it attracts (this year Wein had to fight for a permit to put on an auxiliary concert in the local high school), will not tolerate a lot of loud music. Even more important, amplified music tends to overwhelm everything else. If the festival is to remain a *folk* festival, rock and urban-blues groups cannot be allowed to dominate it. Nevertheless, it is ridiculous to invite electric acts—especially when they are supposed to be the drawing cards—and tell them they can't make music the way they want to make it and the audience wants to hear it. For most of the weekend, amplifiers were kept at low volume. This was especially disastrous for Taj Mahal, who sounded sickly, but all the electric performers resented it; they were not willing to go along with the Newport game, which decreed that they were mere crowd-pleasers and that Libba Cotten, Henry Crowdog, and Buell Kazee were the real VIPs. The staff aggravated the bad feeling by regarding the festival crowd—particularly the hangers-on camping on the hill—mainly as a nuisance and a potential threat to order. There were fences and cops all over the place; the half-empty box seats were guarded from incursions of proles, and God help the unwary spectator who tried to buy a Coke at the performers' refreshment stand. But the weekend passed with only one serious incident: several kids went to the hospital after dropping some unidentified pills, and the rumor persisted, in spite of Wein's denial, that one girl had died. On Sunday, Yippie leader Jerry Rubin was hustled out of Festival Field for giving "pornographic literature" (a Yippie leaflet illustrated with a sketch of a copulating couple) to a nun; the nun took it in stride, but Wein was outraged. Otherwise, things were all too peaceful.

The first evening concert, on Thursday night, was a grim affair called Free Form Folk. Jim Kweskin, a member of the festival's board of directors, had instigated an experiment in spontaneity. There was to be no schedule, no program; a group of performers would get onstage, and the rest would be up to them. "In this new age of LSD, pot, macrobiotics, yoga masters, and the total involvement of psychedelic ballrooms and light shows," he explained in the festival program (why, I wondered, did he leave out Scientology and glossolalia?), "people seem to be no longer satisfied with the old concept of a stage with performers and an audience with spectators." Further on, he declared, "We want to take that step into the void of the unknown." Predictably, the spontaneity that resulted was that of a bad party. ("I was told that a lot of people here don't know what's happenin'," said Kweskin, acting as nonannouncer. "Well, you're not alone, ha ha! We don't know what's happenin', either.") The two dozen or so performers remained on the stage, where they didn't quite know what to do, and the spectators remained in the audience, where they were bored. The only void in evidence was a large patch of empty seats—the weekend influx had barely begun. And, new age or not, the air was permeated with the scent of moldy fig; the performer who copped my Almeda Riddle "Go Tell Aunt Rhody" Folk-Camo Award with a song about the joys of apple picking had plenty of competition.

There were a few happy moments. Eric von Schmidt, the Henry Miller of the folk revival, sang a lusty "London Waltz" ("The Rolling Stones were there / Strapped to the electric chair"); the Kaleidoscope, a rock band strongly influenced by Middle Eastern music, was impressive; and Sandy Bull played, much too briefly. But Taj Mahal, handicapped by a mediocre band as well as anemic amps, was a disappointment. As for the evening's star attraction, Richie Havens, he did his classic, *you*-know-the-words hummed version of "A Little Help from My Friends," mangled a couple of Dylan songs, treated us to the ultimate in folk art—the guitar-strum solo—and got a standing ovation. If he had just stood there, it would have made no difference; the crowd was hungry for someone it knew. The concert lasted much too long; since there was no program, no one knew when to stop. But I was afraid to leave, still tyrannized by stories about Bobby or Joanie dropping in after the tourists had gone and playing for the *real* fans. Finally, all the performers joined in on about ten drippy verses of "At the End of a Long, Lonely Day"—a finale if I'd ever heard one. I had gone as far as the parking lot when Joan Baez made an unscheduled appearance and sang something about lending a helping hand. You can't win 'em all.

Friday night, Streets and Mountains, was better. The draggier part of the program, which included a fatter, louder version of Odetta and a super-annuated mountain singer, was enlivened by Janis Joplin, who breezed through the audience wearing a flowered hat and carrying a champagne glass in each hand. There was a soft buzz—superstar in our midst. Happy and tough and above it all, she stopped in the middle of the aisle, looked around, and disappeared into the performers' tent. Then Arlo Guthrie came on, with his white suit, electric hair, mock-hillbilly-gangster accent, and wide-eyed deadpan, and milked his one joke—the absurdity of the bureau-cratic mind—for fifteen funny minutes of song and monologue. During the second half, Joan Baez surprised me with an imaginative selection of songs, including "Gentle on My Mind" and "Suzanne"; her main faults used to be overseriousness and lack of variety, and she seems to have conquered both. The most interesting act on the bill was the Bread and Puppet Theater, a troupe that blends mime, dance, puppetry, and music into the most polished protest art I have ever seen. At its best, the staging is so tight that you can't tell the giant papier-mâché puppets from the people. But a lot of the effect depends on lighting and on an intimate atmosphere, so in the huge amphitheater it didn't quite come off. At the end of the play, which involved a highly stylized confrontation between young people and robed figures in death masks, a confused audience waited in silence for it to continue, then clapped uncertainly. Joan Baez and the other performers, along with what looked like a large LBJ puppet, came on for a finale, "Down by the Riverside." And it wasn't even midnight.

The high point of the festival was the Saturday night concert, Country Music for City Folks. The performances were almost uniformly good, and, for once, the unresponsiveness of the audience annoyed me. George Hamilton IV (remember "A Rose and a Baby Ruth"?) brought his strong voice and mellow (electric) guitar to Gordon Lightfoot's "Early Morning Rain"; Roy Acuff mugged and twirled his Yo-Yo and did "Wabash Cannonball;" Joan Baez sang—right out there onstage—one of my guilty secret loves, "The Green, Green Grass of Home," which has about as much cachet as "Yummy Yummy Yummy." But everyone waited impatiently for the two big acts, which weren't country at all. B. B. King appeared just before intermission and put on his usual superlative show. I admire B. B. more than I like him. I'd rather watch Willie Mays than Joe DiMaggio, and King's music is too controlled and sophisticated for me. Still, I was a little disturbed when King—perhaps trying to emulate Otis Redding's success at the Monterey Pop Festival—ended his performance with a spiel about how the world needs love. It wasn't like him, and it didn't work. Big Brother, of course, was held till the end, while the crowd grew steadily more restless; people kept walking in and out and bought a lot of hot dogs. Then it was time, and Janis, in one of her great sleazy outfits—a low-cut black minidress with a tinselly bodice, a Dracula cape, and rhinestone arm bracelets—launched into "Piece of My Heart." Her voice was a bit thin (paranoiacally, perhaps, I suspected skulduggery with the mike), but the group played much better than I had remembered. The amps were turned up, and it was good to hear real rock again. Afterward, there was a party in town. B. B. played, Taj Mahal thought his own thoughts, Janis danced and drank ("They don't pay you *nothin'*, man," she said. "But I had a good time tonight, that's what counts"), and the college kids with phony passes gaped. The music was very loud.

Sunday, the last day. The afternoon Fresh Faces concert was entertaining. The most exciting fresh faces belonged to the Kaleidoscope, who did a mordant contemporary version of "Oh Death" and a quasi-Oriental piece, "Taxim." In the evening, it rained; Doc Watson was great; Janis Ian did her best to prove that "Society's Child" and "Janey's Blues" were happy flukes; George Wein announced that this was the best festival ever and that the crowd had behaved beautifully. The second half of the evening concert was dedicated to Woody Guthrie; the performers sang Guthrie's songs and read from his autobiography. I might have enjoyed this more if I had not seen the original Guthrie Memorial, at Carnegie Hall, which was warmer and better organized, and had Bob Dylan besides. Still, it was a good way to end. Guthrie represents the best of what the Newport Folk Festival has stood for; his songs transcend fashion—as all folk music is supposed to do, though little of it does. An hour of "This Train" and "Talkin' Dust Bowl" and "This Land Is Your Land" did a lot to soothe the bitterness of that uptight weekend. At the end, I even wanted to linger, but my friends were anxious to get started, hoping to beat the inevitable jam at the ferry. That transportation problem won't be around much longer—a bridge and an interstate highway are in the works. Neither will Festival Field, which is in the path of the highway. Cheap irony, perhaps, but I can't help hoping that someone will take the hint. The Folk Festival needs more than a new home. It needs a whole new rationale.

The Scene, 1968
NOVEMBER 1968

SAN FRANCISCO

I had been in San Francisco a week, was preparing to visit the new Fillmore West for the third time, and asked a friend from East Bay to come along. He wasn't really in the mood, but he had a hard time saying no. "I feel as if

I ought to go," he said. "As if it's *culture*." I'd been experiencing a similar sense of obligation but dismissing it as a rather banal occupational disease. Yet, after all, it's just a matter of degree: I'm not an art critic, but if I went to Florence I'd feel duty-bound to see a lot of paintings. Rock and roll was the lazy man's music. Who worked at liking Little Richard? You dug him or you didn't. I hadn't quite realized how much things had changed until I found myself going to concerts here and in Berkeley (a) to pay my respects to the cultural capital of white pop music, (b) to gain insight into what the new groups were doing, and (c) to see Steve Miller live, because I was afraid I had misjudged his first album (he turned out to be as bad as I thought—third-rate honky-tonk with a fuzztone—but then the night I was there he had to cope with a bum sound system and was without his rhythm guitarist). The only group I went to see for its own beautiful sake was the Grateful Dead.

Even now there is more and better music going on here than anywhere else in the country. The Bay Area has long been an amazing reservoir of musicians. In 1964, they were sitting around the Berkeley campus playing for fun. Now, apparently, they've all joined rock groups. In the past week or so, at least fifteen local bands, most of them completely unknown elsewhere, have performed at the Fillmore West, the Avalon, the Oakland Coliseum, the Berkeley Community Theater, and various clubs; of those I've seen, the worst are well above the level of the average third-billed act at the Fillmore East, and the best need only practice, good advice, and luck to be really great. But, for all this talent, the cultural capital is not what it was when the earliest groups were defining a new consciousness. Such intensity is always difficult to sustain, and the circumstances have not been favorable. Haight-Ashbury has passed to the hoodlums and the meth addicts, the growing political urgency has made music seem less important, and the media, after publicizing the scene to death, have lost interest in it, which is even worse. It may be that the mystique of community that characterized San Francisco rock was based at least partly on wishful thinking; Grace Slick was never exactly the hippie next door. Yet for me and a great many other people, in and out of San Francisco, it was very exciting, and I am not happy to see it replaced by what amounts to a mystique of musicianship—a reverence of the sort that makes entertainment "culture." This attitude has its roots in the increasing conversion of white rock from a vocal into a primarily instrumental music—a trend that originated in San Francisco, though it is by no means confined here.

(Eric Clapton has said that Cream uses a voice as just another instrument; Ten Years After, the best of the English blues bands, appears to have the same philosophy.) The most striking casualty of this development has been the eclectic sensory experience that dance floors and light shows were set up to provide. At the Fillmore West, almost everyone sits on the floor and watches—one scarcely visible corner is reserved for dancing, as if on principle, just as so many of the groups offer token vocals on principle—and the light show has become an unobtrusive backdrop. The audience wants to concentrate on what the performers are doing with their instruments.

The best and most polished group I've seen here, It's a Beautiful Day, is totally involved with instrumentation. Not one of its six members—four men and two girls—can sing rock.[1] They lack the basic prerequisites of volume and enthusiasm—especially the lead singer, who also plays the violin. But they are excellent musicians (except for one of the girls, whose function is obscure; she shakes a tambourine now and then, but that's about it). Their sound is built on intricate, shifting rhythmic patterns that reminded me of the Kaleidoscope (a band that isn't very well known but should be), and it is so varied and unfailingly interesting that the vocal vacuum doesn't matter. At the other extreme is a group of five girls called the Ace of Cups. Everyone sings, and each singer is better than the last, ending with the bass player, Mary Gannon, who has a perfect rock voice, strong, mellow, and idiosyncratic. She and three of the others are essentially belters, but the fifth voice (the piano player's) is soft and torchy—an effective contrast. Their melodies and arrangements are excellent. But they can't play at all. (This is not surprising. There are plenty of female rock singers but, for some reason, virtually no girls who play instruments seriously.) They pick at their instruments as if at unwanted food on a plate—especially the drummer, who provides almost no beat. The lack of virtuosity is no problem in itself—in fact, given my prejudices, it is refreshing—but the lack of drive is. Their singing is so good that I hope they can overcome this handicap; that they've been performing for a year without learning more is disturbing.

---

1. In 1968, Willis had not yet formed a feminist consciousness around the distinction between women and girls. If she had republished this elsewhere, I'm fairly certain she would have noted this political evolution, much like she did in her collection *Beginning to See the Light* (1981) with the use of *Negro* and *man* in her 1968 essay "Dylan."—Ed.

Other groups I've enjoyed are Creedence Clearwater Revival, a work-manlike hard-rock band that is a bit more established—it has an LP out and a hit single, "Susie Q"—and the Cleveland Wrecking Company, which is in the wall-of-sound tradition, with a lot of well-integrated electronic noise à la Byrds. One group I hated, Black Pearl, is nevertheless provocative enough to be worth mentioning. The group is a better-than-average white soul band, but it is dominated by a lead singer, Bernie Pearl, who comes on like Jim Morrison imitating James Brown. The result is a lot of embarrassing posturing and self-conscious dirtiness. Still, the idea of abstracting the wildness of white bohemian anarchism and combining it with the wildness of black soul has interesting possibilities, if it's handled with intelligence, detachment, and humor. Unfortunately, Pearl displays none of these qualities.

Except for the Dead, the big groups have been out of town. The Airplane has been in Europe with a twenty-seven-man entourage, and Big Brother recently gave its last local concert to feature Janis Joplin, who is going out on her own. The Airplane doesn't belong to San Francisco anymore; it belongs to the world, like the Beatles and white Levis. As for Janis, she has always belonged to herself. I hope she'll be well and not lose her incredible voice too soon. Incidentally, both groups' latest albums— the Airplane's *Crown of Creation* and Big Brother's *Cheap Thrills*—are classics. Not only that, they are pure, immediate pleasure. The Grateful Dead's new album, *Anthem of the Sun*, does take some getting used to, but I find myself enjoying it more and more. Sometimes I think the Dead are the only really happy people left.

Summary of Love in Queens
JULY 1969

Rock fans have certain stock complaints, and one is that there is no decent live rock scene in New York. The Fillmore is a cross between Philharmonic Hall and the subway at rush hour. The clubs offer prohibitive prices and the vibrations of a dentist's drill. Once in a while, something nice happens in Central Park or Tompkins Square, and people talk about it for months afterward. But mostly rock talk in New York is wistful, punctuated by many mentions of Woodstock and (last year) San

Francisco and (this year) Mill Valley. One place nobody muses about is Queens. Queens—yech! A lot of rockheads, including me, have tended to define both their generational revolt and their spiritual progress in terms of their migration from Queens to Manhattan. But a favorite pastime of Americans is rediscovering their origins—that's what the whole rock renaissance is about, after all—and this may be the year we find out that Queens has a soul. Didn't Jimmy Breslin promise, "If elected, I shall go to Queens"? Aren't the Mets contenders? Queens is where the working class calls itself the middle class. It's the scene of the epic teenage rivalry of the fifties, between the "rocks" and the "collegiates." It's the home of the original sawdust pizza. Rock belongs to Northern Boulevard as much as, if not more than, to Second Avenue. And Queens has something Manhattan doesn't have—lots of open space. This fact has not escaped rock promoters. Last summer, two producers brought a number of major groups to the Singer Bowl, in Flushing Meadows. The concerts were an artistic flop; the stadium was too large, the sound was terrible, and the problem of musical theater-in-the-round was solved—or, rather, parried—by means of a revolving stage, which allowed each spectator to get a good look at the performers every three minutes or so, a system that does not facilitate rapport. This year, the Singer Bowl concerts have been taken over by Music Fair Enterprises, the company that runs the Westbury Music Fair. Howard Stein, a young producer who was hired to organize the shows, has screened off a section of the arena and made improvements in the sound system, and prospects look good. At the same time, however, Music Fair Enterprises has outflanked itself by delegating Stein to take on a much more inspiring project—a series of rock dances in the open-air (but roofed) New York State World's Fair Pavilion, also in Flushing Meadows. The first of these was held on Friday, July 11th. It featured the Grateful Dead and Joe Cocker, and it was quite simply fantastic. If the management continues to do the right things, rock at the Pavilion could become an institution. For the sake of the music and the culture—and for the sake of Queens—I hope it will.

I rode to Flushing on a chartered bus that MFE had hired to lure the skeptical press to the outlands. The bus driver got lost, and we took a little tour of Corona (coming within eight blocks of my old junior high school). Then, to make up for his lapse, he began to speed. It was no use—we were late anyway. But by this time the bus had become part of the adventure. It was the Who's Magic Bus, the Magical Mystery Tour Bus. We jounced along eating brownies and shouting instructions to the driver. At the Pavilion, it soon became evident that the rest of the crowd shared our expansive mood. They kept coming in, thousands of happy kids—almost five thousand by the end of the evening. The Pavilion was large enough to accommodate everyone without strain. The ground level served as a huge round dance floor; on the balcony there were tables and chairs, the food concession (the main culinary attraction was tacos, a beautiful idea, though the reality was mediocre), and a nice view of the park. The atmosphere was totally relaxed. As in the San Francisco ballrooms, people were free to dance, crowd in front of the stage, sit in a corner, wander around, eat, or do whatever else impulse dictated. There were no intrusive guards or cops.

The music was great. Joe Cocker and his band did an excellent hard-rock set that included a spectacular rendition of "Let's Go Get Stoned"—redundant advice for most of the audience, which sang along enthusiastically. During the break between sets, someone backstage had the good sense to put on *Beggars Banquet,* and a large core of spectators got up to dance to the Stones. Nothing like that had happened at a rock concert—in San Francisco or anywhere else—for a long, long time. Later, when the Dead were about to come on, there was some squabbling between a solid bloc of dancers who stood in the middle of the floor—and insisted moralistically that everyone else do the same—and the people sitting behind them, who complained that they were cutting off the view. After a few minutes of edgy exchange, Bob Weir came onstage and announced, as the Dead do whenever they can, "The management of this place told us you can get up and dance if you want to, so why don't you get up and dance?" That did it. The dancers won; the sitters got up. They were probably glad they did. The Dead proceeded to perform for more than two hours. They played a lot of new material (notably "Don't Murder Me," a witty country-western song), some standards (including Otis Redding's "Hard to Handle," with Pigpen doing a pretty fair vocal), and several cuts from their new album, *Aoxomoxoa;* my favorite was "Mountains of the Moon." Through it all, Jerry Garcia, in his red polo shirt, beamed at us. It was the season of love all over again.

The Dead were the perfect group to launch this latest and best exercise in the nostalgia that has been hitting the rock community lately. Dancing. The summer of love. *Queens.* We still need that ambience, those memories. It's not enough to stare reverently at Eric Clapton's nimble fingers. I only wish the admission price could be lower. Three dollars is reasonable compared to what city places charge, and you get more for your money; still, it's not exactly proletarian.

I didn't appreciate just how good the Pavilion concert was until the following night, when I attended the Madison Square Garden debut of Blind Faith, the new Eric Clapton–Ginger Baker–Stevie Winwood combine. (The group is rounded out by a relative unknown—bassist and electric violinist Rick Grech.) The best part of the evening was that it was short, although this irritated me, theoretically, as one more example of the promoters' indifferent greed. For the prices the kids paid (the cheapest seats were four dollars), they deserved at least half an hour more of music. They also deserved, and didn't get, adequate sound, an alternative to the atrocity of the revolving stage, and an environment that was not conspicuously hostile and policed. Clapton played well, as usual, but Winwood's voice did not come through, and, as for Baker, his show-offy drumming just makes me nervous. In spite of the shoddy production, the audience was ecstatic. Hundreds of teenagers rushed the stage, screaming like Beatlemaniacs. I don't understand it. I'm sure the Emperor has no clothes, but there must be an aesthetic of nakedness I'm not getting.

Elvis in Las Vegas
AUGUST 1969

Las Vegas is more like Hollywood than Hollywood, because the money is changing hands right out front. Committed to veneer as an art form, over-thirty and relentlessly white in essence, if not always in packaging, Vegas is the antithesis of the cultural revolution. Its hopelessly reactionary nature is best exemplified not by the fountains in front of Caesars Palace, or even by the ethnic comedians, but by the existence of—yes—prominent citizens who want to Make Las Vegas Beautiful, which means toning down the neon on Fremont Street and creating vest-pocket parks. Andy Warhol, tolerant as he is, would have a hard time justifying that. Yet the metaphor of the crap game does have its application to rock: "Just give me money, / That's what I want." The crass determination to get rich has been one of the great unsung forces behind the cultural revolution.

Of course, it has also worked the other way. In the past fifteen years, Hollywood and its variants have bought off plenty of rock performers: the Paul Anka types, who used rock as a detour until the nightclubs were ready for them; black people—like the Supremes—who identified success with whiteness; and, most important of all, Elvis Presley. Elvis, the very definition of rock and roll for its vociferous defenders and detractors, became the first rock-and-roller to switch to ballads for the whole family, and a pioneer (here he had some competition from Annette Funicello and friends) of the unalienated youth movie. You couldn't blame Elvis. In those days, everyone kept speculating about what would happen to punks like him when the rock-and-roll fad was over. It took the Beatles to affirm the first principle of the cultural revolution: the kids have money, and kid music equals kid capitalism. Colonel Parker, meet Brian Epstein.

When I heard that Presley had accepted an engagement at the new International Hotel in Las Vegas and was to give his first concert in nine years, I knew the confrontation had to be interesting. Elvis was at once old money and young money, sellout and folk hero. How would he play it? In his television special last winter, he wore a leather jacket and wiggled his hips. But then he recorded "In the Ghetto," which was weak on beat and strong on slush. It was a No. 1 hit—except in the ghetto—and no doubt met with the approval of the Make Las Vegas Beautiful folks. Now Kirk Kerkorian, who owns the International and apparently wants to become Nevada's other famous tycoon, was energetically promoting Elvis's return to the stage. He invited all the New York rock writers to come out in his plane—the first privately owned DC-9, remodeled to seat twenty people and make the usual first-class accommodations look chintzy. The press releases for the hotel promised that all its features would be the largest, the newest, and the most expensive. Ordinarily, invitations to junkets—a traditional Hollywood institution—are no problem. Who wants to fly to Houston to see Tony Bennett? But in this case I was faced with a dilemma familiar to observers of revolutions and nuclear particles. To participate would compromise my objectivity; to hold aloof would falsify the experience. In a medium as sensitive to context as rock, the hype is an essential part of the message. The story was not just Elvis but Elvis and all of us in Kerkorian's womb. I flashed yes, and, along with other refugees from the cultural revolution, armed with long hair, giant sunglasses, and artificial euphoriants, I set out to dig Babylon: garish is beautiful. There was something to be said for the Las Vegas thing. At the same time, I hoped Elvis would be crude and surly and stomp all over the veneer with his blue suede shoes.

The opening took place in the Showroom Internationale, a two-thousand-seat nightclub whose sublimely irrelevant décor included relief carvings of Greek temples and winged gods and goddesses, and whose menu that night consisted of such tasty items as Aloyau Roti à l'Anglaise Périgourdine and Pointes d'Asperges au Beurre. The audience was 99.44 percent white and predominantly middle-aged and moneyed; the celebrities present ranged from Fats Domino and Phil Ochs to Pat Boone and Henry Mancini. I was surprised at how seriously people were taking the occasion. They seemed to feel that Elvis was theirs, not just a progenitor of the music their kids listened to. A woman of fifty who had come from Los Angeles whispered excitedly, "My husband thinks I'm real silly, but I always wanted to see Elvis in person." It was obviously the raunchy Elvis, not the Hollywood Elvis, that she wanted to see.

We had to sit through the Sweet Inspirations—a great black gospel-rock group that persists in wasting its talent singing "Alfie"—and one of those unmentionable comedians. Then Presley came on and immediately shook up all my expectations and preconceived categories. There was a new man out there. A grown man in black bell-bottoms, tunic, and neckerchief, devoid of pout and baby fat, skinny, sexy, totally alert, nervous, but smiling easily. For some reason, he had dyed his hair black. It was the same length as ever, but combed down instead of back into a ducktail. He started with "Blue Suede Shoes." He still moved around a lot, but in a much different spirit. What was once deadly serious frenzy had been infused with humor and a certain detachment: this is where it began—isn't it a good thing? Though the show was more than anything else an affirmation of Presley's sustaining love for rhythm and blues—we knew it all the time, Elvis—it was not burdened by an oppressive reverence for the past. He knew better than to try to be nineteen again. He had quite enough to offer at thirty-three. He sang most of his old songs, including a few of the better ballads, and a couple of new ones. When he did "In the Ghetto," his emotion was so honest it transformed the song; for the first time, I saw it as representing a white Southern boy's feeling for black music, with all that that implied. "Suspicious Minds," an earthy country-rock song about jealousy, which is going to be Presley's new single, was the highlight of the show. Almost as exciting was his version of "What'd I Say." The only mistake he made was to sing the coda from "Hey Jude"; once a gimmick has been picked up by Eydie Gorme on a cerebral palsy telethon, it loses something. But the gesture was understandable. Elvis was clearly unsure of himself, worried that he wouldn't get through to people after all those years, and relieved and happy when he realized we were with him. As the evening went on, he gained in confidence, and the next night he was loose enough to fool around with the audience, accepting handkerchiefs to mop his forehead and reaching out his hands to women in the front row. During both performances, there was a fair amount of sighing and screaming, but, like Elvis's sexual posturing, it was more in fun than in ecstasy. It was the ritual that counted: "Of *course* I screamed. I'm not dead *yet*." At the opening-night press conference, I asked Presley if he had had trouble relating to an audience of mostly older people. He shook his head and smiled. "The older people have learned, you know. They can do it, too." Yeah, yeah, yeah.

If Elvis continues to perform—he says he wants to—and "Suspicious Minds" is as big a hit as it should be, he could have a significant impact on pop music in the coming months. It remains to he seen whether he can transcend either his grand-old-man image or the Hal Wallis years, but he seems to want to try. I wonder if Colonel Parker approves. Is Parker just an ectoplasmic projection of Presley's Hollywood side? Will he now shrivel up? The night before I left Las Vegas, I saw him drop five hundred dollars at roulette. You can't win 'em all.

The Cultural Revolution Saved from Drowning
SEPTEMBER 1969

You have to give the producers of the Woodstock Music and Art Fair this much credit: they are pulling off a great public relations coup. They have apparently succeeded in creating the impression that the crisis in Bethel was a capricious natural disaster rather than a product of human incompetence, that the huge turnout was completely unexpected (and, in fact, could not have been foreseen by reasonable men), and that they have lost more than a million dollars in the process of being good guys who did everything possible to transform an incipient fiasco into a groovy week-end. Incredibly, instead of hiding from the wrath of disappointed ticket-buyers and creditors they are bragging that the festival was a landmark in the development of youth culture and have announced that they plan to hold it again next year. But before history is completely rewritten, a few facts, semifacts, and strong inferences are in order.

For at least a month before the festival, it was obvious to everyone in-volved in the music scene—industry people, writers for both the straight and the underground press, radicals, and hippies—and also to the city fathers of Wallkill, New York, that the crowd was going to be enormous and the facilities inadequate. The four under-thirty backers of Woodstock Ventures seemed to be motivated less by greed than by sheer hubris: the ambitiousness of the project was meant to establish them as *the* pop pro-ducers, kingpins of the youth market. Their promotion was pervasive. On July 18th, a month before the festival, the *Times* reported that the man-agement expected as many as two hundred thousand people and had al-ready sold fifty thousand tickets. At that time, they were planning to hold the festival in Wallkill, on a three-hundred-acre site—half the size of the grounds in Bethel—linked to civilization by three country roads. When a Concerned Citizens Committee warned that Wallkill's water supply could not accommodate the anticipated influx and that festival officials had not made realistic plans to cope with traffic, health, or security, the produc-ers vowed to fight the town's attempt to exclude them and implied that the opposition came from antiyouth rednecks. When the change of site was announced, just twenty-four days before the scheduled opening of the fair, there was a lot of speculation that it would never come off at all. An expe-rienced promoter told me, "It'll happen, but only because they've got so much money tied up in it. They can't afford to back out. But they'll never finish their preparations in three weeks. Monterey took three months. It's going to be complete chaos." Alfred G. Aronowitz, of the *Post*, one of the few journalists to cast a consistently cold eye on the four young entrepre-neurs, wrote witty on-location reports giving them the needle and adding to the general pessimism. Meanwhile, back on St. Marks Place, Woodstock was rapidly evolving into this year's thing to do. A "Woodstock Special" issue of the underground weekly *Rat*, published the week of the festival, featured a page of survival advice that began, "The call has been put out across the country for hundreds of thousands to attend a three-day orgy of music and dope and communal experience." I left for Bethel in much the same spirit that I had gone to Chicago at the time of the Democratic Convention. I was emotionally prepared for a breakdown in services and a major riot. If I enjoyed the festival, that would be incidental to participating in a historic event. The actual number of people who showed up was a surprise. The only other real surprise was that there was no riot. The extra numbers could not excuse the flimsiness of the water pipes (they broke down almost immediately), the paucity of latrines (about eight hundred for an expected two hundred thousand people) and garbage cans, or the makeshift medical facilities (the press tent had to be converted into a hospital). One kid reportedly died of a burst appendix—an incident that in 1969 should at least inspire some questions.

Although it is possible that the fair lost money, many knowledgeable people are inclined to doubt that the loss was anywhere near the one and a half million dollars Woodstock Ventures is claiming. The corporation should open its books to the public. The thousands of ticket-holders who were turned away from the site because of traffic jams (while other thousands of contributors to the traffic jams got in free) deserve some consideration. So far, the management has said nothing about refunds, and there has been talk of setting up a group suit to demand the money. One complication is that since no tickets were collected there is no way of distinguishing those who made it from those who didn't, but rumor has it that the state may sidestep this problem by suing the producers on the ground that they had no serious intention of taking tickets at the fairgrounds.

If the festival succeeded in spite of the gross ineptitude of its masterminds, it was mostly because three hundred thousand or more young people were determined to have a good time no matter what. The accounts of the peacefulness and generosity of the participants are all true, but they have tended to miss the point. The cooperative spirit did not stem from solidarity in an emergency—the "we all forgot our differences and helped each other" phenomenon that attends power blackouts and hurricanes—so much as from a general refusal to adopt any sort of emergency psychology. The widespread conviction that the Lord (or the Hog Farm, or the people of Monticello, or someone) would provide removed any incentive to fight or to hoard food, and the pilgrims simply proceeded to do what they had come to do: dig the music and the woods, make friends, reaffirm their lifestyle in freedom from hostile straights and cops, swim naked, and get high. Drug dealing was completely open; kids stood on Hurd Road, the main thoroughfare of the festival site, hawking mescaline and acid. But the most exhilarating intoxicants were the warmth and fellow-feeling that allowed us to abandon our chronic defenses against other people. As for the music, though rock was the only thing that could have drawn such a crowd, it was not the focal point of the festival but, rather, a pleasant background to the mass presence of the hip community. Few of us got close enough to see anything, and as the music continued for seventeen hours at a stretch our adrenaline output naturally decreased. (On Sunday, a boy who had driven in from California commented, "Wow, I can't believe all the groups here, and I'm not even listening to them." "It's not the music," said another. "It's—all this!") The sound system was excellent, and thousands listened from camps in the woods, dozing and waking while the music went on till dawn. Everyone was so quiet you felt almost alone in the dark, but you couldn't move very far without stepping on someone's hand or brushing against a leg.

The festival site was like the eye of a storm—virtually undisturbed by the frantic activity behind the scenes. Once the nuisance of getting there was over with (I eventually got a ride in a performers' police-escorted caravan) and the Lord had provided (I just happened to bump into some friends with a leak-proof tent and plenty of food), I found the inconveniences trivial compared to the pleasures. But then I did not have to sleep out in the mud for two nights, and by Sunday I couldn't help suspecting that some of the beautiful, transcendent acceptance going around was just plain old passivity. It was a bit creepy that there was such a total lack of resentment at the fair's mismanagement, especially among those who had paid from seven to eighteen dollars. People either made excuses for Woodstock Ventures ("They couldn't help it, man; it was just too big for them") or thought of the festival as a noble social experiment to which crass concepts like responsible planning were irrelevant. For the most part, they took for granted not only the discomforts but the tremendous efforts made by the state, the local communities, and unpaid volunteers to distribute cheap or free food and establish minimum standards of health and safety. No one seemed to comprehend what the tasks of mobilizing and transporting emergency food, water, and medical personnel, clearing the roads, and removing garbage meant in terms of labor and money. Ecstatic heads even proclaimed that the festival proved the viability of a new culture in which no one worked and everything was free. And in the aftermath anyone who has dared to complain has been put down as a crank. It should be possible to admit that the people created a memorable gathering without embracing those who botched things up. (A letter writer in the *Village Voice* went as far as to say, "Woodstock Ventures should be congratulated and not chastised for giving us smiles, peace, music, and good vibrations." All those paying customers might disagree about being "given" music; personally, I don't see why Woodstock Ventures should get credit for my smiles.) But maybe it isn't. And maybe there is a lesson here about the political significance of youth culture. From the start, the cultural-revolutionary wing of the radical movement saw Woodstock as a political issue. The underground papers made a lot of noise about businessmen profiting from music that belonged to the community, and some movement people demanded and received money to bring political groups to the festival and set up an enclave called Movement City as a center for radical activity. If the festival staff had been foolish enough to try to restrict the audience to paid admissions, the movement might have had something to do. As it was, Movement City was both physically and spiritually isolated from the bulk of the crowd. It was not the activists but a hundred-odd members of the Hog Farm, a Santa Fe–based pacifistic commune, who were the most visible community presence, operating a free kitchen, helping people recover from bad acid trips, and setting up a rudimentary communication system of oral and written survival bulletins. A few radicals talked hopefully of liberating the concessions or the stage area. Abbie Hoffman interrupted the Who's set on Saturday night to berate the crowd for listening to music when John Sinclair, a Michigan activist, had just been sentenced to a long prison term for giving some marijuana to a cop. Pete Townshend hit Hoffman with his guitar, and that is more of a commentary on the relation of rock to politics than all of *Rat*'s fuzzy moralizing.

What cultural revolutionaries do not seem to grasp is that, far from being a grass-roots art form that has been taken over by businessmen, rock itself comes from the commercial exploitation of blues. It is bourgeois at its core, a mass-produced commodity, dependent on advanced technology and therefore on the money controlled by those in power. Its rebelliousness does not imply specific political content; it can be—and has been—criminal, fascistic, and coolly individualistic as well as revolutionary. Nor is the hip lifestyle inherently radical. It can simply be a more pleasurable way of surviving within the system, which is what the pop sensibility has always been about. Certainly that was what Woodstock was about: ignore the bad, groove on the good, hang loose, and let things happen. The truth is that there can't be a revolutionary culture until there is a revolution. In the meantime, we should at least insist that the capitalists who produce rock concerts charge reasonable prices for reasonable service.

Stranger in a Strange Land
DECEMBER 1969

This town is an uptight military reservation. In the vicinity are an Army base, an Air Force base, the United States Air Force Academy, and the combat-operations center of the complex radar-defense system known as NORAD. The local economy is dominated by the military, and the population consists largely of service families, active and retired. The Springs is said to have more Minutemen than any other city in the United States. Because of the presence of Colorado College, a small, nonvolatile, upper-middle-class institution, long hair and weird clothes are a familiar sight here, but the older residents seem able to tell students, whom they don't take seriously, from full-time heads and politicos, whom they regard as a threat. Usually, the hostility is masked by elaborate small-town courtesy, but the mask drops often enough to make dissidents chronically wary. A while ago, some friends of mine from the Springs' small radical community decided to take a walk in the snow at two in the morning. A block from their house, two young cops stopped them and threatened to arrest them for not carrying identification. After all, what were they doing out at that hour? Visiting their dope dealer, no doubt. Nothing really happened. It was just a little reminder.

There is another, pleasanter side to Colorado Springs. To the west, just a few minutes' drive away, are the mountains. It's a tonic to wake up in the morning and face Pikes Peak, which looks a little different every day, as the weather changes. The air is clean and sweet smelling (at least, it seems that way to an expatriate New Yorker; the natives are grumbling about too many cars' causing air pollution), and when the sun comes out after a snowfall the town looks like a Christmas card. The environment provides a continuing natural high, and the slower pace of life provides the time to indulge it. If you can get your mind off the military, it is easy to live in the moment in Colorado Springs, to enjoy simple things. In fact, you have to; there are few complicated things to enjoy.

My reactions to music, and to rock in particular, have always been very much influenced by the context in which I hear it—by the place, by the people, by the medium (records, radio, dances, concerts), and by the variety of music available at any given time. During the past few years, my usual context has been New York City. Because all kinds of music, live and recorded, are so easily accessible in Manhattan, I was becoming increasingly selective about what I wanted to hear and less and less patient with sounds that did not immediately reach out and grab. For me, rock music, to avoid being lost in New York's sensual bombardment and becoming just another city noise, had to be sophisticated, tough, and strong in conception, which is to say very pop. In recent months, in Colorado, my attitude toward rock has changed a great deal. I have new needs that music can fulfill, and some of the old needs are at least temporarily absent. Right now, I am closer to the ecstatic blues freaks at the Fillmore East than I have ever been before. And though I will never really be where they are—and don't particularly want to be—I've learned some important things about music and about my own head.

The most significant change in my perception is that I am much more involved in music as pure noise, which means that although I am by no means completely uncritical, I am more willing to follow a song where it leads and suspend judgment for a while—practically all noise is interesting in some way. When I first came here, a few months ago, I was listening to a record, almost subliminally following the various instruments and doing a little creative drumming with a pencil and an album cover, when I suddenly realized that what was playing was the Vanilla Fudge's *The Beat Goes On,* which must be one of the worst albums ever made. At the same time, I realized that it didn't much matter; I felt like drumming anyway. In the past couple of months, I have begun to enjoy the Crosby, Stills, and Nash album, which I had dismissed as too polished, too sentimental, and too soft, in the Simon and Garfunkel manner. Now the romanticism of songs like "Suite: Judy Blue Eyes" and "Marrakesh Express" doesn't bother me; if anything, it strikes me as a positive quality. I am also more receptive to white blues. I couldn't listen to the Blind Faith album in New York; now I listen to it fairly often.

One reason for these changes is my social and political isolation. Rock, however ambiguous it may be as a revolutionary force, does hold the culture of social rebellion together, and in a town where you can be busted for walking down the street in long hair music is a powerful reminder that you are not as alone as you feel. It was this need to be part of the national counterculture that drew kids from all over the country to the Woodstock festival. In New York, a second-rate white blues band may sound like Mantovani next to B. B. King, but here white blues means kicking out the jams, affirming solidarity with the brothers and sisters out there somewhere. Ironically, many black people here are fascinated by white longhairs, aspire to be "hippies," and identify with white head music. For me, at this point, rock—any rock—has such positive associations that whether it is good or bad is secondary.

The other crucial factor is that Colorado Springs is quiet, both literally and spiritually. My choices don't have to be as rigorous, simply because there aren't a thousand different stimuli competing for my attention. I have time to relax and float downstream. I don't have to be in any special place, physical or mental. Which in itself is a nice place to be—for a while, anyway.

The Return of the Dolls
JANUARY 1973

Last fall, the New York Dolls created the Mercer Arts Center's velour underground. Then they went touring in England, where their original drummer died in a drug-related accident. Now they are back home, where they opened their first return set at the Mercer with, naturally, "Back in the U.S.A."

The Dolls are almost as sensational as everybody has been claiming, but I suspect that that's only one of the reasons I liked their show so much. The other reasons have to do with the way I feel about New York. Like a lot of other people, I found at one point that I had to get out of the city. Also like a lot of other people, I eventually came back, because in my head I'd never really got beyond the suburbs, and I wasn't about to stay *there*. When I got here, one of the first things I noticed was that I didn't have anything to wear, and one of the first places I noticed this was the

Mercer Arts Center. The scene there struck me as a laid-back, somewhat campier version of pop-crazy New York, circa 1966; the natives reveled in their ersatz-ostrich-feather coats and Iranian sheepskins and fifties gold ankle straps and makeup (on both sexes) and everything long instead of short, but without that old naive conviction that as fashion goes so goes the world. In spite of my sartorial inadequacies, I felt more at home with this crowd than with the wined and barbiturated high-school-age Con III rejects that populated such emporia as the Academy of Music. Mercer habitués were a bit older; with an intuitive identification that escaped their British counterparts, they dug irony and revelation-through-artifice and the complex iconoclastic pleasures of cutting with rather than against the commercial grain, and in this context they dug rock and roll. In short, they represented a New York style of convoluted bohemianism that, like Jewishness—and unlike the expansive, evangelistic California variety of hip—you almost had to be born to. I had been born to it—a fact of life and sensibility that no religious experiences in the Rocky Mountains could ever efface—and I had come home.

The Velvet Underground was a New York band in exactly that sense, and now there is a second generation, consisting of the Dolls and a number of lesser-known bands that are beginning to graduate from the Mercer to uptown joints like the Villageast. Unlike the Velvets, however, these bands are devoted to hard rock, which gives them a bit more populist potential. And if the New York band, as a genre, should ever catch on outside Manhattan—stranger things have happened, I suppose—the Dolls will probably be the spearhead. David Johansen, their nineteen-year-old lead singer, looks suitably bizarro in his rumpled Prince Valiant hairstyle, lipstick, shaggy black jacket, and leather pants, and radiates a sulky, leashed sexuality that features the definitive American version of the Jagger sneer; lead guitarist Johnny Thunder is even more striking—a gold-lamé scarecrow who resembles Keith Richard with a tic. The Dolls' songs are about subways, kicks, Frankenstein monsters, rock-and-roll nurses ("Give me a shot, give me a pill, / Got me shootin' this junk against my will"), and other icons of contemporary urban existence; they belong in the "Subterranean Homesick Blues," "Satisfaction," surrealism-in-everyday-life tradition. The songs are exciting—the Dolls belong to that elite category of performers who can afford to do a Chuck Berry song without worrying that their own stuff won't survive the comparison—and

Johansen has a powerful rock-and-roll voice that tantalizes, always keeping something back, as if to say, "I could take you there, but you couldn't stand it." He may be right.

During that first return performance, the audience was as enthusiastic as cults usually are, but on my way out I heard one guy say, "I'm disappointed. It's really nothing—he's just like Jagger." Ah, yes, New York. David Bowie, forget it!

What's the matter with Lou Reed? Here's a man I think is such a genius that once when I was face to face with him in a hotel room I couldn't say a word (what I wanted to say was "Your music changed my life," which would have been most uncool), and his second album, *Transformer,* is terrible—lame, pseudo-decadent lyrics, lame, pseudo-something-or-other singing, and a just plain lame band. Part of Reed's problem may be that he needs a band he can interact with, a band that will give him some direction, as the Velvets did, instead of simply backing him up—in other words, not just a band but a group. (The same can be said about most group leaders who make solo albums, which is why I don't care much for Pete Townshend's and am kind of dreading John Fogerty's.) And I don't think David Bowie is doing him any good, either as a producer or as an increasing influence on his persona. . . . To be fair to Bowie, his other recent production effort, Mott the Hoople's *All the Young Dudes,* is one of the best albums to appear in recent months, and the title cut, which Bowie wrote, and which was a big hit single in England, is the song of the year—maybe of the decade (this one, not the past one). I take it all back, David.

San Francisco Habitat
AUGUST 1973

San Francisco and its environs have never been hospitable to rock and roll. The fabled acid-rockers were folkies at heart, and so were their fans. John Fogerty—who had to swallow that truth harder than anyone—recalls that in 1967 many local freaks were convinced that if the new bands were going to fulfill their destiny and transform the world they had better shed the label *rock,* with all its, ah, bad associations; *head music* was one of the substitutes proposed. I see no evidence that the general attitude has changed since then. Still, the Bay Area does have its unregenerate rock-and-roll loyalists, most of whom (in my fantasy, anyway) are teenage denizens of darkest Oakland who come out at night like the rats near the waterfront. There was a fair-sized contingent at the Long Branch Saloon in Berkeley the night I went to see the Modern Lovers, a neo–Velvet Underground band from Boston. The Lovers (who seem to have acquired the beginnings of a national following; a lot of kids in the audience were shouting out requests) have inevitably been compared to the Dolls, but in some ways they are more like an American version of the pre–Meher Baba Who with John Entwistle singing lead instead of Roger Daltrey.

Early in the evening, during the B-group's set, a strange-looking boy with short hair, bug eyes, and a white T-shirt emblazoned—in pencil— with the words "I Love My Life" danced alone on the periphery of the dance floor, attracting fishy looks and comments like "There's a weirdo in every crowd." The weirdo turned out to be the Modern Lovers' lead singer and guitarist, Jonathan Richman. Unlike the other members of the band, who are hard-edge urban freaks, Richman is an oddball's oddball—the archetypal Queens high-school creep (I guess they have them in Boston, too) who sits in the back of the classroom with his shirttail out, making faces and crass comments, picking his nose, hanging out with other creeps, who share his pain and his anarchic innocence. He is a pure pop relic, the kind of ironist whose self-conscious straightness is the highest compliment to perversity. He also has an evocative, if mannered, voice and plays brilliant, daring guitar.

The Lovers' subject matter is, naturally, love—for the disintegrating city ("I know the modern world is bad, / And it's getting worse I suppose every day, / But that's where we belong today"), for their peers ("Don't die now, / Someday we'll be dignified and old together"), for inaccessible girls. There is anger, too, in both the words and the music, but it is their transcendent agape that may ultimately make the Modern Lovers more than an interesting ripple on the new wave. Though the band has real flash, Richman's persona is so narrowly eccentric that I found it a little boring once the novelty had worn off. At times, his antihip posture flirted with a dubious moralism; in a song about trying to win a girl away from her "hippy-skippy" boyfriend he declaimed peevishly, "If these guys are so great, / Why can't they take the world and take it straight?" But there were other moments during the Lovers' act when I felt truly exalted. Toward the end of the set, they did a song about driving down the highway with the AM radio on. A familiar theme, of course, yet the treatment was intense enough to communicate that old sense of belonging to an eternal rock-and-roll community—which is, after all, a drug we've been digging on for twenty years or so. As Jonathan cried, "Got the power, got the magic," I remembered the first time I ever saw the Who, the night they sang "You are forgiven!"—and I was.

Berkeley is also home base for a new hard-rock group called Eyes, five women who are doing—finally!—what no other female band has managed: integrating a feminist consciousness with a love for rock and roll and an acute fan's sense of their own place in its tradition. They are also angry, sexy, funny; their songs stay in my head; and they have a powerful lead singer in Alicia Pojanowski, a tough-soft woman from a working-class family in Wayne, New Jersey. Both their politics and their feeling for rock history are reflected in their choice of sources (their repertoire includes versions of "Shop Around," "I've Got a Line on You," "Respect Yourself"), their stage act (Alicia may move like Mick Jagger, but she projects an unmistakably female sexuality), and their Dylanesque lyrics, which deal with survival in the face of male absurdity, female vulnerability, and urban insanity ("I asked you over a month ago, please to move out your things; / You say you'd really like to oblige me, but your arm is still in a sling"). The band is managed by a witty, mordant composer who calls herself Ms. Clawdy. Ms. C. not only is responsible for some of Eyes' best material— notably an authentic masterpiece called "Night Blindness"—but has written a collection of terrific songs that have never been performed publicly, including the only song I've ever heard that's about rape from the woman's point of view: "I must have been expecting him, I was so collected and calm, / I even found myself thinking of you as he pinned back my arms."

I've seen Eyes twice; the first performance was a knockout, the second disappointing. The band is still a rough diamond. Ms. Clawdy talks of beginners' hesitations: do we want to commit ourselves to the cutthroat music business *for real*? But the basic talent, intelligence, and energy are there, and I, at least, have been waiting a long, long time for these women and what they represent. I hope to see them in New York someday soon.

Chapter 6

THE SOCIOLOGIST

Pop Blues

APRIL 1968

During the nineteen-fifties, the eagerness of politicians to avow their anti-Communism was matched only by the alacrity with which journalists and celebrity pundits attacked the then new rock and roll. In response to an especially insensitive polemic by Sam Levenson, I wrote him a letter defending the music for its freshness and its exciting beat and added that since (like so many of his allies) he appeared to have reacted less to what he heard than to a general fear and resentment of teenagers, I was enclosing a list of songs I thought he should listen to. I still have a copy of that letter, and though my arguments are satisfactorily prophetic, a lot of the songs on the list make me blush. If we who grew up with rock and have always loved it feel smug these days, the smugness is tainted—at least for some of us. We all knew Elvis was great, no matter what Harriet Van Horne said, but who among us has soul so pure that he never liked Pat Boone? My own taste was not only less discriminating than it could have been but often discriminating in the wrong way. I tended, for instance, to prefer the tamer, white versions of rhythm-and-blues records to the black originals. Partly this was because the imitators were pushed on the radio, but partly it was because Georgia Gibbs *sounded better* to me than LaVern Baker; I was one of the white teenaged reasons the music was being watered down. So for me—as for all the present-day college kids who first came to rock through Dylan and the Beatles—the current resurgence of interest in rhythm and blues means the making of new discoveries.

At the moment, fifties music is an incipient fad: a New York booking agent plans a national tour of oldies acts in conjunction with major radio stations; the Mothers of Invention, noted for devastating Brechtian parodies of rock and roll, are rumored to be recording original rhythm-and-blues tunes under the name of Reuben and the Jets; in England, where old rock records have become collectors' items, boys are trading in their Edwardian furbelows for leather jackets and greasing down their Beatle cuts. And, beyond the inevitable camping, rhythm and blues is being collected and reissued on records. Some months ago, Columbia brought out *18 King Size Rhythm and Blues Hits,* a group of songs that were originally recorded by King, a Cincinnati-based R&B label. Now Atlantic—the company most responsible for bringing black music to the white market—has released a four-album set called *History of Rhythm & Blues.* Though both anthologies are worth owning, I much prefer the former. *18 King Size Hits* makes no claim to completeness, yet, with selections ranging from the Southern blues of Little Willie John, through Bill Doggett's "Honky Tonk" (the best rock instrumental ever recorded) and the New York pop sound of the Platters, to the soul music of James Brown, it demonstrates the scope and variety of R&B better on one record than the Atlantic collection does on four. At the same time, it is short enough not to need padding with mediocre songs, so nearly every cut is special. *History of Rhythm & Blues* is a failure more of showmanship than of substance. It is far too long for what it really is—a history of Atlantic Records—and the misleading title only calls attention to what has been left out. *History* does not even exploit the full Atlantic repertoire. It is very pop oriented, deemphasizing blues in favor of commercially successful rock. (More than a third of the cuts are devoted to the Drifters, the Clovers, and the Coasters.) In principle, this is a perfectly legitimate approach, but again it points up the omissions. The

Atlantic stable contains no examples of the popular Harlem sound—the Platters and all those mythic one-shot groups, like the Heartbeats and the Five Satins—whose sweet, diatonic harmonies appealed to Northern whites because they derived from gospel, a "whiter" music than blues. And although on *18 King Size Hits*—definitely a blues rather than a pop record—the absence of white performers seems perfectly natural, on *History* the gratuitous inclusion of Bobby Darin just begs us to miss Elvis Presley and Buddy Holly. Still, the four records of *History* offer plenty of good music. Volume 1: The Roots 1947–52 is the bluesiest, most diverse, and most interesting of them and contains the two best cuts—the Clovers' tragicomic "One Mint Julep" and Laurie Tate's awesome wail "Anytime, Anyplace, Anywhere." Second choice is Volume 3: Rock & Roll 1956–57, which has a strong Southern contingent—Joe Turner, Ivory Joe Hunter, LaVern Baker, Chuck Willis—and includes the Coasters' classics "Searchin'" and "Young Blood."

Black R&B always had a peripheral position in rock and roll, which absorbed and transformed it for the benefit of whites. These albums right some old wrongs. Now that I have come to demand the harder, rawer voices my teenage ear rejected, listening to Otis Williams or LaVern Baker is a new and gratifying experience, and even the highly commercial groups take on more resonance. The anthologies confirm the superiority of fifties Negro music to most contemporaneous pop.[1] But they also place the music in a historical and developmental context, inviting comparison with earlier blues. And by that stricter standard much of it—especially the more popular Atlantic stuff—does not hold up as well. The lyrics, though they're free of the adolescent self-pity that suffused most early white rock, are sexually and poetically anemic. The music is less basic than the old blues, more ephemeral, more *pop*. It is meant for the radio, not the archives, and, more significantly, it is meant for the marketplace. Which is why R&B is not quite folk music, and why I am afraid all those college kids may in the end be disappointed.

---

1. Willis added a caveat in her collection *Beginning to the See the Light* about the use of *Negro* in her 1968 essay "Dylan." She said that in hindsight, the word "grate[s] on me aesthetically as well as politically," and I'm pretty sure she would have said something similar here.—Ed.

The Ordeal of Moby Grape
JUNE 1968

Many first-rate rock groups sicken and die from too little promotion. Moby Grape, one of San Francisco's finest products, almost succumbed to too much. The most popular San Francisco groups—Jefferson Airplane, the Grateful Dead, Country Joe and the Fish, Big Brother and the Holding Company—have made their reputations largely by word of mouth and unsolicited publicity. Primarily live performers, they had an enthusiastic local following, as well as a host of long-distance admirers in the Eastern diaspora, long before they recorded. Furthermore, this presold audience came from an unusually articulate and evangelistic section of the population—that is, hip teenagers and bohemians. The record companies could not have asked for a better grass-roots promotional apparatus. (Similar conditions have enabled the Doors, a very different sort of bohemian group, to become the hottest pop stars in America without benefit of a spectacular public relations blitz.) But the word-of-mouth process is a slow one, and in the case of Moby Grape, Columbia Records decided to help things along. The Grape's first album *(Moby Grape)* got the full treatment. Columbia spent over a hundred thousand dollars in promotion, flew Los Angeles bigwigs to San Francisco for a party at the Avalon Ballroom, dispatched the group on a national tour, designed a special Moby Grape logo and Moby Grape buttons, and distributed Grape press kits covered in imitation (I assume) velvet. The most interesting aspect of the campaign was the simultaneous release of five singles, each containing two cuts from the album—a highly unorthodox maneuver presumably undertaken on the theory that, with all those Grape records available, one of them had to catch on. I was dubious; it seemed to me that the choice would only confuse the radio stations. Still, along with most other observers of the scene, I expected that in the end Columbia's promotion would get results. After all, the raw material was there. The group was enormously talented. All five members wrote songs, all were excellent musicians (especially the lead guitarist, Jerry Miller), and all had voices (especially Bob Mosley, who may be the best white male blues-cum-country singer around). They were versatile—the music on *Moby Grape* ranged from soul ("Mr. Blues") to country ("Ain't No Use"), from classic hard rock ("Omaha") to soft lyric ("8:05"). Yet it was all held together by the

Grape's distinctive sound, which featured three (!) guitars, a strong beat, tight arrangements, voices recorded way in the background, and a pervasive tension between driving energy and gentleness. The recessed vocals made the lyrics almost unintelligible, which was a shame. The Grape, like the Beatles and too few others, had caught on to the creative possibilities of conventional pop-song diction; they made brilliant use of repetition in "Omaha" and "Changes," and of romantic clichés in "8:05." And—also with little company—they preferred pithy, colloquial prose to poetic adventurism: "Would you let me / Walk down your street / Naked if I want to? / . . . Can I buy an amplifier / On time? / I ain't got no money now, / But I will pay you before I die." *Moby Grape* was not only a very good album; by all the normal standards, it was also very commercial. Few LPs contain more than one or two cuts that can reasonably be released as singles—a single has to be suitable for AM radio, which means it must be short, not too far out, and catchy enough for the listener to remember after hearing it once or twice. Every one of the Moby Grape singles fulfilled those requirements; every one of them sounded like a potential hit. The excitement at Columbia was genuine—Moby Grape seemed a sure thing. The Grape shared the general optimism. One early morning, two of them camped outside Columbia's offices waiting for someone to arrive and give them money for a taxi to the airport: stars do not take the bus.

It never happened. The five-singles ploy did not work at all. The album sold adequately, reaching Top Forty on the trade charts—but then the Big Brother album, an atrociously produced record put out with no fanfare by a small, chintzy company, was to do almost as well. And the promotion campaign resulted in two kinds of negative feedback. On the one hand, the Grape's natural audience was put off by the hard sell; on the other, such close contact between five hippie musicians and the pop establishment made for severe abrasion. During their tour, the Grape managed to offend disc jockeys, writers, and even their own publicity people; a pot and morals bust (the three members involved were eventually cleared) did not help matters. Suddenly no one would touch them, and there was a publicity blackout. The Grape never quite recovered from that turbulent beginning. Today they do not have the prestige their talent warrants, nor are they a top draw at concerts (which is where the steady money is). And now that the San Francisco movement has peaked, they may never make it big. If I could, I'd do something about that. At the moment, all I can do is give their second album, *Wow*, a reserved plug.

Wow is not as uniformly impressive as the first album, perhaps because it is more exploratory. The sound has shifted away from hard rock toward blues and country; the voices this time are emphasized, and Mosley's is heavily exploited. There is a lot of playing around with different styles, most of it unsuccessful. "Bitter Wind," an experiment in noise, is— pretentious noise. A blues version of "Naked If I Want To" smothers that confection in angst. Worst of all is "Just Like Gene Autry; A Foxtrot," a big-band number that includes the voice and ukulele of Arthur Godfrey and has to be played at (remember?) 78 rpm. It's nice that the Grape should be interested in conceptual art, but having to switch speeds soon becomes an intolerable nuisance, and the song is not worth the trouble. My favorite cuts are all mainstream Grape: "Murder in My Heart for the Judge," a superb exercise in controlled violence; "Three-Four," a moving country song; and "Motorcycle Irene," a rocker with beautiful crash noises and a tough lyric: "Dirty, on her Harley, / (But her nails are clean.) / Superpowered, deflowered, / Over-eighteen Irene." "Miller's Blues," a rather dull song, nevertheless shows off some great singing by Mosley and a long Miller guitar solo.

Wow comes packaged with a bonus record of improvisations called *Grape Jam*—evidence that the Grape can (so there) handle the extended instrumentals now in vogue. It's a pleasant extra—particularly since Al Kooper and Mike Bloomfield play piano on two of the cuts—and an interesting counterpoint to the tight formalism of Moby Grape's "real" albums. But it makes me a little nervous. I hope the Grape won't defect to the avant-garde. Someone has to mind the store.

The Star, the Sound, and the Scene
JULY 1968

The sociology of rock and postrock has been based on three concepts: the star, the sound, and the scene. That sociology, like most, is firmly rooted in economics. Since the simplicity that gave rock its mass appeal also made it relatively easy to create, performers and the businessmen behind them faced a problem familiar to the makers of cigarettes and cars: how do you outsell a horde of competitors whose products are as good as yours? The solution was equally familiar: attractive packaging. The crucial elements in the package were charisma and sound—the artist's trademark, the gimmick that unified his work and set it apart (Little Richard's scream, the Everly Brothers' close harmonies, the Beatles' falsetto). If a performer or group did not have a unique sound, it helped to identify with a collective sound—usually that of a subculture (rockabilly, the Mersey sound) or of a creative producer (Phil Spector, Berry Gordy). I do not mean to conjure up the specter of hucksters sitting around the Brill Building cold-bloodedly inventing salable gimmicks. Sometimes it worked that way. But mostly the process was unconscious: performers whose personal style was naturally gimmicky, or whose managers understood intuitively how to get attention, survived and bred imitators. Actually, before rock and roll became self-conscious, commercial and aesthetic considerations were almost indistinguishable; the geniuses of that period, from Chuck Berry to the early Beatles and Stones, owed their greatness to the same qualities that made them best-sellers. (Presley was an exception, and he ended up in Hollywood singing ballads.)

The Beatles were transitional figures. For one thing, their charisma was much more interesting than that of any previous rock-and-roll stars. Their image—that androgynous, childlike insouciance, the way they reveled in their fame and wealth without ever taking it or themselves seriously—sold records, which is what Brian Epstein had in mind when he made them wear mop tops and Edwardian suits. But it was also a comment on success, an embodiment of ingenuous youth in the affluent society—and "comments" and "embodiments" are, after all, aesthetic categories. Similarly, the Beatles' sound—a deliberate attempt *not* to sound black, contrary to custom—was at once a commercial novelty and an artistic self-assertion. These developments fascinated pop artists and others for whom the aesthetic significance of commercial phenomena was a major preoccupation—enter the first self-conscious rock fans. The Beatles were also responsible for the bohemianization of rock. The concept of the rock *scene*—a term borrowed from jazz and implying an elite in-group as much as a place—originated in mod London and spread to San Francisco. Rock became identified less with particular superstars or sounds than with a whole lifestyle; "psychedelic" music was not so much a sound as a spirit. In 1965, the average person asked to associate to the phrase *rock and roll* would probably have said *Beatles*; by 1967 the answer would more likely have been *hippies, drugs,* or *long hair.* When American bohemians took up rock, they brought along their very un-Beatlish distinctions between art and Mammon, and for the first time people talked about *serious,* as opposed to merely commercial, rock. Yet if such talk was possible, it was only because the Beatles (with a lot of help from Bob Dylan) had paced a miraculous escalation in the quality of pop songs. Since *Sgt. Pepper,* few people deny that "serious" pop is serious art. And though there is still some overlap, the split between the AM-radio-singles-teenie market and the FM-LP-student-hippie-intellectual audience is a fact of life.

With this evolution has come a shift in the way the music is perceived. There is, for example, an unprecedented demand for technical virtuosity. Good musicianship was once as irrelevant to rock as it was rare; the whole point of electric guitars and dubbing and echo chambers was that kids with no special talent could make nice noises. But now the music has enough scope to attract excellent instrumentalists, as well as an audience interested in traditional criteria of quality. Not that this audience's taste necessarily lives up to its pretensions; often flash is mistaken for skill. Still, a few years ago it would have been impossible for an Eric Clapton or a Mike Bloomfield to make it in pop music on the strength of fine guitar playing. The new audience also favors complex music and lyrics—a trend that threatened to get totally out of hand until Dylan's *John Wesley Harding* provided some timely propaganda for simplicity. What all this adds up to is an increasing tendency to judge pop music intrinsically, the way poetry or jazz is judged. Social context is still important, as it is for most art. But although social and economic factors were once an integral part of the rock aesthetic—indeed, defined that aesthetic—they are now subordinate to the "music itself."

On balance, in spite of all the good music that would never have happened otherwise, I think this tendency is regrettable. What it means is that rock has been co-opted by high culture, forced to adopt its standards—chief of which is the integrity of the art object. It means the end of rock as a radical experiment in creating mass culture on its own terms, ignoring elite definitions of what is or is not intrinsic to aesthetic experience. The reason the Beatles, the Stones, and Dylan are the unchallenged—and probably unchallengeable—giants of pop is that through and beyond their work their personalities have a continuing impact on the public consciousness that, if it is not aesthetic, is something just as good. (This is especially true of Dylan, an indifferent musician who never bothered to become a studio expert.) The new standards are bound to inhibit further exploration in this area. In addition, lack of a compelling image puts the new performer at an almost insuperable disadvantage in trying to make an impression on a public whose imagination is deeply involved with established artists. At best, new performers are taking longer to be recognized, and fewer and fewer will attain that special relationship to the public psyche that is so often uncomprehendingly dismissed as "mere celebrity." I'm thinking, for example, of the Sweet Inspirations, a Gospel-oriented quartet whose first album came out a while ago. They're great and by all rights should take over the position of preeminent girl group last held by the Supremes and before that by the Shirelles. But though they have a hit single ("Sweet Inspiration"), I doubt that they will make that pinnacle. So what? Well, part of the fun of listening to the Supremes was that they were the *Supremes*.

A related problem is the loss of the mass audience. Whether the upgrading of the music is in itself responsible for that loss is questionable. The Beatles held the loyalty of their original teenage fans long after they had stopped making simple, happy dance music; when the kids finally turned off, it was less because the Beatles were esoteric than because they were old hat. More recently, the Doors and Jefferson Airplane have done very well outside the coterie. Jimi Hendrix, on the other hand, has not, though he has all the accoutrements of the superstar—a distinctive personality (he's the only expatriate black hippie around), a distinctive sound (achieved by choke-neck playing on the electric guitar), and a spectacular live act (he plucks his guitar with his teeth, sets fire to it, and breaks it up). What *is* certain is that the new music has thoroughly confused the record industry; no one can figure out how to promote it. Since the beginning of this year, the sheer quantity of serious pop, as well as its immense variety, has defined sloganeering. Most of the new musicians are not interested in gimmickry or image making; they just want to make music. It's no longer possible to attract notice with a fancy album cover and a way-out name. And the scenes are dying. The Small Faces are the only interesting British group to break since Cream. The best first albums of this year's San Francisco crop come from two of the original underground groups, the Loading Zone and Quicksilver Messenger Service; except for a little-known group called Serpent Power, and Blue Cheer, which has a certain crude energy going for it (what I mean is, it's loud), the "second generation" San Francisco groups are a disaster. Early this year, MGM Records, out of naïveté or desperation, tried to invent a new scene, and a few other companies went along. It was called the Boston sound (though there was no special sound involved) and was promoted as antidrug and antiexotic—rather negative premises on which to build a scene. The groups themselves were a dreary lot, ranging from the competently frenetic Beacon Street Union to the sublimely ridiculous Earth Opera. (By the time the Earth Opera album was released, the vibrations were pretty bad, so the group was billed as a *Cambridge* product. It didn't help.) Moral: scenes may be made, but they have to be born first.

For the sake of completeness, I ought to note that there are two areas of pop music in which sociology still dominates. First, *negative* charisma is very potent. A group that is thought of as a teenybopper band won't be accepted by most serious rock fans no matter how good it is. Ask someone in the audience at the Fillmore East what he thinks of the Hollies or the Young Rascals. Second, there is a minor cult of sensitive adolescent folkies like Tim Buckley and Steve Noonan, for no reason I can discern except that they are probably just like the kids who idolize them. In the case of Richie Havens, the attraction must be that he is black and friendly—an irresistible combination these days.

Roots
FEBRUARY 1969

Right now, the most important phenomenon in popular music is the white-blues band. Technically, the dominant influences are English; Jimi Hendrix, whose wall of noise is the only really original feature of the new blues (predictably it comes from a black American, however mod-ified), and Eric Clapton, the white-blues musician most responsible for popularizing B. B. King's guitar techniques. But the spirit that characterizes the current blues scene began in San Francisco, with the emphasis on live performance, looseness and improvisation, and an antipop, anticommercial ethic. Blues was always integral to the psychedelic sound; less tainted by the Great Society than rock and roll, it fitted Haight-Ashbury's social radicalism. If blues is now the favored form of the hip community everywhere, it is mostly because increasing political desperation is undermining the essentially optimistic pop outlook. For analogous reasons, fans have adopted the pro–avant-garde bias of the fifties jazz audience.

The same forces that led to the white-blues boom have created a small countertrend: the country-music revival. Behind the fascination with Nashville is the need to preserve music as a diversion—a *respite* from high art and political headaches. "Close your eyes, close the door / You don't have to worry anymore / I'll be your baby tonight," sings Bob Dylan on *John Wesley Harding,* the seminal record of the country movement. Of course, since people are pretty schizophrenic these days, the categories tend to blur; most of the songs on *JWH* have political overtones. But in general white blues represents an attempt to figure out where we're going, and in country, an appreciation of where we've been. Country music affirms our Americanness and, coincidentally, our whiteness. Its rediscovery in many ways parallels the rediscovery of fifties rock by folkies and intellectuals; it was in such a spirit that Joan Baez sang the great schlock ballad "The Green, Green Grass of Home" at the Newport Folk Festival. Country enthusiasts are not unaware of the element of puritanical provincialism in the music. Rather, they react to it with ironic affection; that is, in a pop way. Similarly, sentimental pastoralism is indulged consciously—an approach that takes the curse off. Unlike blues devotees, the country audience is not anticommercial. Blues fans' attitudes toward soul music range from hostile to ambivalent: it's black but it's slick; Aretha Franklin is great, but she does those Coke commercials. Country fans dig country-western, which is big business.

Basically, then, the country revival is a holding action, a refuge for the disintegrating pop sensibility. (The recent spate of articles proclaiming the Death of Rock could hasten the death of rock. If magazine editors get nervous and cancel features on rock stars, if record companies get nervous and stop signing so many new groups—well, that's the American way of death. Still, I'm not taking bets. The future of capitalism looks dubious, too, but I wouldn't advise anyone to cash in his General Motors stock quite yet.) The blues thing, for all its regressive aspects—the lionization of inferior musicians, the snobbery, the familiar spectacle of white kids trying to retrieve a form that young blacks have abandoned, no doubt for good reasons—has an air of possibility; it could lead to something better, to the artistic and social breakthrough of our fantasies. Country music is just a pleasant dead end. And yet, other things being equal, I'd rather listen to country than to white blues. Because of its melodic quality, even mediocre country music is easy to take (in fact, there is a fine, sometimes nonexistent boundary between country-western and easy-listening music); a blues band that isn't good enough to get me really involved just gives me a headache. At least half my favorite albums of the past year or so are country-oriented: *John Wesley Harding,* the Byrds' *The Notorious Byrd Brothers* and *Sweetheart of the Rodeo,* and *Music from Big Pink.*

For those who are into country music, an interesting development is the resurgence of the Everly Brothers. Early practitioners of country-based rock and a major influence on the Beatles, Don and Phil Everly are the perfect emblem of a country revival whose purpose is to salvage pop. They embody nostalgia on two levels. Not only do adults who were teenagers when they were first popular—and also younger people vicariously experiencing the fifties—love them for belonging to the pop age of innocence but the brothers themselves are nostalgic about their Kentucky boyhood and the songs their parents taught them. (Back in the early fifties, the family had a morning radio program that featured country and gospel music.) The latter component is indispensable. Without it the Everlys might seem outdated; by participating in a fad—the musical quest for America's rural past—they become contemporary.

Recently, the Everly Brothers spent a highly successful week at the Bitter End. They came here from a Las Vegas engagement and did more or less the same act, with all the silly show-business patter. They wore black suits with velvet collars. Their hair was a lot longer than it used to be, but they had the same sweet smiles and the same sweetly harmonizing voices. They sang their old hits, took requests, got us to sing along with "Bye Bye Love." They announced that they weren't going to plug their album *Roots,* then proceeded to plug it and to sing a song from the album—Merle Haggard's "Mama Tried." Later, they did five minutes of the coda from "Hey, Jude." "Saint Jude is the patron saint of the second chance and of the impossible," Don informed us. The last encore was "Kentucky." All through the set, we sat delighted, digging the naïveté, the show biz, the memories, the *Americana.*

In contrast, *Roots* is the sophisticated product of conscious pop thinking and packaging. The basic idea came from a Warner Brothers executive, Andy Wickham, who is an Englishman turned Angeleno—one of the thousands of upper-class British kids who embraced American vulgarity and American music and became mod London. Like *Sweetheart of the Rodeo, Roots* attempts to survey, with both involvement and distance, tendencies in country music. The Byrds' involvement is manifested in the loving care of their arrangements, and their distance in the gulf between their bohemianism and songs like "The Christian Life." The Everly Brothers are connected to the music by family tradition, but they have come a long way from Kentucky—Dad Everly could never perform in Las Vegas. The album, whose jacket art includes a dozen snapshots of Don and Phil as children, begins and ends with tapes of the *Everly Family* radio show. In between, the brothers cover a lot of ground, including two Merle Haggard prison songs (the rule in country music seems to be that a rebel has to come to a bad end); "Ventura Boulevard," a spare, beautiful evocation of childhood in a small town; "Illinois," a countrified rendition of a song by a very urban composer, Randy Newman; "I Wonder If I Care as Much," their own song and a good example of their fifties style, though this version is much more intricately arranged than the earlier incarnation, on the flip side of "Bye Bye Love"; and "Less of Me," a moral-uplift song that provides the same kind of reference point as "The Christian Life" on the Byrds album.

Dylan's Anti-Surprise
APRIL 1969

> Something is happening, but you don't care what it is, do you,
> Mr. Zimmerman?

"I don't need much, that ain't no lie. / Ain't runnin' any race. / Give to me my country pie. / I won't throw it up in anybody's face," sings Bob Dylan on his new album, *Nashville Skyline*. And, at least on the surface, that declaration sums up the mood of this much more than pleasant record. Dylan has taken a vacation from mythmaking and perversity to relax and fool around with his music. As usual, his sense of timing is perfect. *Nashville Skyline* appears at a moment when the whole rock scene has relaxed; the era of the masterpiece, when everyone waited tensely for the latest miracle to emerge from the studio, is really over. The album also represents the culmination of a year in which Dylan-mongering fell to an all-time low—in which news of our hero was consistently homey and reassuring, like a polygraph finally straightening out. Dylan, as we all know, has been alive and well in Woodstock, occasionally trekking to Nashville and meeting up with Johnny Cash.

So I wasn't even surprised that *Nashville Skyline* wasn't much of a surprise. Dylan has been hung up on country music for a long time—*John Wesley Harding* got everybody interested, but it should be remembered that *Blonde on Blonde* was recorded in Nashville in 1966—and he had given every indication that he was going to keep pursuing it. Much as I had expected, *Nashville Skyline* is a collection of simple, melodic country songs. The one shocker is Dylan's voice. He really *sings*—carries a tune, that is—and, as a result, sounds ten years older and just like a country singer, which seems to be his point. The album is his tribute to a genre, complete with manifesto ("Country Pie," the song quoted above). The usual relationship between Dylan's words and his melodies is reversed. *Nashville Skyline* is primarily *sound*—country sound of several varieties. Most of the lyrics are pastiches of country-western and pop clichés ("I was cruel. I treated her like a fool. / I threw it all away") whose function is to provide the proper setting for the music. In the past, Dylan has used country music as a vehicle for self-expression; in this album he subordinates self to genre. Using examples from his earliest work, he comments on this reversal of values: in the much publicized duet with Johnny Cash, he transforms his old song "Girl from the North Country" from an intensely adolescent, weltschmerzy folk ballad into a stylized, cheerful country-western song; "Nashville Skyline Rag," an excellent instrumental, contains unobtrusive snatches of his unmistakable harmonica, a trademark that hasn't changed in eight years.

Dylan's mood of acceptance, his use of clichés in the attempt to fashion "generic" songs, his revived interest in his past were all evident on *John Wesley Harding*, though here these concerns are treated more casually and playfully. Furthermore, several country records put out by pop performers in the wake of *JWH* anticipated *Nashville Skyline*'s basic musical ideas. Dylan professes not to care that he hasn't presented us with anything startling—he ain't runnin' any race. But, ultimately, his refusal to top himself turns into a new way of topping himself; his acceptance becomes another form of belligerence. Unpredictability, he is saying, is as big a bore as anything else—why should he have to make the revolution every time? *Nashville Skyline* may be a revolt against hipness, but it is sure to be one of the hippest records of the year.

This album is not only about country music. Like *Another Side of Bob Dylan* and *Blonde on Blonde,* it is about women. Dylan has always combined frankness about the power struggle between men and women with reticence about sex—an unusual combination. The conventional approach in pop music is to combine realism with a display of sexual power—indeed, to identify the two—or else to soften the whole male-female relationship with fantasy. The first tendency comes out of blues and is bound up with the myth of black sexuality; the second is the product of white music and puritanism. Before Dylan (and the Beatles), American bohemians and radicals who rebelled against the hypocrisies of white middle-class culture almost invariably used blackness as a central metaphor. Dylan never did. Like all the other folkies, he learned blues riffs and sang about Mississippi, but his radicalism was modeled on Woody Guthrie's and his bohemianism on Allen Ginsberg's, and blues sensibility contributed little to his melodies (diatonic and crude), his rhythms (English-cum-hillbilly), his lyrics, or his sexual attitude. Now he is discovering that romantic fantasy, staple of the white pop tradition, has its place. His attitude toward women, like his attitude toward everything else, has softened considerably. *Nashville Skyline* is an album of tender, humor-filled love songs—not a putdown in the lot. "One More Night" is reminiscent of "Don't Think Twice, It's All Right"— only now Dylan acknowledges it is at least as much his failure as hers that "I couldn't be what she wanted me to be." "Tell Me That It Isn't True" pokes fun at his past mania for uncompromising honesty: "They say that you've been seen with some other man. / . . . Darlin', I'm countin' on you. / Tell me that it isn't true." My favorite cut, musically and lyrically, is "Lay Lady Lay," a low-keyed, delicate sexual invitation backed up by absolutely spectacular organ music.

In short, this record fulfills a promise Dylan made us all a year ago: "Shut the light, shut the shade. / You don't have to be afraid. / I'll be your baby tonight." OK, Bobby.

Elliott Murphy's White Middle-Class Blues
FEBRUARY 1974

As the polarity of Los Angeles and San Francisco in a sense defined the sixties, so the spirit of this sobered-up (or at least hungover) decade can be found, like that young dude in the Dolls song, somewhere between the

Babylon of Manhattan and Babylon, Long Island. Not coincidentally, for the first time since the rock-and-roll era began, a distinctive New York brand of rock is coming into its own, aesthetically and mythically, if not (yet) commercially. New Yorkers embody the contemporary mood because of their dogged belief in original sin, their emphasis on ambition when possible but survival above all, and—perhaps most important—their rootedness. Out-of-towners may come here seeking anonymity, but native New Yorkers are always reminding everybody where they came from— what neighborhood, what class, what family; if their chauvinism is often inverted (my section of Queens is uglier than yours), it is because they are really bragging about their stamina. In palmier days, such parochial attachments had begun to seem a bit cranky; a basic assumption of the cultural revolution was that young (white) people were transcending (read obliterating) their origins, materially through affluence and the endless possibilities of selective consumption, morally and spiritually through one or another variety of expanded consciousness. Although, ironically, this very attempt at transcendence led many people—especially those involved in politics—to an almost anthropological preoccupation with their backgrounds, as a generation we resisted the idea that we might have more in common with our parents than with a great many of our peers. The countercultural ideal rather neatly paralleled the melting-pot myth, even in the racism that gave it the lie. Bohemia was, after all, an alternative to—or a special kind of—upward mobility. It offered all of the cultural and—under the veneer of voluntary poverty—many of the material advantages of upper-middle-class life without the traditional work and family obligations, and it was one possible resolution of the conflict of loyalties often experienced by college graduates from poor and lower-middle-class families. This was all very well in a superheated economy that allowed unprecedented numbers of people to have their freedom and their stereo set, too. Now that we can't always get what we want—and may not even get what we need, a shockingly un-American possibility—it is embarrassingly obvious that the head next door is (and always was) first of all a minister's daughter or a car salesman's son, a Jew or a WASP, a product of Scarsdale or Gary or Flatbush; and that the tensions, prejudices, and limitations of vision these differences imply are ultimately more potent than Orange Sunshine.

All this is natural subject matter for pop music. Much of the power of sixties rock lay in its ability to mediate between white middle-class bohemians and their urban and suburban past. Bob Dylan, the archetypal cultural revolutionary figure—fleeing his home, changing his name, re-creating himself again and again—called his first rock album *Bringing It All Back Home.* Now a kid named Elliott Murphy, an F. Scott Fitzgerald freak who plays a familiar-sounding harmonica; writes lyrics that make *Blonde on Blonde* fans shiver under their leopard-skin pillbox hats; looks—with his long, lank platinum hair, his white Gatsby suits, and his inward stare—as if he just stepped off the *Bringing It All Back Home* album jacket; and has gone the route from Garden City to Max's Kansas City (with a European detour), offers us a contemporary report on the trip.

Murphy's first album, *Aquashow*—consumers of such arcana may recall that his late father ran the Aqua Show in Flushing Meadow—is on one level another end-of-the-dream lament, but his stance is more complicated than that. It is clear to him that we can't really go home again, even though we never really left, because home itself has changed irrevocably: the sixties fantasy and its failures have become part of everyone's everyday reality. In "Hometown," Murphy insists, "Don't tell me you don't hear that small town callin' you, / 'Cause y'know what, baby, you're still doin' all the same things you used to do." But this hometown is a place where "even churchmen are wearin' stripes, / And all the hometown girls are gettin' in much too late tonight"; where "you know they used to say that kid was born with a silver spoon. / He told me that he left his home way too soon, / 'Cause no one ever told him about the power of a real full moon." "How's the Family?" is a dirge-like catalogue of sixties casualties: the wife who realizes her self has been denied, the fifteen-year-old junkie, the estranged old people, the men who "know who they're working for and what's more they know why." *Aquashow* is not kind to the suburbs, but neither is it the usual hip whine. Murphy obviously identifies with the milieu he is describing; instead of the air of moral superiority that was the counterculture's most irritating trait, his suburban songs reveal an edge of self-doubt, even of guilt ("I saw your mother downtown yesterday. . . . / She told me all her kids had run away. / They call at Christmastime"), as well as a healthy sardonic awareness of privilege. His tone is less that of the cultural pundit deploring alienation than of the teenager griping about his high school; as he puts it in "White Middle-Class Blues," "I'm in the middle of Brooklyn, can't see no escape. / They say the South is a bummer, but this ain't that great."

Murphy also avoids the overreaction of some of his contemporaries, who would like to pretend that the sixties were simply a hallucination.

He is still obsessed with pop myths, as any aspiring rock star has to be. "Last of the Rock Stars"—his theme, and the best where-are-we-now anthem since "All the Young Dudes"—is about the power of that obsession. Invoking the death of Jimi Hendrix and (implicitly) his own ambition, he cries out, in an agony of faith and cynicism, that rock is still the best we have yet isn't enough: "Rock and roll is here to stay, but who will be left to play?" Which is exactly the way many of us feel about the state of our music, not to mention the state of our souls. Murphy is less successful with songs like "Hangin' Out" and "Poise 'n' Pen," whose evocations of hip low life can't compete with Lou Reed's or, for that matter, David Johansen's. Somewhere in between is "Marilyn," an interesting try that misses. In it, an ingenuous adolescent persona informs us that "Marilyn Monroe died for our sins" and in the process re-creates the sin that killed her, making her into a symbol instead of a person. I like the idea, and some of the words are great—my favorite line is "Our thoughts were dirty, though she was clean"—but, finally, the song doesn't come off. What's wrong, I think, is that Monroe really did die for male sins, and so Murphy as well as his narrator ends up sounding innocently exploitative.

So far, I'm more impressed with Murphy's album than with his live performance. In spite of his considerable talent, his striking looks, and an excellent backup band, his onstage presence is not as electric as it should be. Though he is cocky enough, I sense a certain lack of divine confidence, which may come of being too cerebral. But whether or not Elliott Murphy makes it as the last, or the next, of the rock stars, he is certainly the best thing to happen to the New York scene since the Dolls. And that, for me, is saying a lot.

Mott the Hoople: Playing the Loser's Game
MAY 1974

On the back cover of Mott the Hoople's new album, *The Hoople*, underneath all the credits, appears the line "It's life and life only." The quote expresses not only Mott's continuing debt to Bob Dylan but the ambition (some would say hubris) of the ideological rock-and-roller. To a band like

Mott the Hoople, rock and roll is life. More specifically, it is structured life: history. Like most critics—and ideological fans—I identify with performers who share that assumption. As a critic, I prefer it to the competing premise—that rock and roll is music—because it's more interesting to write about. As a fan, I perceive that rock and roll and its electric offspring, rock, have provided a spiritual—often literal—record of my life and times, and that the most memorable songs have generally commented on this function as well as fulfilled it. This used to be a natural process; today, of course, it is highly self-conscious. In fact, it seems to me that an obsessive, almost puritanical sense of history is precisely what distinguishes rock and roll in its contemporary version from rock in general. The ironic, though not illogical, result is that seventies rock-and-roll bands, which are in a way the most faithful transmitters of a tradition that united an entire generation, tend to appeal—in America, anyway—to the cult rather than the mass. (The only exception I can think of—given that I consider *seventies* a spiritual and aesthetic rather than strictly chronological qualifier—is Alice Cooper, who parodies the historical sense in his act even as he embodies it in songs like "School's Out" and "I'm Eighteen.") Most American fans—and I guess I can't really blame them—don't want to be burdened with tradition; they want boogie music. British kids are more receptive—largely, I'm convinced, for political reasons: the British class system is still too rigid, or maybe just too blatant, to nurture the sort of classless, escapist fantasy that comes so easily to American bohemians. But even (or especially) for a quintessentially English band like Mott, this is irrelevant. Making it in rock and roll means making it in the USA.

For Ian Hunter, Mott the Hoople's lead singer, chief writer, and dominant personality, the limitation has been frustrating, not only because riches and fame are no doubt as attractive to him as to any other performer but because stardom—not just the respectable popularity he is finally enjoying—has to be an integral part of what he is trying to achieve: rock and roll divorced from a mass audience is at best a shadow of itself. *All the Young Dudes,* the album that established Mott's critical reputation in this country while failing to move the band out of the cult category, conveyed a rootless, defiant bitterness that was attributable at least as much to the gall of thwarted ambition as to the tensions and disillusionments of the seventies. The next album, *Mott,* made that theme explicit, as the bitterness struggled with a kind of tender affirmation: "Rock 'n' Roll's a loser's game, / it mesmerizes and I can't explain." *The Hoople,* which, as the title suggests, functions as a companion piece to *Mott*, doesn't try to explain, exactly, but it's almost a catalogue of pop preoccupations: the drama of youth crushed by authority; young love; gang violence; class oppression; New York; the tenuous line between glamour and sleaze; the relation of self and image; the need to continually re-create the Golden Age of Rock and Roll, which means continually re-creating one's adolescence. The obvious omission is sex. Mott's music has always been ascetic (though Ian, in his understated way, is very sexy onstage), but on this record more than on any other the asexuality seems a concrete expression of the group's alienation. *The Hoople* is the most distanced of Mott's albums. Its subject matter is (deliberately?) more predictable, hence less personal. And Ian's voice echoes from beyond some generational grave, as if attempting to deliver a final message before fading out completely. The effect is weirdly Brechtian, which is appropriate, I suppose, but also disturbing. After all, Hunter can sing effectively about being burnt out only if in some sense he isn't. If he has really stopped caring, why bother? But if he is heading in that direction, he hasn't quite got there yet. In "Through the Looking Glass" (the most honest cut on the album, I think), he tells his mirror image, "I'll never look at you again— / 'cause I'm really not that vain. / Seven years' bad luck ain't too long— / but before I smash you, hear this song." I wonder if the allusion to *Tommy* is intentional.

   The Hoople is not an easy record to like, and on the whole I think *Mott* is better music as well as better life. But I'm looking forward to seeing Ian and the boys when they arrive in New York for a five-day engagement at the Uris Theater, beginning May 7th. There aren't too many rockers who even look in that mirror anymore.

Leo Sayer, the British singer-songwriter who first attracted attention as the lyricist for Roger Daltrey's solo album, is now making his bid with an LP of his own, *Silverbird*. I like a lot of his singing and some of his music, which is composed by Dave Courtney. But his lyrics (often backed by appropriate string arrangements) are soppy, and I can't stand his persona, which is—get ready—the Sad Clown. When I saw him recently at the Bottom Line, Sayer actually performed in clown costume and makeup—a spectacle that almost rendered me nostalgic for Ziggy Stardust. Even his best song, "The Show Must Go On" (Three Dog Night has made it into a great single), doesn't bear too much close listening. It seems there's an enormous crowd of people and they're all after his blood, and he wishes baby would help him escape from this masquerade, and he feels used and abused. Yech. At his best, Sayer shows that he has learned a bit about rock and roll from David Bowie, Mott the Hoople, Slade, and even the Who. At his worst—well, if he can write a song based on the line "Tomorrow is the first day of the rest of your life," can Kahlil Gibran be far behind?

For years, I've insisted that the way to make a great rock movie would be to cut out all the fancy "creative" stuff and just film a concert. So *Ladies and Gentlemen, the Rolling Stones* is that rare treat, a fantasy come true. Visually, it is thoroughly satisfying. (A purist friend of mine argues that there are too many close-ups, that if they were *really* going to film a concert they should have shot everything from the perspective of the tenth row. I'm sure I'd enjoy that movie, too, but as a Stones voyeur I appreciated this one more.) And in spite of my deep suspicion of any technological development that threatens my stereo set with obsolescence, I have to admit that the quadraphonic sound is an impressive bonus. Yep, it really sounds as if you're there. Now, ingrate that I am, I've escalated the fantasy: the movie ought to be shown in a huge dance hall.

Springsteen: The Wild, the Innocent, and the Street Kid Myth
NOVEMBER 1974

That white youth culture has derived much of its ethos, style, energy, and—above all—music from black people is obvious. But I suspect that for many, if not most, white middle-class kids growing up in Northern cities or (especially) suburbs during the early rock-and-roll years the black influence was indirect and subliminal, and the white working-class street kid more potent both as reality (there were maybe fifty blacks out of five thousand students in my Queens high school, but working-class whites, mostly Italian, represented a sizable subculture) and as metaphor. Those of us who had been trained by liberal parents to see blacks as just-like-us-except-for-their-skins had no scruples about projecting our fantasies onto alien whites. (In *Blackboard Jungle*, the Sidney Poitier character turned into an upwardly mobile goody-goody; the villain was white—even, if I recall correctly, blond.) As a further complication, the barriers between middle-class and working-class teenagers were often flexible enough to promote a good deal of identity confusion. I knew a number of middle-class kids who were closet greasers, acting one way on the street, another at home, unsure of where they really belonged. And though I was a class snob—without even knowing there was such a thing outside English novels—I did make some friends across class lines. I realized that there was a contradiction somewhere, but I never confronted it, any more than I questioned how I could love rock and roll and still accept the adult verdict that it was trash. Nor did I make the connection between my own condescension and my discomfort with richer kids who condescended to me.

With the rise of a bohemia dominated by the children of affluent homes and elite colleges, the myth of the white working-class hood declined, except for a vestigial fixation on motorcycles in general and the Hell's Angels in particular. The romantic (and scary) fantasies reverted to blacks, who had revealed that they were not just-like-us after all; the bigotry against working-class whites persisted in more prosaic forms. Those changes, as always, were reflected in pop music. Upper-middle-class radicals and hippies had always been uncomfortable with rock and roll. Before Bob Dylan came along, they had rejected it; afterward, they were tirelessly inventive about merging it with folk, country, blues, jazz, electronic music—whatever was handy. "Pure" rock and roll—the idea of it more than the diminishing number of examples, which too often reproduced every characteristic of early rock except its excitement—became a symbol of protest for fans and performers who resisted the counterculture's aristocratic bias. And as the sixties fell apart rock-and-roll loyalists aggressively revived the white-street-punk myth.

This revolt against elitism was not so much proletarian as lower middle class, its instigators dissident members of the counterculture rather than outsiders. Although, as I've noted, the boundary is not always clear, there is a difference between middle-class kids who identify with street punks and the punks themselves. Since this difference was often denied, nouveau punkism generated its own brand of pretension and dishonesty. At its worst, it became an excuse for blatant male chauvinism and nihilistic trashing of every value and aspiration beyond (male) orgasm and (male) violence. But it has also produced genuine urban-populist rock-and-rollers, like the Dolls—who combine the street-punk myth and the equally antiaristocratic gay-low-life myth without fudging the distinction between the roles they play and who they are—and Bruce Springsteen.

Springsteen's rock and roll is rooted equally in lower-middle-class semisuburbia (he comes from Asbury Park, New Jersey) and in post-sixties youth culture; his particular version of the street kid owes as much to, say, Emmett Grogan as to Terry Malloy. Springsteen is a romantic, with an impressive capacity for verbal and musical excess. His lyrics chronicle urban street life and its denizens—Spanish Johnny, Crazy Janey, Wild Billy—in passionate detail, image piled on image, rhyme on rhyme. His voice assaults and seduces with growls, breaks, laughs, sobs, whispers, and other varieties of exquisitely expressive noise. He is also a funny, affectionately ironic observer of his world (real and invented) and of his own strutting and posing.

If all this sounds familiar, it should. Springsteen looks and sounds uncannily like a younger, non–mellowed-out Dylan, and he has deliberately cultivated the resemblance. This is a nervy thing to do, since it not only tempts people to dismiss him as an imitator but invites comparisons that almost have to be unfavorable. Yet he gets away with it. I think the reason must have to do with the obsessive way so many young men identified with Dylan during the middle sixties. (Not that women weren't deeply influenced by Dylan, but the relationship was of necessity more oblique.) Given that context, Springsteen's Dylan number becomes another way of celebrating all the young dudes still struggling to realize what Dylan represented—the possibilities for surviving a crazy system. And survival—of the body, let alone the spirit—is a concern that threatens to become more and more pressing for more and more people; Dylan has written plenty of prophetic lines, but the one I think of when I watch Bruce Springsteen is "Nobody's ever taught you how to live out on the street / and now you're gonna have to get used to it."

Springsteen's stage act has improved every time I've seen it, and his recent performance at Avery Fisher Hall was the best yet. I especially enjoyed the way he moved, acting out each song (dancing down the street, mounting his Harley) with just the right mixture of drama and self-parody, projecting a sense of maleness that depended not on the exclusion or denigration or conquest of women but on his appreciation of his body and what it could do. His singing was fine, and his band was as powerful and anarchic as ever. Still, there were boring stretches. Though Springsteen has written a few great songs—my favorites are "Incident on 57th Street" and

"Jungle Land" (his "Desolation Row," or is it *Highway 61?*)—he is not a great songwriter. His melodies tend to be shapeless and to sound alike. As a result, his first album, *Greetings from Asbury Park, N.J.,* is virtually unlistenable; his second, *The Wild, the Innocent, and the E Street Shuffle,* is uneven; and when his concerts go on long enough—this one lasted two and a half hours—they begin to drag. Not coincidentally, the high point of the show was the final encore, a spectacular performance of the Gary U.S. Bonds hit "Quarter to Three." As it happened, I had never heard that classic before, and I listened with serendipitous awe. In the middle of the song, Springsteen paused to announce, "I ate a lot of cheeseburgers today. I have a lot of cholesterol around my heart. And my doctor says if I sing 'Quarter to Three' he won't be responsible." Then he drove on toward his heart attack, driving us along with him. I'm not yet ready to endorse Jon Landau's rash proclamation that Springsteen is the future of rock and roll, but in the present he sure provides a good night out.

The Importance of Stevie Wonder
DECEMBER 1974

A few years ago, I saw the Monterey Pop Festival movie for the fourth or fifth time. I had always loved Otis Redding's performance, but this time I heard intimations in his music that I'd never picked up before. Sung by a black man to an audience of white freaks—"the love crowd," he had labeled them (us), with amusement and affection and who knows what cynicism—a ballad like "I've Been Loving You Too Long" became more, much more, than a simple love song. The line "Please don't make me stop now" was both a plea and a warning. It spoke of human relations in general and race relations in particular. It reminded the love crowd that in their naive rapacity they had taken what sustenance they needed from black music and the black outlaw culture without much thought about what they could give back. And it insisted, sadly but firmly, that that one-way transfer of energy—of love, if you will—could not continue forever. This is your chance, Redding seemed to be urging; if you *do* something about love instead of merely talking about it, then maybe—just maybe—we can all make it through. I still don't know how much of this was really Redding, how much a projection of my own frustration, long after the fact, at our bungled historical moment (or the illusion of one), but the experience affected me deeply. As a racial-cultural mediator, Sly Stone was more sophisticated, Jimi Hendrix more profound, but it is Otis's challenge that I think about when I listen to Stevie Wonder.

On a recent Friday at Madison Square Garden, before an audience dominated by white kids in their twenties, Wonder gave a Christmas benefit concert, whose proceeds will buy medical equipment, musical instruments, games, and other supplies for a number of charitable organizations serving the poor, the aged, and the handicapped. His performance, which lasted two hours, was uneven; I felt by turns high and bored, moved and annoyed, and full of doubts and fantasies that were, I suppose, less a product of the immediate situation than a measure of how important Stevie Wonder has become.

Wonder not only has attracted a huge interracial audience and made the cover of *Newsweek* at a time when there is little communication between black and white musical cultures but has engaged our imaginations, made connections, become more than a performer, in a way I was beginning to forget about. At his best, he has the power to make optimism and racial reconciliation marvelously credible. Without denying "the nightmare that's becomin' real life"—pain, anger, bitterness toward oppressors, even the petty spite that can arise out of disappointment in love are all present in his lyrics, in the strange, often tormented sounds he coaxes out of the synthesizer—he can suggest that the joy of being human ultimately prevails. And because the anarchic, exploratory textural busyness of his music enlarges our sense of possibility the way Dylan's words once did, because his pleasure in the exchange between performer and audience both communicates and inspires something like love—perhaps also because we know he hasn't exactly had it easy—we are ready to believe him. But there is a delicate balance involved here, and too often it tips in the direction of romantic and religious sentimentality. Wonder's lapses are disturbing, because they call into question his successes. Does his transcendent joy reflect some sort of reality we can grasp and build on, or is it, after all, just a pleasant distraction? Is there a possibility of racial détente based on hard times ahead, on the common disillusion and defiance expressed in a song like "You Haven't Done Nothin'"? Or will the more fatuous aspects of Wonder's message of universal love simply provide the growing horde of religious escapists with still another focus for their complacency? Is this part of what "Superstition" is warning against?

Given the circumstances of this particular concert, it would have been hard to avoid bathos, and Stevie didn't try. He talked about how this was a very special event, a dream come true; about how much joy it gave him to give to the people; about his vision of love and respect between people regardless of the color of their skin. He mentioned the car accident that nearly killed him a year and a half ago. He sang Christmas songs, an overly self-conscious medley of oldies, and a bunch of the romantic ballads that are my least favorite part of his repertoire. For all that I know how complicated it must be for a man like Stevie Wonder to arrive at simplicity at the age of twenty-four, I couldn't help wishing that his philanthropy had some political content and that he didn't sound quite so much like a 1963 brotherhood speech.

Still, I had a pretty good time. So did Stevie, playing with his synthesizer, dancing (yes) with the women singers in band, chiding the audience for talking during his rap ("Please relax your lips"), goofing around, maintaining a loose, forgivably self-indulgent pace. All through the evening, there were peak moments that made my reservations seem cranky. Toward the end, I began to worry that Wonder would omit "You Haven't Done Nothin'" and "Living for the City" as unsuitable for the occasion, but I should have had more faith. He sang them both, then went on to "You Are the Sunshine of My Life" and, finally, "Superstition." Behind me, someone lit a stick of incense. Maybe we haven't blown it, after all, I thought. And maybe—just maybe—we haven't.

Introduction to Beginning to See the Light: Sex, Hope, and Rock 'n' Roll
1981

Until I started putting this collection together, I did not realize how consistently I've been obsessed with the idea of freedom. In one way or another, my pieces on such apparently diverse subjects as rock and roll and feminism, radical politics and religion reflect my belief in the possibility

---

Originally published in *Beginning to See the Light: Pieces of a Decade,* by Ellen Willis. New York: Knopf, 1981.

of a genuinely democratic culture—a community based on the voluntary cooperation of equals. If this book can be said to make one central assumption, it is that there really is such a thing as liberation, however hard it may be to define or describe, let alone attain.

My definition is political; it assumes the need for organized opposition to the present social system. But it is also psychological; it has to do with self-knowledge, with the ability to make conscious choices and take responsibility for them rather than act compulsively from unconscious (that is, unadmitted) motives. Since on some level we never really believe the illusions and rationalizations we insist on porting around like boulders from some totemic mountain, it is a relief to drop the burden—or so I've always found. Still, I never feel quite comfortable talking about choice and responsibility. Those words usually imply an antimaterialist moral and religious outlook—a fact that, to my mind, reveals the limitations of both materialist and moral/religious vocabularies. I don't believe in "free will," if by that one means choice unconditioned by its material context, but I do regard the idea of freedom as inseparable from the idea of the individual self, the subject who chooses. We are shaped by history and culture, by our economic and social situations, yet we are not just passive recipients—or victims—of external pressures. It is human beings who create history and culture, who change their situation or fail to do so. I think there is an aspect of the human personality, a core of basic—if you will, biological—impulses, that transcends and resists the incursions of an oppressive culture. And I think the craving for freedom—for self-determination, in the most literal sense—is a basic impulse that can be suppressed but never eliminated.

Politically, this view of freedom aligns me with cultural radicals rather than socialists; as I see it, the enemy is not capitalism per se, but the authoritarian structure of all our institutions, including those—the family, especially—that regulate our so-called private lives. From a conventional Marxist perspective the individual is a historical artifact, invoked by the rising bourgeoisie as a rationale for capitalism; since the concept of individual freedom is a mask for the reality of class exploitation, it is illusory, or at least fundamentally suspect. I would argue, rather, that it was in part the impulse toward freedom that led to the bourgeois rebellion against feudalism; that the bourgeoisie did not create the individual, only the conditions for the emergence of self-conscious individuals as a powerful political force. From this standpoint capitalism is a massive paradox, particularly in its later stages. On the one hand, bourgeois democracy represents the first great phase of the cultural revolution; capitalism has instituted certain basic civil rights, supplied the libertarian ideas behind all radical movements, weakened the authority of the patriarchal family and church, allowed masses of people unparalleled personal freedom and social mobility. Yet the corporate state and its global empire are themselves authoritarian, hierarchical structures. Most Americans have little or no control over the conditions of their own working lives, let alone the overall direction of the economy, nor do our formal democratic rights give us real power to determine public policy. The colonized people who have contributed to the enrichment of the capitalist West share neither its prosperity nor its relative freedom. And the imperatives of the marketplace set people against each other; the comforts of middle-class life are bought at the expense of the poor, liberty at the expense of community. Under these conditions our emancipation from the coercive bonds of traditional societies exacts a high price—even for the privileged—in insecurity and psychic isolation.

Obviously, the next phase of the cultural revolution requires a radical alternative to capitalism. But because the socialist-minded left is inclined to focus on the second half of the capitalist paradox while ignoring or discounting the first, much of what passes for a radical critique of this society is insidiously conservative. The tendency to see capitalist individualism solely in negative terms has, for instance, led many leftists to indulge a sentimental view of the family as an oasis of human warmth in the capitalist wasteland, as if the warmth the family offers were any less contingent on conformity to a set of institutional rules than the wages our bosses dispense. At times this "haven in a heartless world" mentality verges on outright nostalgia for tradition, for the lost security of the old organic community—an emotion I find doubly difficult to share, given that women in precapitalist societies were chattel, while Jews were economic and political pariahs. The same brand of selective perception feeds leftist romanticism about Third World dictatorships, also organic communities of a sort. But collective liberation without individual autonomy is a self-contradiction. To be anticapitalist is not enough. Socialist regimes have attacked the grosser forms of economic inequality, yet in terms of the larger struggle for freedom, socialism in practice has been, if anything, a devastating counterrevolution against the liberal concept of individual rights.

Overtly or implicitly, most of the essays reprinted here carry on this quarrel with the left. The first section of the book is, among other things, an extended polemic against standard leftist notions about advanced capitalism—that the consumer economy makes us slaves to commodities, that the function of the mass media is to manipulate our fantasies so we will equate fulfillment with buying the system's products. These ideas are at most half true. Mass consumption, advertising, and mass art are a corporate Frankenstein; while they reinforce the system, they also undermine it. By continually pushing the message that we have the right to gratification *now,* consumerism at its most expansive encouraged a demand for fulfillment that could not so easily be contained by products; it had a way of spilling over into rebellion against the constricting conditions of our lives. The history of the sixties strongly suggests that the impulse to buy a new car and tool down the freeway with the radio blasting rock and roll is not unconnected to the impulse to fuck outside marriage, get high, stand up to men or white people or bosses, join dissident movements. In fact, the mass media helped to spread rebellion, and the system obligingly marketed products that encouraged it, for the simple reason that there was money to be made from rebels who were also consumers. On one level the sixties revolt was an impressive illustration of Lenin's remark that the capitalist will sell you the rope to hang him with.

But the subversive element in mass culture is not just a matter of content, of explicit invitations to indulge and/or rebel; it also has to do with the formal properties of mass art. Here too the left has tended to be obtuse, assuming that because mass art is a product of capitalism, it is by definition worthless—not real art at all, but merely a commodity intended to enrich its producers while indoctrinating and pacifying consumers. And again this assumption betrays a hidden conservatism. Why, after all, regard commercial art as intrinsically more compromised than art produced under the auspices of the medieval church, or aristocratic patrons? Art has always been in some sense propaganda for ruling classes and at the same time a form of struggle against them. Art that succeeds manages to evade or transcend or turn to its own purposes the strictures imposed on the artist; on the deepest level it is the enemy of authority, as Plato understood. Mass art is no exception. It is never simply imposed from above but reflects a complicated interplay of corporate interests, the conscious or intuitive intentions of the artists and technicians who create the product, and the demands of the audience. The distinctive aesthetic of mass art, which is based on images (and sounds) designed to have an intense sensory, erotic, and emotional impact, clearly derives from the necessities of marketing—the need to distinguish one's product from its competitors, to grab and hold the largest possible audience. But the forms invented to fulfill those requirements—the bright colors, bold, linear patterns, and iconic simplicity of advertising art; the sexual rhythms, tight construction, irresistible hook lines, and insistent repetition of rock-and-roll songs—have an autonomous aesthetic existence. They convey their own message, which, like the content of advertising (or the content of pop lyrics) is essentially hedonistic.

Implicit in the formal language of mass art is the possibility that given the right sort of social conditions, it can act as a catalyst that transforms its mass audience into an an oppositional community. This is precisely what rock and roll did for teenagers, and rock for the counterculture, in the fifties and sixties. Logically, the prominent role of pop music in the sixties revolt should have changed the left's attitude toward mass culture. After all, most leftists were rock fans, and even the group that came to symbolize the most uncompromising hatred of America took its name from a Bob Dylan song. Instead, radicals tended to evade the issue by making distinctions between "commercial" and "serious" rock. That serious rock was as commercial as the other kind did not deter some movement folk from making extravagant claims for it as revolutionary people's music. Others, unable to avoid noticing that rock was big business, complained about its "co-optation" by the music industry, as if the two had ever been separate.

For a time the seventies seemed to vindicate the co-optation theory. A lot of things changed—the state of the economy, the structure of the record business, the mood of the audience—and rock became a conservative force, a vehicle for assimilating the trappings of the counterculture into the social mainstream while purging it of threatening content. The dropout posture that had once implied membership in a community of outsiders came to mean no more than a smug upper-middle-class solipsism. But this complacency incited its own rebellion, the rude eruption of the punk movement, which sparked the larger phenomenon of new-wave rock and roll. Compared to the mass audience that standard rock enjoys, new-wave fans are a cult (though a sizable one). Still, new wave is rock and roll, now self-consciously based on the same formal principles that were once a commercial necessity. And it means something that these principles remain a focus for aesthetic and social dissidence.

Of course, rebellion is not the same thing as revolution. It's not only that capitalists are experts at palming off fake rope—as the development of the rock establishment attests—but that revolt does not necessarily imply radicalism, as a long line of rock-and-rollers, from the apolitical Little Richard to the antipolitical Ramones, attests. Which is only to say that neither mass art nor any other kind is a substitute for politics. Art may express and encourage our subversive impulses, but it can't analyze or organize them. Subversion begins to be radical only when we ask what we really want or think we should have, who or what is obstructing us, and what to do about it.

Afterword

RAISE YOUR HAND

Daphne Carr and Evie Nagy

Ellen Willis started a movement when she became the first pop critic of *The New Yorker.* As a fan, as a feminist, as one of cultural journalism's most influential and provocative pioneers, Ellen wrote the pieces that convinced many impassioned writers to commit to this often frustrating field of popular music criticism. Even those music writers who don't know who Ellen was (and there are many, though we hope fewer with the publication of this anthology) owe her for helping to legitimize pop criticism as a space that could be approached with the same intellectual curiosity and social import as writing about politics, religion, or other supposedly weighty cultural topics. For her, popular music writing *was* all of those things. Plus dancing.

Ellen's writing was an immense inspiration for music writers, but she was also a decade-plus faculty member at New York University, where she founded the innovative Cultural Reporting and Criticism program. Her legacy as a program director, instructor, and mentor is rarely part of the narrative of remembering Ellen Willis, but it is clear that she directly shaped a generation of cultural reporters with her rigorous approach. In this essay we (Evie as Ellen's former student and Daphne as a longtime fan of Ellen's work) reflect on these intimately connected and yet distinctly experienced elements of her influence as a writer, editor, and teacher. Through our discussions with dozens of Ellen's students and fans, we have come to understand her as someone who served many as a model for how passionate, progressively minded writers should go about their careers and lives.

Ellen was a foundational writer of American rock and roll criticism in the late 1960s and early 1970s. Like jazz writers in the preceding decades, these fledgling public intellectuals of rock music had few models for understanding the new music's culture or sound, so they had to cobble together critical theories, their own observations and experiences, and their beliefs about the art of writing into a thing that would become the field of "rock criticism." Ellen and her peers saw it as wide open, as she told journalism scholar Elizabeth Weinstein in a 2005 interview: "You got to sort of really invent the genre, because rock and roll was really considered junk and there were no articles on it except for columns saying rock and roll causes juvenile delinquency."

Whereas Robert Christgau forged legions with his dense, literary style of criticism and Greil Marcus inspired sound-driven historical narratives, Ellen's contribution to the origins of pop criticism was in her unyielding challenge to the sociology of mass culture (with its negative views of the commodity and fear of large spectacles) and through her feminist, new journalistic inquiry. In her work she wove together sound, performance, and the audience's bodily affect with radical cultural critique and her own ever-present quest for pleasure, freedom, and democracy. These ideals she saw flourishing amid and around pop music "junk"—its records and big concerts. For Willis, writing was a public space to draw attention to, and shift, the very foundations of culture. Like all great writing, hers is an argument for something, and that something is only music inasmuch as music is the sound of the good life.

"Ellen was a slow writer and had a disciplined intellectual process," Donna Gaines says. "And she wasn't fucked up." In other words, there were material and spiritual reasons for Ellen's style difference. She was not a high stylist, not obtuse or literary. Unlike her gonzo peers and followers, she wasn't trying to make her language re-create the experience of the music. Likewise, her first-person voice promoted ideas, not herself. Her style was almost invisible, and if all her fans and mentees would use one word to describe it, that word would be *clear*.

But clear is much harder to write than it is to read. Ann Powers was among many to remark that Ellen's brilliant intellect was intimidating. "She didn't confront the neurosis of a woman writer that much. A big question for my generation of '80s feminists was, 'How do we know we have a right to speak?' With Ellen there was such a strong assertion: 'Yes, I am going to speak.'" A next-generation critic Jessica Hopper mirrors Ann's anxiety: "I have a hard time reading more than a few pages in one sitting because her writing makes me feel like I'm not doing the heavy lifting I should be. Her writing is a dare as much as it is a lens."

Ellen was hired at *The New Yorker* in 1968 after publishing exactly one piece of popular music journalism—her Dylan article, the first piece in this anthology. William Shawn brought her in to write a new column on music called Rock, Etc. and asked if she wouldn't mind writing as E. Willis, since there were at that moment too many women's bylines in the magazine (such as that of one of her major influences, P. Kael). "Yes, I would mind!" she said. So started twenty-six-year-old Ellen Willis in her seven-year, fifty-six-piece run as the first pop music critic of *The New Yorker*.

There she wrote about her favorites often and neglected whole segments of popular music entirely. She often fought with Shawn about her fan-oriented and personal tone, as did Kael at the time. Karen Durbin remembers one such story Ellen told of a struggle around a description for the song "The Bloods" in coverage of the first National Women's Music Festival in June 1974. Shawn thought "menstruation" to be a distasteful word and wanted it out. "It's not either. It's natural," Ellen said. And it stayed.[1]

The year Ellen quit *The New Yorker*, she became *Rolling Stone*'s first female contributing editor under that magazine's first female editor, Maryanne Partridge. Willis wrote about topics as disparate as chauvinism, pornography, politics, baseball, and Janis in her Alternating Currents column between 1976 and 1978. Former *Rolling Stone* books editor Sarah Lazin remembers her as the writer who inspired the women in editorial—overqualified and languishing in lowly jobs until Partridge's arrival—to stop being "groovy chicks who hung out with the great writers" to become "great writers and editors ourselves."

Ellen wrote a brilliant piece for Greil Marcus's 1979 desert island disc essay collection *Stranded*, but by the 1980s she had basically ceased

---

1. This anecdote was taken from rock critic Georgia Christgau's paper "Just Like a Woman: The Rock Criticism of Ellen Willis," read at the EMP Pop Conference 2008.—Ed.

music writing, going on to become a major feminist activist writer, cultural critic, and cherished editor at the *Village Voice*. Her leaving the field affected writers. "I remember feeling discouraged that she felt the subject had been exhausted for her. Maybe because in that first generation the women hadn't hung on," says Powers. Still, "to be able to give up a subject on which you're an authority because you're unsatisfied with the way you're writing about it is pretty gutsy." For a while after Ellen stopped writing music criticism, the lore of her, proximity to her, and some library archives were the only way to know of her influence.

Current *Maxim* editor and former *Blender/Voice/Spin* editor and writer Joe Levy read a piece in the 1980s in the anthology *The Anti-Aesthetic* in which Edward Said walked through a book fair wondering who wrote all this stuff and for whom. "It became a really important question for me to ask about music criticism: *Are we writing for other music critics or are we writing for a general audience?* And the reason I loved Ellen's work so much was because it answered that question so well. When I became an editor, I xeroxed her work and gave it to other writers."

Ann Powers and Evelyn McDonnell were two of the *Voice* writers who got Levy's Xeroxes, and together with an editorial room that included many writers who had worked with and/or read Ellen (Barbara O'Dair, Joy Press, Donna Gaines, Donna Minkowitz, Alisa Solomon, and Joan Morgan) they made the 1990s a decade in which women's voices would flourish and be taken seriously in cultural reporting and criticism. Powers and McDonnell included Ellen's work in their anthology of women music writers, *Rock She Wrote*, while O'Dair had Willis write the introduction to the 1997 collection *Trouble Girls: The Rolling Stone Book of Women in Rock*. By that time, Ellen had had a column but was no longer editing at the *Voice*. A regime change within editorial had shifted away from the type of "thumbsucker essays" of which "Ellen was a virtuoso," remembers McDonnell. The journalism business was changing, but Ellen's reputation and influence still loomed large among *Voice* writers and editors.

Besides *Beginning to See the Light*, Ellen's work circulated most widely in the form of her Velvet Underground essay in *Stranded*. Pop music scholar and former indie rocker Matthew Bannister remembers it as a revelation while living in Dunedin, New Zealand, in the 1980s: "Because a lot of music wasn't available to me in NZ, I spent a lot of time reading about music that I had not heard yet and fantasizing about what it was like. So rock journalism really shaped music for me." He happened on a copy of *Stranded* and was thrilled to find a truly critical voice on one of the scene's most romanticized icons. "It was the first thing I read about the Velvet Underground that wasn't pure hagiography."

Bannister believes that Willis's experience of being a woman in the counterculture also helped her clarity of vision: "Because she was a woman in a male-dominated medium, she could see the attraction but she wasn't buying in like the guys were—perhaps she couldn't." Ellen was at once immersed in the culture while also critically distant, an outsider who calls bullshit on those so-called bohos who would seek to exploit innocence for profit. This is most evident in her Woodstock piece, which *Pitchfork* editor Amy Phillips praised as a classic "myth-bust." That unflinching portrayal of the hopes, contradictions, and failures of the counterculture is the antithesis of the romance and nostalgia with which the era is now coated, and from which so much pop music writing emanates. As we move away from the reality of that time, the critical voices from within it become even more important.

Writers from our generation got their first read of Ellen in *Beginning to See the Light* and *Stranded,* but it was too little. Thus far her few reprinted music pieces read only like a major intervention on someone else's history of music writing. So much so that a lifelong feminist and writer like Jessica Hopper hadn't known of Ellen's impact: "When I first started rock-writing seriously, not just fanzine-spitting, I bought big on the Lester/Christgau/Greil/Tosches/*Crawdaddy!*—the much mythologized first-wave boy-genius canon. It wasn't until a few years ago that I realized Ellen was a part of that, was instrumental and influential to her peers. It's validating that she was so major—it makes me wish for more, for all of us now."

In the last decade of her life, Ellen trained a new generation of cultural critics—many of whom never knew of her music-writing career—as a professor of journalism at New York University. In 1995 she founded the Cultural Reporting and Criticism program (CRC) around the idea that there is no separation between thinking and writing, a concept not as obvious as it seems. According to the program's codeveloper and current director Susie Linfield, "there was and still is this idea that you could teach a 'skill' of journalism devoid of ideas, that you could teach people to write without having anything to write about. And Ellen of course came from the exact opposite viewpoint, that the way you learn to write is the way you learn to think; that your thought process and your writing process are one and the same."

CRC students experience this through a rigorous curriculum that falls somewhere between philosophy, cultural theory, social science, and media studies (and the uniqueness of the program within journalism education is one of the reasons that many alums say it is the only place they applied). But for those of us who had Ellen in the classroom, just as there was no separation between thinking and writing, there was also little distinction between teaching and writing. All of our interaction with her, all of her feedback, was on the page or potentially on its way there.

As a social being in the class, Ellen was almost a nonentity. Even if one had no knowledge of her extraordinary body of written work, she was intimidating not for the force of her presence but for its almost spectral stoicism—"understated to the point of being utterly inexpressive," as her former graduate assistant Kate Bolick wrote in the literary journal *n+1* when Ellen died in 2006. Students looking for an authoritarian figure to guide them through the interpersonal negotiations of reporting would not find it in Ellen. Unlike other great teachers whose personality and charisma inspire others by example, Ellen could be maddening in her reserve. Not that she wouldn't get passionate and frustrated—but her passionate frustration was always about the process and work of making an argument or telling a story. As writer, editor, and former student Lauren Sandler describes it,

> she was so grounded philosophically, in everything she wrote, and taught, and said to you casually over a burger. She wouldn't say anything at all unless she had completely thought about it, unless it fit into a larger way of thinking that she had developed over years, based on an ethic and a way of respecting and unmaking and remaking the world, and a way of challenging the way we approach everything. There was never a moment of hypocrisy.

This is not to say that she was predictable. CRC graduate Priya Jain remembers a shocking meeting of Ellen's Sex and American Politics class where she challenged liberals who argued that it was absurd to think gay marriage could lead to legal plural marriage or bestiality—her suggestion, to everyone's extremely awkward horror, was that legally, perhaps it could. "What Ellen did was say those things with the full confidence that your liberal beliefs could withstand some of the more taboo arguments," says Jain. "It's not good enough to say there are areas where you're not supposed to make an argument—all she really wanted you to do was articulate it, and once you articulate it, you realize how shaky it is, and from there you figure out how and where to draw the lines. And it doesn't mean you can't continue thinking that gay marriage, for example, is a good thing." For Ellen, as Lauren Sandler says, "there was no party line." Her consistency was in thought, not personal ideology, and it was one of the reasons she was so effective at putting herself in her work without indulgence, and teaching others to do the same.

Music writers accustomed to the field's typically thick, sonic prose have a lot to admire and learn from the bold, unselfconscious language of Ellen's *New Yorker* columns, wherein she referred to herself and other rock critics as "fans" and wrote sentences like "Part of the problem is Bowie's material"—a simple grievance about an artist who, in the rest of rock criticism's canon, is virtually unassailable. But when she opened her 1972 piece about Creedence Clearwater Revival with an account of dancing to all five of her CCR albums, in succession, by herself, a first thought to someone who knew her from the classroom was, "She did *what??*" Until reading more of her work, and discovering how intricately she connected body, mind, and music, a solo living room dance party seemed completely out of character.

What Ellen modeled as a teacher was how to be an unmatched thinker, writer, and editor; that she didn't fit the Dynamic Professor prototype only meant that all of her time, effort, and concern was focused on training writers to explore connections between culture and self, and with that understanding say something new and important. Many of us who were lucky enough to learn from her, and who continue to learn from Susie Linfield and others who share her ideals, are finding fewer and fewer opportunities in the current media industry to do the kind of writing that Ellen championed. But that doesn't mean that we can't try to emulate her standards of thought and intellectual persistence—not that any of us, anyone we've talked to anyway, feels that we'll ever achieve them.

Ellen unknowingly described her own legacy in her 1971 *New Yorker* essay "But Now I'm Gonna Move," where she dissected the distinction between the sexism of early rock and roll and the more insidious version that took over after rock was supposedly more liberated. At one point, she matter-of-factly credits Janis Joplin's groundbreaking social and cultural rebellion not to her rage, circumstance, or force of personality, but to how these things connected to her intellect:

> In an overwhelmingly male atmosphere, female performers have served mainly as catalysts for male cultural-revolutionary fantasies of tough chicks, beautiful bitches, and super-yin old ladies. Janis Joplin half-transcended this function by confronting it, screaming out the misery and confusion of being what others wanted her to be. But she was a genius.

Never a romantic, Ellen still used the term *genius* to describe Janis. Perhaps it was because she saw in her a woman not divinely but humanly gifted, a person who put all of her self into her art, connected with her fans, and with it made something fantastic and new from what others thought was merely junk. Janis worked for the term, and so did Ellen.

Ellen Willis (1941–2006) was a groundbreaking radical leftist writer and thinker whose true loves were rock music, feminism, pleasure, and freedom. She was the first pop music critic for *The New Yorker* and an editor and columnist at the *Village Voice*. She wrote for numerous publications, including *Rolling Stone*, the *New York Times*, the *Nation*, and *Dissent*. She was the founder of the Cultural Reporting and Criticism program at New York University, and she published three books of essays, *Beginning to See the Light, No More Nice Girls,* and *Don't Think, Smile*.

Nona Willis Aronowitz has written about women, sex, music, technology, film, and youth culture for publications such as the *Nation*, the *New York Observer*, the *Village Voice*, and Salon. She is coauthor of *Girldrive: Criss-Crossing America, Redefining Feminism*.

Sasha Frere-Jones is a musician and writer from New York. He is a staff writer for *The New Yorker* and a member of the bands Calvinist and Piñata. He can be found on the Web at sashafrerejones.tumblr.com.

Daphne Carr lives and writes in New York City. She is editor of the Best Music Writing series and author of *Nine Inch Nails Pretty Hate Machine*. She is the cofounder of Girl Group, a listserv for and about women in popular music writing. Find her at funboring.com.

Evie Nagy is the editor of Billboard Pro and writes about music, culture, and comic books for several publications. A former administrator at Harvard University, she switched careers upon learning about Ellen Willis's Cultural Reporting and Criticism program at New York University.